ROBBIE
& GARY

ROBBIE
& GARY

IT'S COMPLICATED

THE UNAUTHORIZED BIOGRAPHY

PAUL SCOTT

SIDGWICK & JACKSON

First published 2011 by Sidgwick & Jackson
an imprint of Pan Macmillan, a division of Macmillan Publishers Limited
Pan Macmillan, 20 New Wharf Road, London N1 9RR
Basingstoke and Oxford
Associated companies throughout the world
www.panmacmillan.com

ISBN 978-0-283-07147-8 HB
ISBN 978-0-230-75967-1 TPB

A CIP catalogue record for this book is available from
the British Library.

Typeset by Ellipsis Digital Limited, Glasgow
Printed by CPI Mackays, Chatham ME5 8TD

Visit www.panmacmillan.com to read more about all our books
and to buy them. You will also find features, author interviews and
news of any author events, and you can sign up for e-newsletters
so that you're always first to hear about our new releases.

Contents

Life Through a Lens

There is a particular type of isolation that really high-end celebrity buys you. On the balcony of an upscale West London apartment, the brawny, messy figure of a man is perched on the edge of a patio chair fifteen floors up, an unlit cigarette hanging limply from his lower lip, elbows on knees, hands supporting an oversized pair of binoculars. From time to time he will stand unhurriedly, lean lazily against the glass safety screen and scan the ground below in wide, slow sweeps in the lacklustre manner of a bored watchtower guard. During the height of the madness surrounding him, Robbie Williams will come out here every day for hours on end to watch a world that he increasingly feels safe observing only from a distance – viewed warily through the magnifying lenses of his field glasses.

In the dark days of spring 2006, Robbie's latest attempt at making any sort of half-decent life for himself in London was not going well. Two years earlier, he had paid £2.5 million for an open-plan apartment high up in the Belvedere building at Chelsea Harbour. The move had been forced on him not least because the simple act of going out of the front door of his previous home in

Notting Hill had meant running the ragtag gauntlet of jostling paparazzi, hyperventilating fans, gawping passers-by and swivel-headed crazies, all of whom, for reasons stretching from the purely financial to the certifiably psychotic, have long since been inexorably drawn to the top tier of stardom inhabited by Williams.

For months Rob had been waking in a panic from dreams in which he had been stabbed or shot by a deranged fan on his doorstep. Paranoid and scared, his relocation to the Belvedere, with its private lobby and security, was meant to free him from the daily terror of having to come anywhere near those who so obsessively worshipped him, but the experiment had simply replaced one set of neuroses with another. Now lonely and disconnected in his rock-star eyrie, he mirthlessly christened his new home 'Alcatraz', and unwittingly cast himself in the role of his own jailer.

One day in early May, Williams resumed his vigil on the balcony of his flat, but on this particular occasion his binoculars were focused solely on the Thames-side frontage of the Conrad Hotel, on the opposite side of the marina. All day long, squinting into the sunlight, he trained the glasses on the windows of the building, looking for any sign of movement behind them.

From his sixth-floor suite in the Conrad, Gary Barlow was looking out too. Gary had heard that morning from his Take That band mate Jason Orange, who was back in touch with Williams after a long hiatus, that Robbie was to be found in residence at the Belvedere. As Gary prepared for the group's barnstorming appearance that night at Wembley Arena as part of Take That's sell-out reunion tour, he stood for a full fifteen minutes on the balcony outside his room, watching. He imagined, illogically, that somehow he would intuitively know behind which of the scores of panes of glass opposite he might spot his one-time cohort in Britain's biggest ever boy band and – for the past eleven years – his sworn nemesis. Both men, who had not laid eyes on each other, let alone spoken, for a decade, would eventually give up without catching sight of their respective enemy.

There are metaphors here, of course: those of the 'look but don't see, listen but don't hear' variety, which have come to characterize the complicated backstory of Williams and Barlow. Theirs, after all, is a tale of love and loathing, of devotion and destructive obsession, which continues, after more than twenty years, to be the defining relationship in both their lives. Their fractured 'bromance' has shaped the often-tortured history of one of the world's most successful bands. It has truly been a love–hate relationship that has at times been so visceral, so deep-seated, that it has come close to threatening the sanity of both men and led to one of the most caustic feuds ever known in show business. Then, like all great stories, it had in its third act an unlikely twist of reconciliation and redemption, but still left the open-ended question: given their incendiary history, would the détente last? Could it last? Or would the old tensions and vying for power that exploded so destructively before serve to tear them apart once again?

In many ways it is tempting to see Robbie and Gary as one another's muse. Not in the classic sense, as a positive source of inspiration and encouragement, but in the way both have focused every last ounce of energy on obdurately refusing to submit to their respective rival. There have been dark days for both men over the years. For Gary, there have been times when he has been flat out on the canvas, his career reduced to rubble, ridiculed and despised by those who once feted him. Aside from a passing phase of self-pity, however, he insisted on getting up and putting the gloves back on, unwilling to acquiesce to his foe. Likewise, down the years

Robbie has successfully managed to turn his destructive hatred of Gary into a positive. He distilled and bottled his anger at his former band mate and drank shots to give him courage, to make him work harder, write more and strive to grind his enemy into the ground. In the same way that the slights against him, real or imaginary, served to fuel his creative output, so too did the spite, long reserved for Barlow, fortify him at his moments of greatest weakness, when addictions and depression threatened to submerge him.

Then, like their burning loathing, their eventual reconciliation ignited a creative spark that, in the case of Williams, had been virtually extinguished by the weight of his myriad problems: his battle with drugs, his isolation and his artistic malaise. In the case of Barlow, it freed him from the weight of his past mistakes and allowed him to fulfil the role to which he came late: that of mentor and creative facilitator.

Both men have cast a shadow over one another during the moments of rawest contrasting emotions, at the happiest and saddest of times, and in doing so, they have combined – together and apart – to spur the other on to great things.

CHAPTER ONE

Camp Commandant

Given all the nudge-nudge tittle-tattle and the gay whispers that continue to surround Take That to this day, it is perhaps fitting that the first person to come between Gary Barlow and Robbie Williams was not some nubile groupie or starlet du jour, but a homosexual man. In November 1990, Gary, then a nineteen-year-old wannabe, sporting an androgynous spiky peroxide hairdo that had been newly teased by Manchester's most theatrically flamboyant of stylists, Pierre Alexandre, excitedly boarded a flight from Ringway Airport to Orlando. Accompanying him on the week-long holiday to Florida was model-agency boss Nigel Martin-Smith, who three months earlier had put together Take That after advertising for budding pop stars in a newspaper.

During their holiday in the sun, the pair covered all the usual tourist bases: trips to Sea World, Epcot, Disney World, Universal Studios and Wet 'n' Wild were arranged. Gary did all the driving in their hire car, and at night the two men would take long strolls together on the beach. When Gary arrived in the hotel room he would share with Martin-Smith, he was taken aback to find a handwritten note in the back pocket of his jeans that his mother,

Marjorie, had left for him to find on his arrival in the States. The Barlows, a working-class family from Frodsham, Cheshire, were not the types to do touchy-feely stuff, but in the heartfelt note his mother opened up about how proud she was of him, how she and Gary's father, Colin, had always hoped that one day they could take Gary and his older brother, Ian, to Disney themselves, but had never been able to afford it. She ended by saying that it was now Nigel who was going to make all his dreams come true.

Why did the normally buttoned-up Marjorie, who had never done anything like it before or since, feel the need to put her feelings down on paper for her teenage son? Was this traditional Northern mum facing the fact that her younger child might well be gay and letting him know in her loving, roundabout way that she was happy so long as he was?

Surely nobody, it has to be said, would have blamed her if she had jumped to the wrong conclusion. For starters, her son's companion on his first holiday without his parents was a very openly gay man, who, at thirty-two, was thirteen years older than Gary. So open, in fact, that Nigel Martin-Smith was already a renowned member of Manchester's 'gay mafia'. To this day, Nigel, who is on his third or fourth facelift, depending on who you believe, remains a regular fixture on the thriving late-night gay club circuit of the city, owns two venues of his own and is the director of a Manchester-based bar called Queer. At the time he put together the group, he was better known in Manchester as a talented and ambitious, if acerbic, small-time businessman who surrounded himself with a band of cronies from the gay scene who spent much of their time bitching about each other. He ran the Boss Agency, based in Manchester's Half Moon Chambers in the Chapel Walks area of the city, which represented local models and a few singers. His knowledge of the music business, however, extended not much further than signing a singing drag queen and a long-forgotten would-be pop star called Damian who had once got to number seven in the charts and been on *Top of the Pops*.

Nigel Martin-Smith's reputation had not reached Frodsham, 21 miles away, but Mrs Barlow was well aware that her son's new manager was not straight. There were other telltale signs that must have made her wonder about Gary. Not least was the fact that to all intents and purposes Take That were not then the band they would later become, with hordes of screaming schoolgirls constantly following them. Instead, the band had been set up with the express purpose of exploiting something Martin-Smith was altogether more au fait with: the gay market and the pink pound.

Even though the early history of Take That has been well trawled, it is worth revisiting if only to establish how the fault lines between Robbie and Gary were set in place from the very beginning. Whether by accident or design, as we shall see, the dynamics were such that there was a predisposition towards the conflict that would blight their relationship during the first incarnation of the band and beyond.

Anyone familiar with the group's birth in summer 1990 knows that there was nothing auspicious about it, nothing to suggest the stellar success Take That would go on to achieve. In the years after the five were chosen by Martin-Smith, attempts were made by some surrounding the band to rewrite the story and make it seem less manufactured, more organic, less cynical. One of several different tales put out to the press about the beginnings of the group was that Howard and Jason were already friends, had formed a dancing duo called Street Beat and had been spotted by Martin-Smith performing on Pete Waterman's TV show *The Hitman and Her*.

Mark, it was claimed, was a budding singer who had become mates with Gary a year before Take That was founded, when they met in a Manchester studio where Gary was recording and Mark was the tea boy. Mark began helping Gary, so the story went, to lug his gear to his gigs and they formed a band together called the Cutest Rush. In reality, prior to replying to Nigel's newspaper ad, the five had barely laid eyes on each before they pitched up at his offices. They were then shepherded into the nearby gay nightclub La Cage, where, with the exception of Barlow and Williams, who both had decent voices and singing experience, they attempted – with varying degrees of tunelessness – to sing their way through rather haphazard versions of the Jason Donovan hit 'Nothing Can Divide Us' in front of Nigel and a few bored staff who were getting the club ready for the evening rush.

Aside from Gary, on first inspection there was not any indication that the five strangers were exactly overflowing with communal musical talent. The only previous claim to fame of Mark Owen, then an eighteen-year-old bank worker, was that he had won a smiling contest in his native Oldham when he was five. Wannabe dancer Jason Orange, then twenty, from Wythenshawe, Manchester, had finished school with no qualifications and started work on a YTS scheme as an apprentice painter and decorator with the local council. Fellow Mancunian Howard Donald, the eldest at twenty-two, was a keen amateur break-dancer who had left school at sixteen and done a YTS course as a car sprayer.

The youngest, sixteen-year-old Stoke-born Robert Peter Williams, had his mother, Jan, to thank for getting him the job in the band. Hearing that Martin-Smith was putting together a group, Jan persuaded a local boxing promoter, Pat Brogan, to ring a friend at the BBC in Manchester who was able to make the introduction to the would-be impresario. Jan typed out Rob's CV, in which she proudly detailed her son's appearance as the Artful Dodger in the North Staffordshire Amateur Operatic Society's production of *Oliver!* She also wrote that he had won his first professional acting role at the age of nine, as the lead child in a production of *Hans Christian Anderson*, and had appeared in *Chitty Chitty Bang Bang* at the Theatre Royal, Hanley. Rob had then played the king's son in *The King and I* and, when he was eleven, starred as the fiddler in the Theatre Royal production of *Fiddler on the Roof*. At thirteen, while he was a pupil at St Margaret Ward High School in Stoke, he played the part of Fat Boy in a stage production of Charles Dickens's *The Pickwick Papers*. Jan said he had done work experience at Stoke's commercial station, Signal Radio, where they had let him record a couple of voiceovers. At the same time, he had applied to be a presenter on hospital radio and was also writing his own rap and hip-hop songs. She signed off with a quote from her stage-struck son: 'I have only one ambition, which is TO BE FAMOUS.'

Jan found out that Rob had been selected for an audition for the band while he was on holiday in Wales, staying with his father, Pete, from whom she had split in 1977, when Rob was three. Pete, an itinerant comedian, singer and compere, was entertaining the campers during the summer season at the Carmarthen Bay Caravan Park. A panicking Jan started trying to get hold of her ex-husband to tell him to bring Rob back home to Stoke asap. When eventually she tracked down Pete, he then had to do likewise with his son, who had licence to roam the campsite all day and often went hours without running into his father. Pete put the word out and Rob was finally located. Pete got Rob's gear packed up and in his car and they raced off to nearby Carmarthen, where the teenager could catch a bus home. En route, however, Pete ran out of petrol and, terrified he would incur the wrath of his ex, begged a lift from a local pub landlord to the bus station.

Jan took Rob to the audition in Manchester and Nigel Martin-Smith remembers that she had obviously trained him to leave a room properly, like they teach girls at finishing school. His voice was nice enough, and despite his young age, he had charisma to burn. In fact, Martin-Smith decided even before he heard Rob sing that he had to be in the band, which he had originally planned to call Kick It, but settled on Take That after seeing a Madonna poster emblazoned with the words 'Take that and party'.

Martin-Smith also decided unilaterally on a name change for his youngest band member. From now on, he announced, Robert Williams would be Robbie. Nigel said 'Robbie' sounded more playful, more cheeky and would fit better with the joker role that he wanted him to fill in the band. Rob wasn't keen, but went along with what his future boss told him. At the audition proper, Rob impressed with the dance moves he had been practising in the mirror at home for months.

A sixth hopeful at the try-out, who wore short trousers, had acne and looked a bit like Robert Smith from the Cure, was summarily dismissed by Martin-Smith when it quickly became apparent that his tilt at boy-band stardom would be severely hampered by tone deafness and serious coordination issues. Gary and the others quietly registered the way Nigel gave the lad the brush-off, dismissing him without any apparent concern for his feelings. It seemed cold and hard. Nigel then took the five successful candidates to celebrate in the cafeteria of British Home Stores.

Martin-Smith already knew Gary. The manager had invited him to his office earlier that summer after the nineteen-year-old budding singer-songwriter sent out pictures of himself to a bunch of local managers in the hope of finding someone to represent him. At the end of their first meeting, Nigel half-heartedly agreed to listen to some of the teenager's songs, which he'd handed him on a tape. The next morning, as Gary was washing his car, the call came through from an impressed Nigel. He invited Gary back in that afternoon and announced he was going to build a band around him. Gary was not short of offers. He had just been given the chance of a twelve-month contract performing on the SS *Canberra* and was already a veteran of the Northern club circuit.

He had acquired a taste for performing by doing magic shows for his family at home in Frodsham and won the lead role in *Joseph and the Amazing Technicolor Dreamcoat* during his last year at Weaver Vale Primary School. Later, after hearing synth band Depeche Mode singing 'Just Can't Get Enough' on *Top of the Pops* in October 1981, he pestered his parents for a Yamaha PS-2 keyboard he had seen in Rushworths music shop in Chester. Discovering that he had a flare not only for picking out chords and melodies, but also for programming simple drum patterns and bass lines, the ten-year-old Gary soon realized he had grown out of the PS-2, with its limited two-octave range, and set about an almost constant process of upgrading his musical and recording equipment. By the time he was in his early teens, his distinctly nerdy obsession with the latest technology meant that Gary had so much hardware in his tiny bedroom at the family bungalow that there was no room for his bed, so for three years he slept downstairs on the sofa.

Mornings before school, lunch hours and every evening were spent practising and writing songs, and by the time he was thirteen, Gary's expensive hobby had already begun to pay for itself. In early 1984, his mother entered him for a talent contest being sponsored by the *Chester Observer* and the Greenall Whitley brewery. He was pipped to victory by a husband-and-wife duo, but his performance was enough to land him the job of resident organist at Connah's Quay Labour Club in Flintshire, North Wales, earning £18 for his 8 p.m. to 10.30 p.m. spot. Gary, in his red shirt and black dicky bow, entertained the pint-supping punters with Paul McCartney's 'Pipes of Peace' and 'All I Have to Do Is Dream' by the Everly Brothers.

The next six years would see him learn his trade in the workingmen's clubs and nightclubs of Widnes, Runcorn and Liverpool, and backing visiting comics like Bob Monkhouse, Russ Abbot and Ken Dodd. His few free evenings were rarely spent revising for the six O levels he would eventually scrape together. Instead, he passed the time writing songs in his bedroom, including, at the tender age of fifteen, 'A Million Love Songs', which would go on to reach number seven following its release as Take That's sixth single in October 1992. By the time he left Frodsham High School, Gary was earning more than his dad, regularly doing three nights a week in Blackpool for £50 a time and spending Fridays, Saturdays and Sundays closer to home at the Halton British Legion, for which he could expect to pocket between £90 and £120 a night. He invested in a Ford Orion to transport his gear between venues, and at the point he joined Take That, three years after leaving school, he had saved £4,500 to see him through the financially straitened times of the group's early days. Crucially, as well as his modest financial cushion, Gary's years of honing his act on a nightly basis also gave him a professionalism that was then woefully lacking in the other four, who were, in the case of Jason and Howard, hired for their skills as dancers and, in the case of Mark, cherubic good looks.

Over the years there has been a certain amount of revisionism at work when it comes to the early history of Take That. What is beyond doubt is that when Nigel Martin-Smith found out by happy coincidence that his five boys were suddenly as interesting to gingham-wearing teenage girls as they had been to the moustachioed leather-clad brigade, he was not slow to bring all his entrepreneurial and managerial brilliance to bear. But when Take That were formed, in August 1990, the simple fact was that Martin-Smith had yet to see beyond cashing in on the pink pound when it came to his handsome, fresh-faced young charges. Their first gig, shortly after the band was formed, took place in an almost empty straight nightclub called Flicks in Huddersfield. The band came away from the night with £20 between them. The gay clubs Martin-Smith immediately began booking them into paid substantially better.

In the early days, those responsible for the band's publicity had a knack for tailoring the 'facts' of the birth of Take That to whichever media outlet they were talking to. In the years to come, however, Martin-Smith would claim that his intention had always been to play with the issue of Take That's sexuality, to leave the audience guessing about which side the boys batted for. In order for this to work, so the history goes, Nigel famously decreed that the members of the group should observe the most draconian of morality clauses. A strict edict was issued to the five that they must on no account ever be seen with girlfriends or even discuss having them, in order to maintain the 'are they, aren't they?' mystique.

Surely, though, it is not a strategy that stands up to the most cursory of dissections. What possible benefit could there be in attempting to convince a young female fan, high on hormones and adolescent longing, that the object of her affections might prefer to get into her older brother's Calvin Kleins? Wouldn't she be inclined to move her affections on to someone who – in theory at least – was a bit more attainable? The whole thing simply does not stack up.

Nigel's tactic was just as confusing to the band members. 'Gay clubs were such a key component of the plan for Take That's world domination,' Gary wrote in his 2006 autobiography, *My Take*. 'I for one had never considered who our audience was going to be – if asked, I would probably have said people our age and younger. We didn't care who they were – gay, black, straight, bisexual or whatever – just as long as we had a following. Nigel's route into the music scene was through the gay clubs. In one sense, it was a mad approach (the gay market has its limitations).' But as Gary was the first to acknowledge, the gay clubs did pay, albeit only up to £80 a night.

Nevertheless, Gary was not exactly comfortable with having to maintain the ambiguity. 'I'd come out of interviews and realize I'd not said a word of truth,' Gary said later. 'We were told particularly never to mention girlfriends, or any girls at all in fact – it seemed ludicrous and made us look daft.'

In truth, early on there was precious little ambiguity on show, particularly in Take That's maiden television appearance a month before Gary's American holiday with Nigel. Miming to a tape in a dance studio in Manchester on the local BBC evening news programme *North-West Tonight*, Take That could not have looked more gay if the five of them had minced around Union Square, San Francisco, clutching Abba albums, whistling show tunes and shrieking, 'You bitch!' at each other. Gary, with his newly blond hair spiked, went topless, a red hanky tied round his neck, and wore three-quarter-length red satin cycling shorts and a black leather belt. For his part, Mark appeared to be going for Central Casting's stock rent-boy look, all peroxide and body piercing, while Howard wore tiny cut-off denim shorts and a baggy T-shirt. Not to be outdone, Robbie donned a shrink-wrap cycling top and shorts emblazoned with the Pepsi logo.

So, added to the fact that Marjorie Barlow knew the recently formed Take That, of which her son was a key member, had spent the previous weeks trawling their brand of blatant turbo-charged gay fetishism around the gay clubs of the North, it is fair to assume that she would have needed to have been in possession of very few of her faculties not to have had her suspicions about her son's sexuality. Either way, as Gary enjoyed his holiday with his new manager in Florida, she wanted him to know she was proud of him. If she was concerned that Gary was bunking down with an older man, she certainly did not let on. For his part, Gary was quick to point out that although he did share a room with Martin-Smith, he was relieved when they arrived at their Orlando hotel to find that Nigel's intentions were honourable and the accommodation he'd booked contained twin beds.

Previously that year, Gary, with boyish certainty, had drawn up in his Filofax a roll-call of the things he expected to achieve in life. One of the items on the wish list was going to Disneyland. (The others included appearing on *Top of the Pops* and owning a Ferrari Testarossa.) He was, it seems, more than happy to tick off one of his ambitions.

At home in his mother Jan's house in Stoke-on-Trent, Robbie was far from happy. Gary's holiday with Nigel had served only to crystallize his nascent antagonism towards Barlow. Even during their very first meeting at the Take That auditions, Williams had eyed Barlow with disdain after spotting him sitting in an alcove at the nightclub wearing glasses, holding a briefcase and sporting a seriously uncool pair of Converse trainers. His jealousy over the Florida trip would establish a template for not only his future volatile relationship with Gary, but also his dysfunctional and obsessive relationship with Martin-Smith. It lit the touchpaper of a burning, corrosive resentment that would eventually lead to the demise of the group. Later, long after leaving Take That, Rob would reflect on his feud with Nigel: 'I hated him because I loved him so much and I just wanted him to love me back.' For his part, Gary gave every sign of revelling in Nigel's attention. Barlow would later admit that he was well aware that those surrounding Nigel, including the girls who worked in his office, thought Gary was gay, and that he enjoyed playing up to it. It was, as far as he was concerned, just a harmless charade.

So was there more than just a professional aspect to Rob's jealousy of the close, though entirely innocent, relationship between Gary and Nigel? There is little doubt that the sixteen-year-old Williams had become infatuated with his manager. He quickly became drawn to Martin-Smith's confidence, certainty and power. Martin-Smith, who was sixteen years his senior, must have seemed endlessly sophisticated to a naive kid from Stoke. Nigel drove a flashy Ford Escort XR3i, sipped Bacardi and Coke, and was rarely seen before eleven in the morning because he would be out almost seven nights a week clubbing it in Manchester city centre. Rob has since spoken to friends about initially being 'mesmerized' by Nigel, of being simultaneously drawn to, repulsed and frightened by him, but of willingly becoming the disciple of his charismatic and Svengali-like manager. At the same time, however, he felt an almost instant and overwhelming desire to rebel against the strictures imposed on him by Martin-Smith. Rob hated the regular bollockings for being late, for messing around during rehearsals, for getting harmonies wrong or for it taking the group too long to lug their kit into the Salford Van Hire Transit that was their second home at the beginning. He railed against the regular threats that if he or the others didn't pull their weight, they would be out and some other kid would get the chance to cash in the golden ticket.

All the boys were scared of Nigel, wary of being on the end of one of his withering put-downs, almost always delivered in little more than a whisper of cool disdain, and Robbie was not the only one singled out for Nigel's regular verbal volleys. Jason, who was universally accepted among the members of the group to be the one Nigel had the hots for, was perversely also one of those most likely to receive a tongue-lashing. Gary was quickly established as top of the Take That pecking order so far as their manager was concerned, closely followed by the quiet Howard, but that is not to say that even Gary was not in constant fear of getting on the wrong side of Nigel. Tellingly, years later, after notching up countless million record sales, Ivor Novello awards and a stack of Brits, Gary would admit that he still got nervous whenever he phoned his office. While it is clear, however, that the early Take That regime under Martin-Smith was no picnic, it is worth reminding ourselves what the manager was having to deal with. Here, after all, was a bunch of lads who barely knew each other and had no immediate sense of communal responsibility. Without the discipline that Martin-Smith imposed – his constant cajoling and insistence they put in the hours on their singing and dance moves – it is highly unlikely they would have succeeded to the degree they did in such a highly competitive market.

So what of Robbie? For their part, few people I have spoken to

who surrounded the group in those early days did not think that
Rob was struggling with issues surrounding his sexuality. One of
those convinced that Robbie was gay was apparently Nigel himself.
Years later, Williams told his biographer, Chris Heath, that
although Martin-Smith never made a pass at him, Nigel was 'definitely, definitely sure, because he told people that I was gay. I was
definitely gay.'

Given the environment in which he had found himself, it might
seem surprising if a boy who had left school just a couple of months
earlier had not questioned his own sexuality. It goes without saying,
however, that being in the band and performing at gay clubs with
their occasionally seedy clientele was a highly unusual education
for Rob. It has to be stated on the record that Williams has always
maintained he found the experience of playing to gay audiences
nothing but fun, and there is clear evidence that Nigel, who took
a paternal approach to the boys, did his best to protect his young
charges from unwanted attention. Nevertheless, songwriter Ray
Heffernan, who was to befriend Robbie some years later and write
an early version of his hit 'Angels' with him, insisted in conversations with me that Rob told him he had been scarred by the
experience.

What is certainly true is that, for whatever reason, Rob was
almost immediately unhappy in Take That and considering quitting
the group. Within months he went to his father, Pete, to tell him
he wanted out. Pete, a show-business stalwart himself, was well
placed to offer his son advice. Rob asked his father if he could get
him a job as a Blue Coat at one of the holiday camps where he
worked, but Pete persuaded him to stick with it. 'I told Rob to
imagine how he'd feel if he left that group and they went on to
have a number-one hit without him,' Pete told me. 'I'd worked with

a lot of gay people in the clubs down the years and always got on great with them. That's the business and I didn't have a problem with him mixing in those circles.'

Pete's pep talk convinced Rob to stay put for the time being, but his conflicted feelings about Nigel and Gary remained. In its most basic form, Robbie's early antipathy towards Gary could be traced back to a simple clash of egos over the clearly defined pecking order that was set in place by Nigel Martin-Smith when he formed the group.

Gary knew from the outset that he was the top dog and it quickly became evident that he was Nigel's favourite – his holiday à deux with Martin-Smith serving as concrete evidence to Rob if any were needed. From the beginning the two teenagers had been vying for Nigel's attention. Indeed, it became fairly common practice for all the members of Take That to attempt to use their charms to butter up their demanding boss. Gary would later confess: 'In the same way that pretty girls use their beauty to get their way, I think we'd all started to realize that we could manage Nigel a little if we played up to him. Giving him the odd kiss, hug or bit of attention would give us some leverage.' It was a tactic that Robbie was certainly not immune to employing with Nigel when he wanted something.

According to both Robbie and Gary, however, from the outset Martin-Smith skilfully employed a policy of divide and rule between the five wannabes. The fact that they had been thrown together as strangers meant there was little scope for solidarity among the boys. Soon after the group was formed, Jason was a few minutes late for a rendezvous where he was due to be picked up by the van carrying the lads to a photo shoot in London. With Jason finally on board, Nigel's annoyance over his tardiness festered until he ordered the van to turn round and dump him back in Wythenshawe, where Orange lived. The group, Martin-Smith announced, were from that moment forward a four-piece. Although he would later relent and reinstate Jason, not one of the others stood up for him. Even worse, as soon as they were back en route to London, Robbie was rummaging through the stage gear of his sacked colleague looking for something he could wear to the shoot.

'It seemed that Nigel's big anxiety was that we would become too independent,' Gary says, 'or get close to someone other than him. He kept close tabs on all of us; I suppose we were like five monkeys in a cage all going off in different directions. If so, he was the ringmaster.' Gary now candidly admits that he 'played the game' by making Nigel feel he was always on his side. It is worth pointing out, however, that in recent years, when truth and reconciliation have been the buzzwords among the five, Martin-Smith has become the fairly convenient fall guy.

Oddly, given the mayhem they would soon provoke among the nation's young females, Take That somewhat stumbled into their collective roles in a million schoolgirl fantasies. To begin with, Nigel had been struggling to book them two gigs a week at the gay clubs he still believed offered the band their biggest audience. The realization that they just might be barking up the wrong tree came several months after their formation, when the lads were booked to do an early evening show at a club in Hull called Lexington Avenue. They spent the trip in the van bitching about Nigel for booking them to do a 6 p.m. show, fully expecting the place to be empty. To their puzzlement, they found the venue crammed with eleven- to fifteen-year-old girls. In the interests of decorum, the band made an executive decision to wear a few more clothes than they would have for one of their usual gay-club shows, but still there was enough Lycra and skintight shorts on display to send their young audience into a frenzy of hormones and hair gel. After the show, the group rang Nigel at home in Manchester and told him to get them into every under-eighteens club he could find. Later Nigel booked them on a tour of schools in conjunction with the Family Planning Association to promote safe sex. It meant long days, often performing three shows. They could expect to appear at a school in the morning, then do a matinee show, an under-eighteens club and an over-eighteens club all in the same day, before getting back in Nigel's car or the Transit and heading home or to a cheap hotel. It was hard work, but Take That had at least found their metier.

Even so it would be two years of relentless grind before the breakthrough hit came, and the band's gay image wouldn't be discarded wholesale for some time yet. In fact, it was still very much in evidence when Take That released their first single, the Barlow-penned 'Do What U Like', in July 1991. Without a record deal, Martin-Smith founded his own label, Dance UK, to put out the song, a lacklustre attempt to cash in on the house-music craze. He also invested £5,000 on an unashamedly lowest-common-denominator video that featured the lads frolicking naked in gallons of multicoloured jelly. Nigel was determined to get the video banned in an attempt to procure some cheap PR for the band, but despite his best efforts to drum up publicity, it only helped the record enter the UK charts at number eighty-two.

The song was, however, enough to get them a deal with RCA in September of that year, and two months later, a second single, 'Promises', entered the charts at number thirty-eight. Ecstatic at having a top-forty hit, the five lads excitedly jumped up and down on Howard's bed at the Regency Hotel in London, breaking it, but the single disappeared out of the chart the following week and their third offering, 'Once You've Tasted Love', which was released in February 1992, only reached a disappointing number forty-four.

During the recording of the song, Gary was despatched to London for three weeks to work sixteen-hour days in the studio with producer Duncan Bridgeman, while the others remained in Manchester. Only in the last three or four days of recording were the others finally sent for to add their backing vocals. It was an early sign not only of the faith Martin-Smith put in his talented front man, but also of the extent to which Gary was content to take on the mantle of the band's leader. Unsurprisingly, Robbie, with his aspirations to sing lead vocals and contribute to the writing of the songs, was riled by Barlow's position as top dog, but the jealousy was not a one-way street. As they slogged up and down the country trying to build a fan base, Gary watched with a combination of awe and covetousness the unforced way Rob found an instant rapport with their audiences, how, while the others stuck rigidly to the meticulously rehearsed dance routines, he would throw in a few pratfalls, ad-lib easily with the crowd and in the process steal the show.

It was a symbol, too, of how even early on Williams was constrained by the rigid Take That policy of corporate responsibility. He would drive the others, and particularly Martin-Smith, mad by constantly getting his dance moves wrong or messing about on stage. A psychoanalyst would probably say he was already set on a course of destruction, of himself and the band itself. The truth was that as well as being driven by envy when it came to Barlow's position as Take That's unrivalled focal point, Williams considered the whole boy-band concept to be lame, had found the dancing embarrassing even as far back as his audition for the band and cringed inwardly on stage. His play-acting and horsing around were simply an attempt on his part to wrest back some control, to take on, if only subconsciously, the implacable Take That dogma.

By the time 'It Only Takes a Minute', released in May 1992, become the band's first hit, reaching number seven in the UK and number eleven in Ireland, the eventual spontaneous combustion of Rob's relationship with Martin-Smith and the others was already set on its inexorable path. If the single's success brought a belated end to the manager's strategy of aiming the band at the gay market, it also shone a spotlight on the fissures that were opening up between them. Rob, who had taken his first Ecstasy tab at a gay club when the band were in Spain, had begun drinking, often alone in his hotel room when they were on the road. Martin-Smith took to holding regular 'behaviour meetings' at which Robbie's misdemeanours would be picked over. Williams even got into trouble with his boss when his grandmother Betty Williams let some of the first Thatters – the band's fanatical girl fans – into her home in Stoke for a chat about Robbie. In return, Rob christened the management, with its multiplicity of rules, 'Take That Towers'. Meanwhile, he got on the wrong side of Martin-Smith for breaking the strict no-girls code. In Monte Carlo at the plush Loews Hotel, he was so desperate not to be spotted by his manager sneaking out at night to meet a girl fan that he drunkenly took his life in his hands by negotiating his way to her room via a series of balconies high above the Mediterranean.

The situation only became more problematic once it was complicated by the arrival of fame and, like an invading hormonal horde, the sudden appearance of legions of sexually flowering schoolgirls, brandishing Sony Walkmans and rolled-up copies of *Smash Hits*. The phenomenon of the Thatter only grew with the next single, 'I Found Heaven', and with arguably the group's first classic, 'A Million Love Songs', the Barlow-penned tear-jerker that got to number seven in October 1992 and also managed to dent the Dutch charts.

Robbie was allowed to take over the lead-vocal duties on a remake of Barry Manilow's 'Could It Be Magic' in February 1993, which got to number three in Britain and charted in Germany, Australia, Sweden and Ireland, but ironically that only served to intensify his sense of discontent and yearning to take what he believed was his rightful place centre stage. The follow-up, 'Why Can't I Wake Up With You?', established Take That as the next big thing in British pop. Rob's home in Greenbank Road, Tunstall, where he lived with his mother, became an instant shrine for up to 300 girls at a time. They came bearing life-size posters of their hero and tubes of Clearasil to mount messy vigils on the pavement outside. It signalled the onset of age-of-twilight living for Jan, who would later flee the house; she drew her curtains and refused to open them again for the next three years.

In an exhilarating period of five months between July and December 1993 the band scored their first three number ones. First came another Barlow classic, the ballad 'Pray'. It was followed by the ridiculously camp 'Relight My Fire', which inexplicably contained three minutes of banshee-like screeching from former Eurovision Song Contest winner Lulu. Another of Gary's songs, 'Babe', on which Mark took the lead vocal, topped the chart at the end of the year.

By early 1994, and a dozen singles into their career, four members of the band were still surviving for the most part on the £150 a week they were paid by their management as they waited for the serious royalty payments to kick in. One, however, was doing decidedly better.

CHAPTER TWO

His Master's Voice

Two in the afternoon and a liveried butler bearing a silver breakfast tray is navigating an obstacle course laid out on the plush carpet of a well-appointed bedroom. Pairs of trousers, T-shirts, socks and shoes, and a couple of carrier bags stuffed with clothes dot the floor like a messy archipelago as he tiptoes his way stealthily around in the semi-darkness of the room. Spreadeagled naked on his front on the large double bed is Robbie Williams. The previous evening, he was clearly too tired even to pull back the covers before collapsing into sleep and is now snoring noisily, his fingers still clutching a half-open pack of Silk Cut. Through the open door, drifting in from the hallway, can be heard the distant stop-start tinkling of a piano.

In early 1994, Gary paid £300,000 for a house called Moorside in the Cheshire village of Plumley. With its private driveway and gates to keep out fans, the house was, in Gary's eyes at least, a baby-grand version of Woodside, the lavish pile in Old Windsor, Berkshire, that had been Elton John's home since the mid-seventies. In reality, nice as it was, Gary's new des res owed about as much to Elton's lavish estate as Subbuteo does to Wembley

Stadium, but nonetheless it gave Gary the chance to own what he christened his 'mini-me mansion'.

Indeed, he had taken rather effortlessly to his newfound role of landed gent. It was Elton who not only provided the inspiration for Gary moving up in the world, but also put his impeccable credentials to use as principal mentor in his new protégé's steady progress towards genuine rock-star excess. For his part, Gary, who had worshipped Elton ever since he could remember, was a more than willing student. The older man, in the role of spiritual and material guide, had devoted hours to showing Gary around his huge collection of art, which included works by Magritte, Picasso, Bacon and Warhol, as well as photographs by Helmut Newton.

Gary and Elton had first met in summer 1993, when Paula Yates, who somewhat bizarrely had attached herself to Take That as their oldest and most famous groupie, brought Elton backstage to introduce him to the boys on the last of three nights the band performed at Wembley Arena in July. The Party Tour, which began the previous November, had been the band's first national tour and progressed quickly in the period of a few months from modest venues like Scarborough's Futurist Theatre to arenas such as Glasgow's 8,000-seater SECC and the NEC in Birmingham. Yates, who was at the time married to Live Aid founder Bob Geldof, developed such a near obsession with Jason Orange after she interviewed the five lads on her bed on Channel 4's *The Big Breakfast* that Jason's worried mum had felt it necessary to warn Paula off her son. Undeterred, Yates followed the band all over the country and they once got off a flight in Amsterdam to find her excitedly waiting for them on the tarmac. Indeed, in the end she became something of an irritant and was routinely the subject of derogatory stage whispers from some of the more outspoken of Take That's backstage crew. For the most part, however, she was tolerated by the band, although Gary disapproved of her leaving her young family behind while she humiliated herself chasing the boy band up and down the country.

Paula also turned up as an uninvited guest when the five boys and Nigel were invited for dinner at Elton's house for the first time at the end of July 1993, their bus being met by two uniformed butlers at the front door. After dinner, the other four persuaded a nervous Gary to play one of his songs, 'The Party Is Over', on their host's white grand piano before Elton, keen to show off his own skills, serenaded the rapt contingent with 'Your Song'. Later, Elton, with the trained eye of an ex-junkie, focused on Robbie as he issued his young guests with the warning: 'After twenty-five years in the business, there's one thing I can tell you: stay away from fucking cocaine. Don't go near it. I can't even begin to add up the money I've spent on that drug. It can ruin your life.'

It was the beginning of a warm friendship between Gary and Elton, though Nigel Martin-Smith had been suspicious to start with that Elton's then manager and former lover, John Reid, was angling to take over the management of the band – a fear that turned out to be groundless. Before long, Gary was regularly pitching up at Woodside, where he and his hero would sit in Elton's Rolls-Royce and listen to the maestro's latest recordings through the car's finely tuned speakers. Gary quickly became seduced by the older man's lifestyle and set out to emulate his idol. So it was that Barlow came to hire, at Elton's suggestion, a butler to take care of his every whim. The servant, a slightly fey but thoroughly efficient man named Maurice, was taken on shortly after Gary bought the house in Plumley. At the end of the day, the gentleman's gentleman would return to his own humbler digs nearby – a three-bedroom postwar prefab bungalow in Bexton Road, Knutsford. It had briefly been home to Gary, who bought the house two years earlier, soon after Take That's fourth single, 'It Only Takes a Minute', was released, in spring 1992. Gary got his elder brother, Ian, a builder, to do it up for him, but soon outgrew it.

Now with his own butler in situ, Gary chose to add to his staff by taking on his father, Colin, recently retired from his job as a project manager for a fertilizer company, to become the full-time gardener. For Gary, it was the start of a wave of big spending that was, while rampant by everyday standards, nonetheless conducted with the eye for financial caution that has been the bedrock of the Barlow approach to money. Simply put, in the eyes of the others at least, Gary was at the time a bit tight. His excesses, therefore, must be considered in the context of his reluctance to part with his cash. As an example of his carefulness, during the early days of Take That Gary invested in an early brick of a mobile phone and insisted that Robbie pay him £1 up front to borrow it to call his mum. To add insult to injury, Gary would also insist that after gigs their van would drop Rob off at the Trust House Forte services on the M6, from where he would have to wait to be collected by Jan, rather than taking the short detour to drop him at her front door in Stoke. The issue of Gary's inflated wealth when compared to his band mates was increasingly to become a source of discontent among the other four, particularly Robbie.

But while Gary's undoubted musical superiority was, for the most part, accepted in those first years by the other members of Take That as being a simple matter of fact, it was his exalted status as the major breadwinner in the group that quickly became a source of simmering dissatisfaction for them. When, after more than a year of trying, the band was signed by RCA in September 1991, they were paid a £75,000 advance, but that figure had to be divided between the five members; plus Nigel, according to Gary, was at the time taking a 25 per cent cut of the group's earnings (though later he would offer to reduce his commission to 20 per cent). Then there were the expenses that were owed to Martin-Smith, who for more than a year had put his hand in his own pocket to keep them on the road. He had even remortgaged his house to set up his own record label to release Take That's first single, 'Do What U Like'. Suffice to say that once everything had been taken into consideration, their individual cheques were not the small fortune they had been banking on.

Not that Gary need care. A month after doing the deal with RCA, he signed his own publishing contract with Virgin Music Publishing for £150,000. A stipulation of the deal was that the other four would also have to sign up, but because Gary was the group's sole songwriter, only he would be paid the advance. Already Barlow was in a different financial league to the others and over time the issue of cash would become an open sore. In his autobiography, Gary conceded that it must have rankled.

Not, it should be said, that, to begin with at least, Gary was one to flash the cash. At Nigel's suggestion, the sensible Barlow put his nest egg in a NatWest Money Market account that he could only access with Martin-Smith's countersignature. Instead of spending his earnings, Gary would occasionally go to a hole-in-the-wall machine just to marvel at his bank balance without drawing a penny. Meanwhile, the other members of the band would seethe over the £1,000 a week Barlow charged Take That for using his own keyboards when they were on tour. Gary's off-hand response to their complaints was that it was cheaper for them than if they rented the gear from a music shop.

Legends quickly grew up among the band about Gary's thrifti-
ness. Robbie, who dubbed him Ebenezer Barlow, would visit Gary
at home in the winter and find him sitting at his piano in a duffel
coat so he didn't have to put the heating on. He also insisted on
re-boiling a kettle instead of refilling it with cold water in order to
save on energy costs. According to Williams, Gary would not always
use his indicator lights when driving because, he claimed, it saved
the battery, and would keep his specially ground Arabica coffee for
himself, while offering visitors to his home instant from an
economy-sized tub of Nescafé. On another visit to Gary's house,
Rob noticed that his rival had bought a Mercedes 350 but had put
the badge from the more expensive Mercedes 500 on it. Gary also
left his cohorts, who were making more modest sums, spitting blood
during one band meeting by announcing: 'I don't believe it, lads!
I've just been given a cheque for two and a half million pounds.'
Given Gary's tender years and his relatively humble background,
he can, of course, be forgiven for his excitement at his sudden
wealth, but his careful approach to money would not be shared by
Robbie when his own not insubstantial earnings began to filter
through. Some years later, when he was handed a £500,000 cheque
by Take That's management, Williams would settle on an infinitely
more rock-'n'-roll course of action and use it to snort a line of
cocaine.

Gary's investment in his new house in Plumley was to be the
beginning of his own flirtation with decadence. With at last some
serious wall space at his disposal, he set about purchasing the sort
of sculptures and paintings he had seen displayed in Elton John's
place. Before long, Gary would be trawling art galleries all over
Europe in search of finds. His taste for high art, first acquired under
Elton John's tutelage, only intensified thanks to another new

friendship, this time with Gianni Versace, whose spendthrift nature even eclipsed that of Elton. Take That were invited to Versace's lavish home, Villa Fontanelle, on Lake Como following the release of the band's fifth UK number one, 'Sure', in October 1994 after he announced himself to be a fan. Inspired by the Italian designer's ornate digs, Gary began shopping with a new vigour. Innumerable Italian oils of battlefields and cupids by Panini and Giordano were snapped up, and bronze and marble figures were regularly crated up to be shipped from Milan and Rome to Cheshire. In Paris, Gary, who Rob recalls commenting on his excess if he spent anything over £50 on an outfit, would think nothing of splashing out £75,000 on a pair of paintings.

Years later, and by now living in Los Angeles, Williams took to playing home movies to his friends shot by Gary in their Take That days. With Barlow as cameraman and director, the majority of the footage would more often than not linger proudly on the latest antique addition to Gary's home, with Barlow himself giving a suitably reverent voiceover about some aspect of its provenance. Invariably, however, the screenings would be accompanied by the sound of Rob wetting himself with laughter and shouting: 'Look at his fucking candlesticks!'

After Gary moved into Moorside, Robbie became a regular overnight visitor. Rob had begun taking flights to Dublin for weekends with his mum or on the lash with his mates, and when he returned to Manchester Airport, he would often take a cab to Gary's and crash out for a couple of nights to get over the excesses of the previous days. Barlow's butler would make him toast and flit around tidying up the mess that Rob routinely made of his bedroom. While Robbie slept well into the afternoon, Gary would spend his days downstairs at the piano penning the latest Take That hit. On other evenings, Robbie and his then girlfriend, actress Samantha Beckinsale, would pop over for dinner.

It is a picture of the apparently close relationship between the two men at the time that flies in the face of Williams's later assertion that they had never been friends. After leaving the group, little more than a year later, Robbie was saying in interviews that his relationship with Barlow had been so distant and strained from the outset that he would feel immediately uncomfortable if he had to sit next to Gary on a flight. Shortly after quitting Take That in July 1995, Williams told one interviewer: 'The fans think they know the guys, but they don't, no one does. We used to tell people in interviews that if we weren't in Take That, we would still have been mates. Well, I'm sorry to say that just isn't true. What we had was strictly business.' In a prelude to the conflict to come, Rob said that, despite living and working with Gary Barlow almost every day for five years, he still felt he didn't know him.

Little wonder, then, that Barlow would feel with some justification that Robbie had quickly set about rewriting the history of their relationship, with Gary conveniently painted as remote and unapproachable. Barlow's version of events is markedly different. He remembers well how he would call Rob and, no matter what time of day or night it was, his band mate would always be up for coming over to Moorside to lay down a rap or lyrics on a new Barlow composition. Gary is also adamant that if there was bad feeling between the two men, it was never, ever expressed by Rob. Indeed, others within the Take That set-up corroborate Gary's assertion that there weren't many signs to spot and that Robbie had always been one of his biggest supporters, constantly complimenting him on his songs.

Given that Rob would later issue a damning assessment of Barlow's talent as both a songwriter and a vocalist, there was all the more reason for Gary to be confused. But it is here that one of the principal flaws in Gary's ability to relate not only to Williams, but also to Owen, Donald and Orange during Take That's first incarnation is most glaringly displayed. Naively and thoughtlessly, Gary laboured under the false impression that if the others were not complaining about his behaviour to his face, then they must, surely, have been content with the situation. Increasingly, however, they were not. Indeed, there is evidence that Barlow's leadership of the group was not half as benign as he was prepared to admit to himself during that period.

Almost from the outset Gary had fallen relatively easily into the role of Nigel Martin-Smith's eyes and ears within the quintet. More damagingly for his relationship with Williams, he had also acquired some of the darker character traits of the band's manager – the very ones that Robbie had quickly grown to hate. Egged on by Nigel, Gary soon began to gossip behind the backs of the other boys. Such was Martin-Smith's influence over him that those friends who had known Gary before his days in Take That were taken aback by how effortlessly he slipped into the stereotypical speech patterns and constant bitching of some of the more flamboyant members of Nigel's camp clique. For the record, it should be pointed out that Gary was not alone in turning on his band mates if it meant currying favour with Nigel. The success of what Rob describes as their boss's 'divide and conquer' policy was such that although there were friendships of sorts within the band, with Robbie and Mark frequently partners in crime, particularly in the early days, and Gary and Howard regular drinking buddies, there remained at the core of their relationship the ethos of 'every man for himself'. And in

Gary's defence, it is important to remember that he was just nineteen when he was thrown into the unreal world of life in a pop band. His teenage ego couldn't have failed to be inflated by the fact Martin-Smith made it perfectly plain that as far as he was concerned, Gary was the real talent of the band.

Nevertheless, Nigel could not be blamed for the stranglehold on the recording process that Gary exerted from the outset. One early bone of contention between Barlow and Williams emerged over the recording of 'Once You've Tasted Love', a Gary composition that would become Take That's third single. The song features a rap by Robbie that was incorporated into the recording by one of their early producers, Duncan Bridgeman. Later, Rob approached Nick Raymonde, the band's A&R man at RCA's parent company, BMG, and asked if he could have a writer's credit for his rap contribution to the track. Gary's response was uncompromising. 'Well, if he wants a credit, let's just take it off the song,' he told Raymonde. In the end, the track appeared with a sleeve note that read simply: 'Words and music by Gary Barlow.' Williams was convinced that Gary not only did not want to share the credit for the song, but resented having to part with the 5 per cent of the royalties Robbie's involvement would earn him.

Likewise, Rob was left furious and deflated when, on another occasion, Gary phoned him one evening in late 1993 to say he had a song, called 'Lady Tonight', that he felt could be improved with his input. Delighted that the front man finally seemed prepared to give him a taste of the creative process he desperately craved, Rob, who didn't have a driving licence, waited excitedly for Gary to collect him from his mum's house in Stoke. On the way back to Knutsford, Gary played him the track and Robbie wrote a rap to go along with it, which they recorded back at the house, Rob standing in the bathroom with a microphone to get better acoustics. Again, he would receive no writer's credit when the track was eventually released on Take That's third album, *Nobody Else*, though this time Gary was adamant that he had instructed Nigel to include Robbie's name. It is tempting to see the relationship between the two band members as classic big brother–little brother terrain, with Robbie desperately seeking the older Gary's approval and continually feeling ignored and rejected.

Given Barlow's territoriality, it was perhaps unsurprising that Rob was quickly demoralized. After writing his first ever song, he phoned Gary and sang it to him. Granted, Rob's tentative first effort at composing lyrics concerned that most un-Take That of subjects prostitution, but when he had finished, Williams was crushed to hear a chilly silence on the other end of the line.

'What d'ya think?' Rob asked eventually.

'Well,' Gary replied, 'it'd be all right if you were in Nirvana.'

Other than collaborating with Mark Owen on the bridge of 'Sure', it was to be Robbie's last attempt at writing for the group.

Even so, if Gary's failure to nurture the younger Robbie's as yet unformed talent as a lyricist was regrettable, there were mitigating circumstances. Since the group's inception, Gary had been expected to churn out hit after hit at a pace that would test the creativity and sheer mental endurance of a songwriter of even his undoubted talent. And, as a survivor of the hard knocks that can be dished out on the tough Northern club circuit, he had, peculiarly for his age, an adherence to an old-school mentality that meant if he thought something was crap, he wouldn't hold back from saying so. Not an approach, admittedly, that was likely to bear fruit with the fragile self-confidence of his junior partner Robbie. But then Gary had also been subjected to his own share of blows at the front end of the band's history. After Take That's first two singles for RCA – both written by Barlow – only managed to make the lower reaches of the charts, the band was immediately under pressure. To make matters worse, early on there had been a change of management at RCA's parent company, BMG, when 150 people were made redundant and the jungle drums were beating that Take That's spell on their roster of talent was threatened with an abrupt end. After the euphoria of landing a record deal, there was for the first time among the band (and Nigel Martin-Smith) a sinking feeling that they might be dumped by the record company before they had even had a chance to get going.

Gary took the relative failure of the singles personally. More importantly, he felt that as the one who had been chosen not for his looks or dancing skills but for his ability as a singer and songwriter, he had failed the others. Deep down he feared that his music was not hip enough for a nineties audience and now the rest of the group were on at him to ditch the ballads and love songs that came easiest to him and write more urban songs with attitude in the vein of the hugely successful American boy band New Kids on the Block. He began arriving on the doorstep of Howard's parents' house in Droylsden and hanging out in Howard's bedroom listening to the hip-hop records that his far cooler band mate was into.

Worse was to come when BMG's new president, Jeremy Marsh, issued a damning appraisal of the music Take That had produced thus far. It was on the advice of one of the company's A&R men, a pre-X Factor Simon Cowell, that the powers that be at the label decreed that the band's next single should be a cover of someone else's record. Their version of the 1975 Travares hit 'It Only Takes a Minute' would go on to be Take That's breakthrough single, reaching number seven in the charts, but Gary was initially devastated by the temporary decision to relieve him of his song-writing duties. 'To me, it felt like everyone had lost faith in me as a songwriter,' he admits. 'I'd believed that we had at least partially got our record deal on the strength of my songs. We had built our hopes on my writing and in turn it had got me a publishing deal.'

And if Gary did not have the time for Rob or anyone else, it was, in part at least, due to the fact that he was perennially knack-ered. The band's capacity for work throughout their six-year history was something of a legend in the music business. From their incep-tion Nigel Martin-Smith pushed the five lads hard. Their days consisted of a never-ending round of concerts, recording and promotion that would drain them physically and emotionally. They would often find themselves performing up to four shows a day in a bid to build a fan base.

Between albums they would be packed off to the country in North Wales or Sussex and put up in a farmhouse for weeks on end while they were drilled on their new dance routines for nine or ten hours a day in a marquee erected in the garden. Meanwhile, on tour in Europe and the Far East, they would regularly be required to perform five or six consecutive high-energy shows. Days off were earmarked for travelling to the next gig and started with 6.30 a.m. wake-up calls to catch a flight or climb back on the tour bus. At the beginning of every day on the road, each member of the band would be given a minute-by-minute itinerary detailing yet more interviews, TV performances, signings and meet-and-greets with record-company staff, christened 'grip and grins' by the band members.

What's more, somewhere in this uncompromising schedule, Gary was also expected to find time to write the band's next album. From the outset Gary had taken on the responsibility of not only writing Take That's original material, but of being highly involved in the recording process. It was to set a pattern, with the obsessive Gary relishing his role as Take That's hands-on musical guide and creative force, but such was the scarcity of time that Gary would find himself trying to write songs in hotels after shows or in cars on the way to gigs. One early example of the pressure he was under came with tours to Germany, Holland and Scandinavia that were immediately followed by a promotional push in the US and Canada before heading to Japan. In America, Gary bought an Apple laptop and loaded it with Cubase, the recording and editing software. Then, at the Capitol Hotel in Tokyo, the record company arranged with Yamaha to have the use of five keyboards, all of which were installed in Gary's bedroom. At the end of long, tiring days on the sofas of TV shows, giving interviews in radio booths or performing gigs, and while the other four partied or went to bed, Gary, fortified by peanut butter on toast, would set to work writing the songs for *Everything Changes*, the follow-up to Take That's debut album, *Take That and Party*.

From Gary's perspective, then, he had undoubtedly paid his dues and taken his knocks. Not only that, he had survived the reverses of their disappointing first singles. The simple Barlow logic, therefore, was that if he could use the experience to come back better and stronger, then so could Rob.

For his part, even though Rob was jealous of Gary's unrivalled position as main man and, to a large extent, Nigel's representative on earth, he was also hugely impressed with Barlow's talent. Having said that, it was always in Rob's nature to want to dislodge Gary from his position as numero uno. He was also acutely aware, particularly in the early days, that while he was undoubtedly the more popular with the fans – only the angelic-looking Mark's pile of fan mail was bigger than his – he was in no position to compete with Gary musically.

Rob's sense of discontent and frustration reached critical mass in summer 1995. Ironically, his meltdown came as Take That reached the zenith of their popularity, becoming the most successful male pop band since the Beatles. For several months his drinking had scaled new, worrying heights. He had also supplemented his taste for booze with that most showbizzy of stimulants, cocaine. In early June, the band flew to Berlin to appear in the MTV Europe Music Awards, but Williams spent his time there partying with the other acts and disappearing to the hotel rooms of Kate Moss and Naomi Campbell, in whose starry circle he had been moving for months. By the time rehearsals for the show were due to start, Robbie was off his head and had gone twenty-four hours without sleep. After puking all over his room at the Hilton, a doctor was called to give him an injection of penicillin so he could at least go through the motions on stage.

At the same time, Rob had fallen in with a pretentious band of liggers, hangers-on and thrill-seekers. Calling themselves the Diamond Dogs, after the David Bowie album, the bunch abused his open chequebook by getting him to pay for their hotel rooms, heavy partying and small mountains of coke. Gary attempted to take Rob to one side to warn him that his new group of friends were nothing more than a band of poseurs and parasites, but predictably, Barlow's disapproval only served immeasurably to elevate the Dogs in Robbie's eyes.

Relations between Williams and Martin-Smith were also severely strained by Rob's mother, Jan, taking an increasingly hands-on role in her son's career, not least because Rob had made a point of avoiding where possible any involvement in the business affairs of the band. Important band meetings invariably ended with Rob's pile of papers untouched other than for the doodles of giant pairs of boobs he was inclined to draw to alleviate the tedium of discussing money matters. Jan, who had agreed to be a cosignatory to the contracts when Take That was formed because Rob was still a minor, began taking an interest in his financial affairs on his behalf. She started making appointments to visit the band's accountants to question them about Rob's earnings. Quite understandably given the horror stories she had heard about other artists being ripped off in the music business, Jan decided to make it her job to check that Rob was getting every penny he was entitled to. To Martin-Smith, however, who was equally understandably protective of his unimpeachable reputation for financial propriety, the involvement of Robbie's mother was taken as a show of aggression.

Rob says that it was when he was in Australia with Take That, a year before he left the band, that he first became aware of the problems between his mother and Nigel. According to Williams, the other boys told him they had all been faxed a letter from Martin-Smith that threatened Jan with legal action. He would later describe the letter as condemning Jan and making him out to be the black sheep of the band. He also claimed Martin-Smith was so wary of his mother he made a point of trying to turn the rest of Take That against her. Later, he would describe the falling-out with the other four members of the band in 'No Regrets', which discusses the tensions between the band and his mother.

The inevitable happened in early summer 1995. Robbie announced out of the blue his intention to leave Take That during a meeting at Gary's house after rehearsals for the band's upcoming tour of Britain, Australia and Asia, which was due to kick off at the beginning of August. He informed his band mates and Nigel Martin-Smith that he wanted out and was only prepared to stay to the end of the tour, for which he would earn £1 million. The others responded by telling him how he was letting the band down with his slapdash approach to the dance routines they were supposed to be learning. They pleaded with him that if he would just concentrate on work, keep his head down and play the Take That game, they could walk away in two years' time with £2 million each.

Later, after the five had taken a competition winner out for a curry and Rob had gone back to the room at Manchester's Midland Hotel where he was staying during rehearsals, he claims the other four had another meeting about his future with the band. It was not simply a case of him turning up drunk and uninterested to rehearsals, which were taking place in a Territorial Army barracks in Stockport, Cheshire. It was not even that he had begun refusing to do some of the dance moves he deemed naff and had announced he would do his own dancing on the tour. The other four could simply no longer trust him. One of the more complicated sequences for the upcoming shows involved Rob catching Jason after Orange had performed a daring backflip. Robbie was often so out of it that Jason was terrified he would drop him and that he'd break his neck.

The final straw was Rob's drunken unscheduled appearance at Glastonbury in late June 1995, during which he appeared on stage with Oasis while he was still nominally a member of Take That. It was his way of quite blatantly giving notice that he intended to terminate his employment. Earlier that day, Williams had loaded sixteen bottles of champagne into a borrowed Jaguar and headed off to the Somerset musical festival. Once there, he proceeded to break every Take That convention: he gave slurred and wide-eyed interviews to anyone who asked, was photographed by the paparazzi sprawled on the grass and pissed with a front tooth blacked out, and in an instant blew apart the clean-living, whole-some image that Nigel had so carefully constructed for the band. When he returned to rehearsals the following week, Gary and – more particularly – Jason, working on instructions from Nigel Martin-Smith, told Rob he needed to commit to the band or leave. Williams told them bluntly he no longer intended to be 'Gary Barlow's backing dancer' and walked out.

Amid the warm mood of forgiveness that surrounded Robbie's reunion with Take That in 2010, Jason would say during an ITV documentary, *Look Back, Don't Stare*: 'If you could really and truly measure the reasons why Robbie Williams, at twenty-one, left Take That, you could probably say half and half. Half because he wanted to go and he needed to go and fulfil his destiny, and half because people got annoyed with him and encouraged him to go and effec-tively threw him out. My main feeling was one of relief because it wasn't me. And I beat myself up for a good couple of years for being the spokesperson when Robbie was leaving. In my efforts to ingratiate myself with the management, I joined with the lads in suggesting to Rob that he should go now.'

However, as Williams himself would point out in the same programme, he had not really given the rest of them much of an option other than to demand he walk. 'I did make it easy for them,' he admitted with hindsight. 'It was difficult enough for them without one-fifth of the team self-destructing. We didn't need such a tight rein. We were all desperate. We were all working-class lads, all teenagers given the golden ticket. And you believed that to be the golden ticket, your one chance to not fuck your life up, to make something of yourself. You sort of follow blindly. You don't realize that you're a backing dancer until a few years in. Hang on! I didn't sign up for that. I would have done. I would have signed up to be Gary Barlow's backing dancer, but that was not my understanding of the gig.'

Later, in the immediate wake of Williams's departure from the band, Take That's tour manager, Chris Healey, was absent-mindedly sifting through some papers in his office when he came across several abandoned sheets of A4 paper. He instantly recognized the handwriting as Robbie's and read through the lyrics to two songs. By the time he was reading them for the second time, he was picking up the phone to dial Nigel Martin-Smith. 'They're bloody good,' he told him.

'The songs were about me and the other boys and how unhappy he was,' says Martin-Smith. 'When I saw them, I was gobsmacked. They were clever lyrics.'

If we are seeking clues as to why Rob's feelings towards Gary were deeply conflicted and why ultimately the situation between them became so flammable and destructive, it is worth exploring here Williams's relationship with his father, Pete. There are similarities between Barlow and Williams senior that are hard to ignore. Principal among them was that they were both proud of their apprenticeships on the tough Northern club circuit. Likewise, there was always and there remains now an inherent competitive streak between father and son that mirrored Rob's relationship with Gary. To this day, Williams's relationship with the father he followed into show business – and far eclipsed in terms of success – is based in almost equal measure on Rob's awe of his father as a performer and a sense of competition. This rivalry has at times meant the relationship has fallen victim to hurtful and damaging periods of tension and estrangement.

Like Gary, Pete, who changed his name to Conway at the start of his career in entertainment, was a product of the once thriving working men's clubs, of smoky cabaret-night spots and British Legions, where he learned his craft after an unfulfilling stint as a policeman and a nine-to-five job with English Electric. The year Rob was born, 1974, Pete was appearing in front of 2,000 people a night alongside big clubland stars like Frankie Vaughan and the Barron Knights. He also had a residency at the giant Talk of the Midlands in Derby. In 1973, Pete had become a local hero in Stoke when he won TV's *New Faces*. When, a year later, he appeared in the *New Faces Grand Final*, the news of the young Robert's birth was announced on screen. Pete came third, one place behind Les Dennis.

One of the first things Pete ever said to me was that if he had stayed a policeman, Rob would be walking the beat now in Tunstall. It was said with a wry smile, of course, but Pete was deadly serious. That Rob idolized his father is beyond doubt, but it was always less of a father–son relationship than it was mates, later drinking buddies and – most significantly – master and apprentice. Pete, who was already divorced from his first wife, local beauty Barbara Eeley, when he married Jan in 1970, became a stepfather to Jan's young daughter, Sally. After Jan had Robert, in February 1974, though, she soon got sick of her husband spending days and weeks away performing up and down the country. She persuaded Pete to give up showbiz so they could take up management of a pub, the Red Lion, in the Potteries town of Burslem, when Rob was eighteen months old. The way Pete tells it, the marriage was already in trouble. The long hours running the pub and Pete's bitterness over being talked into giving up his career as an entertainer only made matters worse. In May 1977, he went to Wembley to watch Manchester United play Liverpool in the FA Cup final and did not come back for three months.

With the marriage over, Pete began an itinerant existence, travelling between holiday camps around the country entertaining the punters, and had to make do with occasional weekends with his son. In the school holidays, however, Rob would spend the summer living in Pete's dilapidated caravan at the likes of Perran Sands, in Cornwall, Cayton Bay, Scarborough, or Haven Holidays, Yarmouth. During their long enforced separations, the young Rob used to imagine he had a magic chair that could transport him from his mum's living room in Stoke to whichever holiday camp Pete was working at. When he did finally get to spend time with his father, Rob would have the run of the camps and was let loose in the amusement arcades or to hang around with the Blue Coats. Pete and Rob would play the odd game of pool or table tennis during the day, Pete never letting his son win. Every night Rob watched his father's act, sucking it up, memorizing it and clocking the way his old man held the audience.

It was no surprise that when Rob was ten, he told Pete he wanted to be a Blue Coat, but Pete wasn't happy. He told his son to forget it. Larking about and having a laugh with the punters was one thing, but what he really needed to do was learn his trade, like Pete had done (and like Gary would do) by serving his apprenticeship in the clubs. 'I wanted him to do it properly and learn from all the terrific people who were out there playing to audiences in those days,' says Pete. 'I came from the old school that said you can't do it without going through the training.' The rebuke from his father would not go down well with the young Rob and would have damaging consequences for their relationship in the years to come.

With Robbie's departure from the band, Take That went ahead with what would become the highly successful Nobody Else Tour, which sold an unprecedented ten nights at the newly opened Nynex Arena in Manchester, plus ten nights at London's Earls Court in August 1995. The group's first single promoted as a foursome, 'Never Forget', went to number one, as did their cover of the Bee Gees song 'How Deep Is Your Love' the following February, selling 670,000 copies and going platinum in the UK as well as topping the charts in Denmark, Ireland, Italy and Spain. During a tour of Australia in autumn 1995, however, they had played to arenas that were half empty or worse.

The sense that Take That were reaching a natural conclusion was only intensified by the persistent rumours that Gary had signed a solo deal with their record company almost immediately after Robbie's departure and was also being courted by Clive Davis, the mercurial head of Arista Records in the US, who had earmarked Barlow as the next British singer to break the States. Meanwhile, relations between Nigel Martin-Smith and Jason Orange had broken down over the increasing involvement of his brother, Simon Orange, a successful financial adviser, who had started making investments for Jason and Gary. Finally, says Gary, Nigel came to him and told him he needed to go solo because he was no longer prepared to manage the band. When Take That called a press conference at the Manchester Airport Hilton on 13 February 1996 – Rob's twenty-second birthday – the rumours of their imminent demise had been doing the rounds for weeks.

Gary would later admit that he was spurred on to bail out sooner than he had planned by his concerns that Williams might get a head start on him and the two men prepared to make their individual assaults on the charts. But would there be enough room for both of them?

CHAPTER THREE

Going So Low

In summer 1996, a year after Robbie walked out of Take That amid a mood of acrimony and recrimination, Gary received a phone call from Beechy Colclough, the celebrity therapist and sometime TV personality. He announced that Rob wanted to speak to him. A second later, Williams's croaky contralto was on the line. 'Hiya, mate. I just wanted to talk to you,' he slurred. 'Just wanted to say, you know, that I'm sorry for all the shit, all that stuff I said. I didn't mean it. It's just . . .' He tailed off and started to cry. 'Mate,' he began again, 'I have got to get well and sort myself out, but when I'm better, I want us to meet, to sit down and just talk.'

Gary's response was friendly enough, but concise. 'No problem, mate,' he said. 'I haven't got a problem with any of that. Good luck. I hope it works out.'

Later, when Rob replayed the conversation over in his mind, he asked himself why Gary had seemed so keen to get him off the phone. Even after twelve months of consuming as much alcohol and weapons-grade narcotics as was humanly possible, he was, he imagined, still compos mentis enough to know when his olive branch was being given the brush-off. Was it that Gary, who was never much good at opening up, was embarrassed to have been put on the spot and felt awkward to be faced with the obvious evidence of Rob's addictions? Maybe Gary actually couldn't care less whether he wanted to make amends or not. Or maybe it was simply a case, Rob had to concede, that he was so out of his tree he didn't have a clue which end was up any more.

Colclough, an Irish-born specialist in treating addictions, had not so much been invited into Williams's distinctly spaced-out orbit as parachuted in on the orders of Elton John. Elton credited Colclough with saving his life by helping him beat his own reliance on booze and cocaine. Now he wanted him to perform a similar minor miracle on Robbie. And while Williams was yet to hit rock bottom, he knew he needed help. Earlier that summer, Rob had woken alone in his new flat in Kensington still drunk and stoned from the night before. The plan had been to begin the usual topping-up process when instead of reaching for the vodka bottle he kept within arm's reach of his bed, he'd picked up the phone and dialled Elton.

As we have already seen, with his instinct for spotting a fellow potential addict, Elton's antennae had been alerted to Robbie during their first meeting at his home in Windsor, three years earlier. Rob had been a semi-regular visitor to Woodside since then, but on the last occasion, at a garden party a couple of months previously, he had been so drunk that he had thrown up in front of Elton's embarrassed guests. When Rob finally decided, on a whim, to ask for his help, Elton was at his house in Atlanta, but within thirty minutes he had responded to Rob's worrying answerphone message and arranged for him to be collected from London and taken to Windsor to recuperate. Robbie would spend two weeks there drying out and playing the occasional game of tennis with the son of the couple who looked after Woodside when Elton was away.

Elton arranged for Colclough to visit the patient every day, but from the outset Rob was apparently unimpressed by his new therapist, recalling that Colclough brandished an expensive-looking watch and told him it had been a present from Elton. As part of his treatment, Colclough did agree that he would talk to Gary on Rob's behalf to let him know what a pitiful state he was in. In truth, Gary would have had to have been holidaying on Pluto not to have been aware of the broad details of his sparring partner's journey into oblivion. Ever since Rob's departure from Take That, the newspapers had delighted in giving a running commentary, often with Rob himself as principal narrator, of his slide into the bottle and his increasing taste for just about any drug, legal or otherwise, that he could get his hands on. To add spice to the story, for a while it had been Noel Gallagher and then his brother and Oasis band mate, Liam, who had been Rob's partners in excess, but gradually they had both become bored of him. More to the point, the 'mad-for-it' brothers had started to think that Rob, who had been following them around like a puppy since his impromptu and shambolic on-stage appearance with Oasis at Glastonbury the previous June, was gay and fancied them.

Williams's falling-out with the Gallaghers would spark a public slanging match similar to the one he had with Barlow. It was Rob's outspoken interview with gay magazine *Attitude* in July 1996, given to coincide with the release of his debut solo single, a ropy cover version of the George Michael hit 'Freedom '90', that sounded the starter's gun on the real internecine hostilities between Robbie on one side and Gary and the rest of Take That on the other. He had used the previous months to aim subtle digs at his former friends, but now Rob came out with all guns blazing. He claimed he had been a 'prisoner for six years' in the group, and it was Gary who got it with both barrels. Rob called his former band mate a 'clueless wanker', 'really fucking dated' and 'selfish, stupid and greedy'.

The interview was a declaration of intent following the lull of the previous twelve months since Robbie's departure from Take That, when both sides had, publicly at least, maintained the pretence that they were still the best of buddies. The interview had given the lie to that illusion, but it was also a premeditated and tactical response to the generally held assumption that now Gary had gone solo, there was only room for one ex-member of Take That in the singles chart. The smart money was on the talented and together Gary taking over the Elton John/George Michael mantle and selling bucketloads of records. Williams knew he had a fight on his hands and, as the underdog, decided there was nothing else for it but to fight dirty.

He also knew that the record industry, the press and the public love nothing better than a good slugfest. The so-called Battle of Britpop between Blur and Oasis the previous summer, which had been packaged in the media as a straight choice between a bunch of working-class Mancs and some nice posh boys from the South, had grabbed the attention. Robbie's highly tuned natural instincts for exploiting publicity told him that he too needed to get the record-buying public to choose sides.

In theory at least, Rob had been given a seven-month head start on his rival, but the reality was that Gary did not really view his ex-cohort as much of a threat. In the time that Rob had officially been a solo artist, he had displayed precious little sign of doing anything halfway creative. His inertia was in part due to his increasing problems with drink and drugs, but it was just as much the result of his failure to put any thought into what he would actually do once he had extricated himself from Take That. These two factors had combined to make his first year of freedom utterly shambolic so far as his career went.

Central to his malaise was the lack of a coherent management strategy. On his departure from the group – and twelve months before Elton stepped in to help – Robbie had fallen in with Kevin Kinsella, a wild-haired Irish-born West London-raised former boxer who had been a fairly peripheral character in the music business since the sixties. Kinsella, who had a taste for half-mast trousers and multicoloured stripy socks, was a Manchester-based celebrity fixer and independent-record-label boss. He had come into contact with Williams earlier in 1995, when Granada Television asked if he could secure the services of the then Take That star to host his own chat show, with the plan that it would be recorded in Malibu and be called *Robbie on the Beach*.

Kinsella had spoken to Rob's mother, Jan, in the hope of arranging something, but nothing had come of the plan because Rob was still contracted to Take That and Nigel Martin-Smith. After his departure from the band, Jan called and told Kinsella that Rob had been sacked from Take That and had gone to spend time at George Michael's house in the south of France, where he was hanging out by the pool with Dodi Fayed, Michael Hutchence and Paula Yates. Jan asked Kinsella if he would take charge of her son's new career now that he'd gone solo. Later, Kinsella told me that when he first met his prospective client, having gone with Jan to collect him from Manchester's Ringway Airport, Rob was in a terrible state. He immediately broke down in tears in the car as the three headed to Kinsella's home in Knutsford, Cheshire, where Rob would live for the next four months. As far as Kinsella was concerned, his new client was at that time little more than a wreck who spent much of his time weeping and grieving over his lost career with Take That.

Given Rob's problems, he was in no fit state to make decisions for himself. For his part, Kinsella, who was considered anything but a big player in the music business, was already privately convinced that his best bet was to move Williams on to some other manager at the first opportunity, resolving to keep Robbie out of the spotlight until he could decide what to do with him. Certainly, Rob wasn't in any condition to start rebuilding his career. Kinsella described those first few weeks to me as a dark time, with Robbie lying around on his new manager's sofa all day, drugged up and drunk, dressed in only his Calvin Klein underpants. With Kinsella keen that the press should not see him so messed up, Rob would sleep in till lunchtime and would then send Kinsella's daughter out to buy him two bottles of vodka, which he would polish off by bedtime.

'He was going through a breakdown,' says Kinsella. 'He had been kicked out of Take That and had no idea what to do with himself. Being famous had been his life since he was a teenager. It is what he did. I really don't believe he knew how to be a real person. He was terrified by the idea of it.'

In the absence of any musical strategy, Kinsella signed Rob up for a guest presenter's spot, sitting in for Lily Savage on Channel 4's *The Big Breakfast*. He was bloated, podgy and panicky, with a desperate Kinsella having to talk him round for twenty minutes after Rob had a panic attack and announced he could not go through with it. On the plus side, Kinsella was able to sign a £100,000 deal for Rob to become the 'freaky face' of 7 Up Light. To add to his problems, however, Williams was entering a hugely expensive legal battle with Nigel Martin-Smith and Take That's record company, for which he was clearly not fighting fit.

It was apparent to Robbie that given his accusations that he had been sacked from the band and had not walked of his own accord, his future was no longer with RCA. Also, even in his chemical haze, Williams was acutely aware of the fact that once Gary launched his own much-vaunted solo career, there was little doubt which of the two of them the suits at the record company would be backing. Meanwhile, Rob's lawyer announced that he was considering a case of constructive dismissal by the band and Martin-Smith.

While Kinsella began talks with Virgin about signing Robbie, the singer himself quit the North for London and put on three stone thanks to a toxic combo of comfort-eating and heavy boozing. His mother, frightened that he was drinking himself to death, took to travelling from Stoke to the capital in the hope of rescuing him, but he would refuse to let her into his flat in Kensington, too ashamed to face her. Occasionally, after a night boozing and drugging at the Met Bar or the Atlantic Bar and Grill, Rob would get on the 7 a.m. train from London to Stoke and would arrive at her door, his clothes ripped and shoes missing, having drunk a four-pack of Special Brew on the journey, washed down with sleeping tablets.

Kinsella, now keener than ever to dispense with his troublesome new charge, tried and failed to persuade U2 manager Paul McGuinness to take Williams off his hands. Kinsella told me that the final straw in his relationship with Rob came when Jan, who was having an increasingly big say in her son's career, became jealous of the closeness that had developed between the two men. As if Rob did not have enough on his plate, Kinsella's departure would result in yet more legal action, with his now ex-manager suing him for what he claimed was unpaid commission.

Tim Abbott, a former marketing man who had worked with Oasis at Creation Records, took over from Kinsella and succeeded at least in extricating Williams from RCA, although it would cost £800,000 to buy Robbie out of his contract with the label. In late June 1996, Robbie signed a £1.5-million deal with the formerly defunct label Chrysalis, part of EMI. Now he was free for the battle ahead with Barlow.

In the event, Gary would beat him in the race to release his first solo single by two weeks, because a stipulation of Williams's parting from RCA was that Barlow's record must be allowed to come out first. Gary's debut, 'Forever Love', would reach number one in the UK in July of that year and would also hit the top spot in Spain and make the top ten in Germany, Italy and Australia. In stark contrast to Rob's dissolute and shambolic appearance, Gary, who had kept on Nigel Martin-Smith as his manager, made sure he was in peak physical condition for his first foray into life as a solo artist. He had been on an intensive diet in the run-up to the end of Take That and had taken on a personal trainer. By the time of his first single, he had lost a stone and a half. He was also keen to move away from the teeny-bopper look of Take That and cultivate a more mature image. By way of announcing his new incarnation, he appeared looking rugged and film-star handsome in *Arena* magazine.

Despite Gary's success, Robbie responded by publicly slating his rival's song. 'I know Gary's talented and he's got many brilliant songs, but I just don't understand that track,' Williams said. It was certainly true that while 'Forever Love' was slick in an American AOR (album-oriented rock) kind of way, it was still a bit of a clunker and sounded like it had been written for a Disney soundtrack rather than the pop charts. At least Gary had come up with his own material, though. By contrast, Rob had spent some of his very few sober moments in the last year writing poetry, much of which he had read to Kevin Kinsella. Kinsella, not being naturally predisposed to sweetening any pill, had pronounced his efforts as 'shit'.

Nor was Gary, despite Rob's attempts to talk up their rivalry in the papers, particularly concerned by any threat posed by Williams, on the basis that in recent times Rob had done next to nothing in the band. Gary, however, would soon come to regret underestimating him.

Robbie's first single, renamed 'Freedom '96' for its debut that August, was widely seen as lame. Even George Michael, who had befriended Williams in the wake of his Take That departure, was dead set against the idea of him recording the track and had to be talked round by Rob into giving his consent for him to release it. The contrast between the videos for the rivals' respective songs was marked too: Gary, all buff and moody in his sophisticated black-and-white promo for 'Forever Love', and Robbie, fat and gurning manically in a puddle-strewn back alley in Miami. In fact, so shambolic had the planning been for the single that when the video was shot, Rob had still not actually got round to recording the track and had to mime to George's version. In a major setback for Rob and EMI, despite the huge hype around the single's certainty to hit the number one spot, the single only managed to reach a disappointing number two in the UK. Crucially, however, with his attacks on Gary, Rob had – consciously or not – sown the seed in the mind of the record-buying public that he, Robbie, had been the beaten puppy in the band, and that he had been ignored and victimized by the steely Barlow, with his cold-eyed determination to take the spoils for himself. Central to this strategy was Williams's claim that he had been sacked by the band in summer 1995 rather than walking out in a fit of pique after failing to challenge the band's strict hierarchy.

But if time is a great healer, the initial reaction of the band was one of fury that Rob was telling anyone who would listen that he had been slung out by his one-time friends. Privately, Gary was less than convinced that his ex-band mate's very public battle with alcohol and drugs was not simply another headline-grabbing tool by the increasingly media-savvy Williams. Gary was also openly suggesting that Robbie's jealousy of him might be partly financial, rather than wholly creative. 'I do wonder if that's the source of his feelings,' he said at the time, 'because I probably made more than six times more than they [the other members of Take That] did.'

Not only did Robbie's growing reputation as pop's latest wild man instantly give him a new, hipper persona at odds with the butter-wouldn't-melt image of Barlow, Robbie's attacks on him served to paint Gary as the pantomime villain of the piece. Alcohol would make Williams increasingly loose-tongued. After yet another drinking session, he would regularly come out with more reckless accusations and slander. Once under the influence, he was likely to say almost anything. New friends would be made over ten pints of Guinness with brandy chasers and regaled with stories about Gary's holiday with Nigel to Florida and how they had both conspired to force him out.

Williams, however, was to find the most unlikely of accomplices in his bid to snuff out his rival's career at birth. Following the success of 'Forever Love', the way had seemed open for Gary to release a solo album and tour on the back of it, but crucially, Barlow and his record company, RCA/BMG, now began to make mistakes. Gary had come up with a debut solo album that both he and Nigel

Martin-Smith believed would be a massive hit, but the release was suddenly and unexpectedly delayed. The reason for the postponement was that RCA was attempting to get Clive Davis to sign Gary to Arista, part of the BMG conglomerate in the US. Davis had been sent the new album and wanted to do the deal, but had said he did not like some of the tracks and wanted the album re-recorded. BMG agreed to the plan, but it would mean going back into the studio. A series of high-profile dates at the Albert Hall that Gary had on hold now had to be put off indefinitely, and the momentum he had gained from his first single was wasted.

Barlow's problems should have presented an open goal to Williams, but Rob was busy dealing with his own local difficulties. Like Gary, he had no album to release. Tim Abbott and EMI came up with the plan of sending Rob to Miami to work with the hugely successful writer Desmond Child, who had produced a string of hits for the likes of Bon Jovi, Aerosmith and Cher, but from the outset the experiment was a disaster. Williams soon began complaining to his long-suffering EMI A&R man, Chris Briggs, that he did not just want to be the latest in a list of artists for whom Child had produced one of his hits-by-numbers. Instead, he demanded that EMI find him someone like-minded, someone British who understood the whimsical lyrics he was writing and with whom he could form a long-standing writing partnership of equals. Almost immediately Rob was pleading to come home from America. Only the personal intervention of EMI president J. F. Cecillon persuaded him not to get on a flight and come straight back. Even so, the trip produced only one usable song, the sub-Oasis rocker 'Old Before I Die', which got to number two when it was released in April 1997.

Meanwhile, the lyrics and melodies Robbie set about writing himself for an album he planned to call *The Show-Off Must Go*

On were – by his own admission – not up to scratch. Depressed and ever more in hock to his addictions, he began talking with apparent seriousness to his circle about his suicidal thoughts. It didn't help his friends' nerves when, after a night of partying, he stepped off the balcony of a Cologne hotel room, several storeys up, and somehow managed to land on top of the veranda of another room.

To compound the issue, the bad influence that was the Diamond Dogs had followed him from Manchester to London and the group of hangers-on shamelessly continued to exploit his generosity to fund their debauched lifestyles.

For his part, even by the time that 'Forever Love' was released, Gary was already beginning to pull his hair out over the hiatus created by BMG's prevarication over his much-vaunted debut album. With Clive Davis demanding changes, suddenly Barlow noticed a definite froideur in the company's attitude towards his material. Davis's interest in Gary's career was slightly baffling anyway, given that the company's head honcho, who was already in his mid-sixties at the time, had been decidedly lukewarm about Take That. But given his track record of signing an A to Z of pop and rock glitterati, including Billy Joel, Bruce Springsteen, Whitney Houston and Barry Manilow, RCA executives in the UK were reluctant to question Davis's unenthusiastic reaction to much of Barlow's new material.

Gary was summoned and he duly headed off to Los Angeles for what would be a disastrous meeting with the record boss in his bungalow at the Beverly Hills Hotel. First, Gary overslept and nearly missed the morning meeting. Then he mistakenly ate Davis's breakfast while the American took a phone call in the other room. By the time he left the meeting, a horrified Barlow had somehow been bamboozled into agreeing to record some country-and-western songs that Davis insisted on playing him. Davis also decided that in order to make an album that could break him in the States, Gary needed to collaborate with a writer with a proven track record, such as the Canadian David Foster, who had worked with Mariah Carey, Gloria Estefan and Prince, or the deeply eccentric Diane Warren, who had recently written the international hit 'Un-Break My Heart' for Toni Braxton.

In the weeks that followed, Gary was publicly talking up the new material he was working on, saying it would help him become a star in the US, but privately he was complaining to Nigel Martin-Smith that he was being coerced into making music he did not believe in and was getting no backing from BMG in the UK or, indeed, Nigel himself, whom he accused of failing to stand up for him in the face of such blatant corporate interference. With their relationship deteriorating by the week, Gary eventually sacked Nigel by a fax sent from his lawyers and hired the manager of the Spice Girls, Simon Fuller. Barlow would later admit that, whatever their differences, it had been a shameful way to treat Nigel, who, for all his faults, had worked tirelessly (and often brilliantly) to help make him a star. Worse was to come, though, when, in early 1997, Davis made an eleventh-hour request that Gary play at his hugely influential pre-Grammys party in New York. Given no time to rehearse, his haphazard and embarrassing performance of 'Love Won't Wait', a song Davis had persuaded Madonna to write for Barlow, was received in stony silence by a star-studded audience that included George Michael, Bobby Brown and Aretha Franklin.

As Gary began his fruitless conquest to break the States, Rob's crumbling relationship with his own manager, Tim Abbott, had reached the point of no return and, like Martin-Smith and Kinsella before him, Abbott began expensive litigation against his now ex-client. Unable or unwilling to control his spending, which included a taste for marathon clothes-buying jaunts, Williams became used to his credit cards being rejected as he rapidly ran out of cash. Abbott had also become the victim of the fast-developing enmity between Rob and Abbott's old muckers Noel and Liam Gallagher.

Managerless once again, Robbie's accountant, Richard Harvey, was given the task of finding him new representation, and in late 1996, Rob was introduced to Tim Clark and David Enthoven of IE Music. Old Harrovian Enthoven had previously managed prog rockers King Crimson, and Clark was a former executive at Island Records. Together they had also managed Roxy Music, Bryan Ferry, T Rex and, more recently, Massive Attack.

Clark and Enthoven listened to some of the demos Rob had made of his own music and groaned inwardly, but when they read some of the poetry he had been writing, they were impressed by its humour and rough-around-the-edges charm. A search was begun to find someone to put their new client's unpolished lyrics to music. A few tentatively suggested collaborations fizzled out and finally they introduced Williams to Guy Chambers. The well-spoken thirty-four-year-old Chambers came with a fine musical heritage, his father being a flautist with the London Philharmonic and his mother having worked at record label Decca. He had been in a series of low-key bands, including Hambi and the Dance, who had managed to get signed to Virgin but were almost instantly forgotten. He had then done a music degree, begged for gigs around London, gone on the dole and subsequently played keyboards for the Teardrop Explodes, Karl Wallinger's World Party and the Waterboys before forming his own band, the Lemon Trees. Guy sent a tape to IE Music, and Clark and Enthoven arranged for a meeting between the serious musician and the car crash that was the most recent edition to their roster.

Williams would later claim that the meeting with Chambers was pure kismet, that he had seen Guy's name on a piece of paper in his managers' office and proclaimed, 'That's him.' What was certainly true was that the collaboration was instantly and wildly productive. For the next few days, in early January 1997, the pair sat locked away in Guy's house. By the time they emerged, they had written Robbie's next single, 'South of the Border'. Three more tracks, 'Killing Me', 'Teenage Millionaire' and 'Life Thru a Lens', were also finished. On the second day, they sat down with Rob's rough version of 'Angels' and completed it in twenty minutes.

Just as Williams's career suddenly got a much-needed shot in the arm, Barlow's was beginning to follow a distinctly downward trajectory. The Madonna-penned 'Love Won't Wait' did eventually reach number one in the UK when it was released in April 1997, but failed to make the top ten in Germany, Holland or Sweden. It would be another two months before his long-awaited album, *Open Road*, now heavily re-recorded in America and London, and boasting no fewer than fourteen producers, would be released nearly a full year after his debut single, 'Forever Love'. Although the album went on to sell more than two million copies globally, it was instantly savaged by the critics. One British paper described it as containing 'thuddingly dull ballads and lacklustre cover versions aimed at the US market', adding that it sounded like 'the feeble ramblings of a washed-up old crooner in a cardigan'. To make matters worse, the blatant pandering to the US market proved to be in vain, with none of the singles from the album reaching higher than a dismal forty-two in the American Hot 100 – despite Barlow's months of soul-destroying promotion, during which he visited every backwater and two-bit radio station in the union in a bid to make a name for himself across the pond. *Open Road* did reach number one in the album chart for a solitary week in the UK, but two subsequent singles, 'So Help Me, Girl' and the album's title track, 'Open Road', which was released in November 1997, barely made the top ten, while a further three embarrassingly failed to chart at all. For Gary, it was a worrying portent of things to come.

CHAPTER FOUR

Feud's Corner

There is nothing like tragedy to bring out the best in the showbiz brotherhood. In December 1997, Gary, taking on the mantle of Bob Geldof, organized the Concert for Hope in London in support of World AIDS Day. He had come up with the idea of a gig in memory of Princess Diana in the days after her death at the end of August that year. By the time of the show, Gary himself, Boyzone, Peter Andre and one Robbie Williams had quickly been confirmed as the headlining acts. The occasion was meant to feature a one-off reunion of Take That, but Mark Owen, who was busy with his own solo career, was unavailable and the idea was scrapped. Backstage at Battersea Power Station, where the extravaganza was being staged, the countdown to the show was an orgy of air kisses, bear hugs and mutual backslapping. Gary, who was being followed around for the day by a camera crew, talked about how great it was to see Robbie. In turn, Williams playfully stuck a tongue in Gary's ear, said how nice it was to catch up with him again and how when his old friend had asked him to appear on the bill, he had agreed on the spot. After the two men performed their own sets, they joined the other acts on stage for an air-punching and suitably tear-jerking communal version of 'Let It Be'. Straight after the show, Robbie, who had not spoken to Gary since he had drunkenly offered him an olive branch via Beechy Colclough nearly eighteen months earlier, went outside, found the nearest camera crew and proceeded, unprompted, to slag off Gary.

Later, Rob would admit that he was not brave enough to confront Barlow face to face, saying: 'I was still pretty much scared of him.' That Williams found it impossible, however, to call a halt to hostilities even for one night was hardly surprising. Three months earlier, his debut solo album, *Life Thru a Lens*, had been released at long last to a lukewarm reception. One of the tracks, 'Ego a Go Go', was a deliciously premeditated and unvarnished attack on his rival which taunted Gary about where he had been since going solo.

In truth, at the time, Gary was not exactly losing any sleep over the barbs, given his more pressing concerns over his stalling career. Nor, to be brutally frank, was Rob in a position to gloat. Two singles from *Life Thru a Lens* had already been released. The first, 'Lazy Days', which was another Williams attempt to mimic the Manc swagger of Liam Gallagher, reached number eight when it came out in the middle of June 1997. Even more disappointingly, the next, the forgettable 'South of the Border', only managed to get as high as number fourteen. Already there was talk in the industry that EMI were thinking of jettisoning their newest star. Nor was it simply a case of him not selling records. It had not escaped the company's notice that Robbie was mentally and physically a mess. His parlous state was evidenced by the fact that immediately after he finished recording *Life Thru a Lens*, he was shipped off by his new managers to start his first spell in rehab. As a result of his condition, the recording process had been like pulling teeth. There would be days when Guy Chambers and his co-producer, Steve Power, would wait in vain for Williams to show up for a planned recording session. On other occasions, he would arrive completely wasted and have to sleep off the booze and drugs on the studio sofa. The sessions would set the pattern by which Rob and Guy would work on his first three studio albums, with the singer showing next to zero interest and the producer's primary concern being to find a take in which Rob did not sound like a city-centre drunk at kicking-out time.

In June 1997, he was admitted to Clouds House, a drying-out clinic in Wiltshire, for a six-week stay that saw him leave only once, in order to shoot a video for the new album. There he began a twelve-step programme to help him deal with his alcoholism and drug addiction. Meanwhile, the attempts of his handlers to keep his illness quiet were becoming ever more farcical. Finally, Tim Clark was forced to admit Robbie's problems publicly, confessing that he had gone missing after returning from a weekend in Ireland with his then girlfriend, the actress Anna Friel (whom he had begun dating two months earlier after inviting her to see him appear on *Top of the Pops*) and had been close to taking his own life. In desperation, his managers had been forced to call Jan down from Stoke in the hope that she could persuade her son to seek help.

As if his personal issues were not problem enough for him, within days of his release from rehab Rob faced the ordeal of his first face-to-face encounter with Nigel Martin-Smith since he had quit Take That two years earlier. They met in London's High Court, where Martin-Smith was suing Williams for the percentage of his earnings he claimed he was owed. The court case, coming as it did on the back of Robbie's hugely expensive legal action to break his RCA contract, was the last thing he needed given his perilous financial predicament. As the wrangling with Martin-Smith dragged on, he was served with another writ for £70,500 of unpaid fees by Tim Abbott.

Martin-Smith's writ claimed that Robbie owed him £31,881 of a £135,000 royalty payment his ex-client had received for his final days with Take That. On top of that, he also claimed he was due £47,000 from a £200,000 advance that had been paid to Rob for Take That's *Greatest Hits* CD. Nigel also insisted that as part of their deal, he was entitled to 20 per cent of Robbie's earnings until 2001, and 10 per cent for a further 5 years after that. In court, the muck was beginning to be thrown, with tales of Robbie's 'glamorous and flamboyant company, alcohol and narcotics'. As he waited for the court to rule on the case, Rob said publicly that if he lost, he could be crippled financially. Following his fiscally draining attempts to free himself from his contract with RCA, this was no exaggeration. In the event, the judge, Mr Justice Ferris, ordered him to cough up an interim payment of £90,000 to Martin-Smith, but more worryingly demanded an inquiry into exactly what the singer had earned since leaving the band.

The three legal disputes had all but wiped out Rob, and the noises off from EMI about the chances for his continued survival with the label were not good. The only glimmer of hope on the horizon was that Robbie had 'Angels' in his back pocket. The song had started life during a holiday Rob took with his mother and sister, Sally, to Dublin at Christmas in 1996. In the Globe pub in the city, Williams met a would-be songwriter called Ray Heffernan, who had recently returned from Paris, where he had been living with his French girlfriend when she miscarried the baby son they were expecting. The Irishman returned home alone and on meeting Rob they struck up a friendship and became instant and close drinking buddies.

Heffernan played Rob a song he had written about the death of his unborn son and together they worked on the lyrics. How much of what finally ended up on record was the work of Heffernan is arguable. Certainly, in all my conversations with him, Heffernan has never accused Rob of stealing the song, saying openly that the chorus and arrangement of the song as a ballad are nothing like the early single verse that he and Rob wrote together. As it was, Heffernan was later paid a £10,000 one-off payment for his part in it and agreed to forego any claim to future royalties. He does, however, remain angry to this day that he was not given a song-writing credit on the album, although Rob did include a dedication on the sleeve notes of the single, which read: 'Even fallen angels laugh last, thanks to Ray Heffernan.'

Despite the high hopes of Rob and his team over 'Angels', it was far from a given that it would be the song to breathe new life into his career. He certainly needed a boost, as more than two months after its release, *Life Thru a Lens* had managed to sell only 30,000 copies and by December 1997, when 'Angels' was released as a single, the album had slipped to 104 in the charts.

After the disappointment of Gary's recent single sales, he too realized he desperately could do with a great song to lift his flatlining career. The problem was, he knew for sure he did not have one on his album. Now, however, he was painfully aware that Robbie did. Barlow first heard 'Angels' at the end of November while he was in Frankfurt for a German TV appearance. Backstage, someone was playing the video of Robbie's soon-to-be-released next single. Gary and Chris Healey, who had previously been Take That's tour manager, stood and watched the new slimmed-down Rob in the black-and-white Vaughan Arnell-directed video, with its sweeping aerial shots of Williams walking along a deserted beach at Saunton Sands, Devon. Barlow's heart sank into his boots.

'That's pretty good, isn't it?' Healey said finally.

'Chris, it's very, very good, and that's what's worrying me,' replied Gary.

'At that moment,' Barlow would later admit in his autobiography, 'I was both happy and sad. Sad because I didn't have anything like "Angels" in the bag and happy because I thought that maybe now Rob had a smash hit on the way, he would leave me alone.' Not for the first time, it would prove to be a case of wishful thinking on his part.

If anything, Robbie's success with 'Angels' – which in spite of only reaching number four in the UK went double platinum and was played 42,000 times in the first year of its release on UK radio – only served to intensify his attacks on Barlow. Rob again went back on the offensive in *Attitude* magazine, calling Gary 'a wanker in a tracksuit'. What had changed now, though, was the dynamics. With a huge hit on his hands, Robbie, instead of being magnanimous and calling a ceasefire, used his elevated platform to launch wave after wave of humiliating broadsides at his nemesis. Out with a blonde he'd picked up the previous night, Rob, whose relationship with Anna Friel had collapsed after only three months because of his addictions, decided on the spur of the moment to seek out an espionage shop in the West End. There he bought a gadget that changes the sound of your voice. Then, giggling like a couple of schoolkids, they headed to the Met Bar in Park Lane, where Williams proceeded to make a series of prank calls to Gary.

If there was a strategy involved in his continued assaults on Barlow, it was nonetheless a tad risky. Given the British public's inclination to side with the underdog, would Robbie risk a backlash for kicking Gary now he was down? Not a bit of it. The public, it seems, was quite happy for the suddenly mismatched contest to go a few more rounds. In fact, the general population seemed to have come to the conclusion, fair or not, that Gary was a smug, self-satisfied, half-arsed facsimile of Elton John and were content to join in the fun.

Gary began a tour of the UK in spring 1998, but now the brickbats were coming thick and fast. The *Guardian*'s reviewer Dave Simpson described his show at Sheffield City Hall as having 'everything you'd expect from a chicken-in-a-basket circuit-club band on a wet Saturday night – places where, incidentally, a teenage Gary learned his trade'. Barlow, he went on, was 'an unfortunate coupling of Cliff Richard and Alan Partridge'. Not that Gary was helping himself. During one segment of his live show, he laid on the cheese by lighting three candles – one for Princess Diana, whom he had met no more than a couple of times, one for the recently murdered Gianni Versace and one for his recently deceased grandmother – before launching into the schmaltzy 'Forever Love'. He also made himself look showy by being photographed on his tour bus in the *News of the World* with the £1,700 Versace duvet he had bought specially for his bunk.

The press were not the only ones getting in on the act. Gary was left raging after the Spice Girls, with whom he shared the same manager, Simon Fuller, took the piss out of him in their movie, *Spice World*. On another occasion, he was invited by Elton John to a lunch at the Ivy to celebrate Elton's partner David Furnish's birthday. George Michael, who had always been a hero of Gary's, was seated at the same table but studiously blanked him throughout the meal. It was not until the following day that he found out the reason why. 'Gary Barlow doesn't have any talent,' George had declared in an interview with *Q* magazine.

Gary was shaken by the backlash against him and was acutely aware that he was ill equipped not only to rebrand himself, but also to compete with the heady combination of flaws, angst and redemption that Robbie's story offered. Suddenly, Gary had to become used to the words 'pop flop' or 'has-been' being inserted before his name in the tabloids. Meanwhile, his attempts to stem the tide of public ridicule backfired pitifully. In a bid to distance himself from his pipe-and-slippers image, he gave an interview to the *Sun*'s pop editor, Dominic Mohan, in which he boasted that he had binged on cocaine and Ecstasy. Elsewhere he bragged about driving his Porsche 911 at 170 miles per hour on the motorway and how he had made conquests of hundreds of Take That fans. Instead of making him appear more hip, however, the effect was simply to make him seem all the more desperate.

'The bile and vitriol worried me,' Gary admitted later, 'and I wondered what I'd done to deserve it, but I didn't comment. I kept my mouth closed, soldiered on and in doing so lost the public sympathy.'

Meanwhile, the effect 'Angels' was having on Robbie's career was dramatic. Within a month of its release *Life Thru a Lens*, which had been languishing in the outer reaches of the charts, sold 210,000 copies. The following month, 'Angels' sold 600,000 and the album went double platinum. (In the UK, an album must sell 300,000 to be awarded a platinum disc.) He might have been selling records at last, but Rob continued to act like he was on an inevitable path to fairly imminent destruction. He appeared on *Top of the Pops* in early 1998 in a gold crocheted dress and a thong, but the public loved him for it.

For them, it exemplified the fundamental difference between the two men. Aside from the charisma deficit, Gary gave every impression of revelling in his gilded lifestyle. Shortly before the break-up of Take That, he had bought an archetypal rock star's mansion, the cavernous Delamere Manor in Cheshire, which was five times the size of Moorside. It came complete with a lake and 117 acres of grounds. It was so big he moved his parents and his brother, Ian, and his wife, Lisa, into two separate houses on the estate. Barlow had achieved money and success, and had the temerity actually to seem to enjoy it.

Robbie, on the other hand, had skilfully given himself an altogether different USP. He might have been living the dream with fame, looks, cash and girls camping on his doorstep, but it was clearly driving him demented and making him miserable. And there, in a nutshell, was the twisted essence of Robbie's appeal. He made us feel better about our own humdrum lives and minor failures. Yes, he had won the golden ticket, but he was still a mess. For him to have been happy to boot? Well, that would just have been rubbing it in.

Professionally, he went from strength to strength. Williams released his second album, *I've Been Expecting You*, in October 1998. It went to number one and would ultimately become a ten times platinum seller in the UK. The single 'Millennium', inspired by the John Barry theme to *You Only Live Twice*, became his first to top the charts. He followed up 'Millennium' by having top-five hits with 'Let Me Entertain You' and 'No Regrets', the latter laying bare his falling-out with Take That and Nigel. At the same time, he was nominated for no less than six Brits, eventually walking away with three, including Best Male Solo Artist, Best Single and Best British Video. He also began an arena tour of the UK that would see him play twenty-four gigs in thirteen cities, all of which sold out in less than four hours. The new album would also offer him the chance to get even with Martin-Smith on record. The simmering loathing was evident on the raging 'Karma Killer', in which a ranting Williams questions why his ex-manager hasn't died yet, compares him to the devil and says he hopes he chokes on his favourite tipple of Barcardi and Coke.

As things went from bad to worse for Gary, he split with Simon Fuller, whose relationship with Barlow had not recovered from the *Spice World* embarrassment, and took on BMG's head of marketing, Kristina Kyriacou, in a bid to give his career new focus. He was increasingly of the opinion that it was simply not possible for both himself and Williams to have successful futures as solo artists. It would be a case of to the winner the spoils. Gary began working on material for a second album and once again Clive Davis insisted on suggesting songwriters who, he promised, would help him find that so-far-elusive winning formula. Creatively, however, Gary was going backwards. A series of meetings with other writers failed to ignite the spark everyone was looking for. He could feel his confidence ebbing away. The misery weight Rob had put on after leaving Take That, and shed as his career soared, now landed on Gary. In America, where Barlow was still expected to travel on promotional tours, Arista employees were ordered to keep tabs on his ever-expanding waistline.

In the absence of a new album to promote, BMG stalled on releasing a new single that Gary had written called 'Stronger'. The song would eventually be put out six months later, coinciding – with comic mistiming – with Robbie's new single, called 'Strong'. While the lyrics of Gary's effort spoke of an inner strength at odds with his private unhappiness, Williams sang, 'You think that I'm strong. You're wrong, you're wrong,' and with it let the listener into his angst-ridden inner sanctum. 'Strong' got to number four in March 1999.

Williams's success coincided with him losing his long-running court battle with Martin-Smith. As the date for the court judgment approached, Robbie went on stage in front of 16,000 fans in Manchester and shouted: 'Nigel Martin-Smith, I know you can hear me. I am your worst nightmare. Yes, Nigel, I have come into Manchester and I have reclaimed it.' Days later, however, Martin-Smith was vindicated by a panel of Court of Appeal judges who rejected Robbie's attempt to have the verdict of the earlier hearing overturned. To make matters worse, the initial £90,000 he was ordered to pay his ex-manager had grown to more than £1 million thanks to the legal costs that had been racked up during the years of wrangling. Outside court, a triumphant Martin-Smith took a pop at both Williams and his mother, saying: 'Robbie has now had two attempts at trying to persuade a court of law that I acted badly towards him. He has now failed twice. My only hope is that, in time, Robbie will come to see things as they actually were, not as his mother has chosen to see them. On a personal level, I am pleased that Robbie has had continued success after Take That, but I feel that those fans who have only heard Robbie's account of events would be very disillusioned if they knew the whole story. I have great pity for Robbie. I really was very fond of him, but he is not the same lad that I took off the dole and made into a star all those years ago.'

Gary was in no position to gloat. His woes continued as he limped to number sixteen in the UK with 'Stronger' and only managed to get to a lamentable seventy-three in Germany. Now, while Rob was playing to packed houses, Barlow was even struggling to get gigs on local radio roadshows. During one pitiful meet-and-greet at Edinburgh's Forth FM, Gary arrived to find his welcoming committee consisted of three mums, a sixteen-year-old bunking off school, a muscular dystrophy sufferer and a traffic warden who, to add insult to injury, proceeded to slap a parking ticket on his Mercedes once Gary had gone inside. He had come full circle since the early Take That days when they had to beg, steal and borrow for any offers of promotion.

In spring 1999, he was embarrassingly forced to cancel a show at Glasgow's SECC just weeks after Williams had performed four sell-out shows at the 10,000-seat arena. A planned tour of the country was twice rescheduled in the hope that Gary would actually have an album ready to promote. Eventually, Barlow had to admit he had no more than six new songs. When at last he did take to the road at the end of the year, thousands of tickets remained unsold.

His failing career put Gary in the mood to fight back against Robbie. After almost four years of biting his lip at the constant carping from his former friend, he decided enough was enough. In an interview with the *Birmingham Post*, he said: 'I'd like to sit here and tell you that all the comments he made about me didn't bother me, but it's so annoying. I always think if there was one thing Robbie learned from Oasis it was how to pick a good feud with somebody. Unfortunately, it was me who he decided to have a go at. All his comments are very hurtful for me personally because it has nothing to do with music. It's all just bitching about me, which I have taken very badly. It's crazy. I honestly don't understand where all these stories came from about how life was so horrible for him in Take That. If his life was so horrible, I never saw any of it. Robbie was always fun and he had a great laugh with us. I have really good memories of that time.' Elsewhere Barlow accused Williams of engineering the rivalry. 'Robbie has made good records and is on the crest of a wave, so good luck to him,' he said, 'but it's very difficult for me to say all this because I don't like him because of the situation he has put me in. He has come out on top and here I am. I've never been vindictive because I don't believe in a war of words in music.'

But nobody, it seemed, was listening – least of all to his music. Now Gary was joining them. He could no longer bring himself to listen to *Open Road*, symbol that it was of his creative inertia and his pandering to a US market that could not give a stuff about him. Barlow retreated to his Cheshire mansion with his girlfriend, model and dancer Dawn Andrews, whom he had first met before his Take That days, when they both appeared in a video for his early solo pop incarnation as Kurtis Rush, Gary's short-lived pseudonym back in Manchester in the late eighties. The blonde, willowy and pretty Dawn had increasingly become one of the only sources of contentedness in Barlow's fraught existence. After their first meeting, the couple had bumped into each other on several occasions down the years. They eventually became a couple once Robbie left Take That and the band were beginning their final UK tour.

Dawn had left her family home in Worcester at the age of fifteen to go to dance school in Surrey and had been modelling and dancing ever since. She was hired as a dancer on Take That's Nobody Else Tour, but she had only had one serious boyfriend and, unlike the band's raucous groupies, was shy, down-to-earth and reserved. Shortly after they became an item, Gary decided it was time to come clean about the girl fans who had warmed his bed and announced gravely that they needed to talk. Suddenly, he was rambling clumsily about the different lives they had had, and how being a pop star meant there had been temptations. Before he could get to the point, Dawn called a premature halt to the discussion.

'Well, of course you have,' she replied matter-of-factly. 'You've been in Take That for five years.'

From the outset the eminently sensible Dawn insisted on imposing an element of normality on her boyfriend's life. On an early date at his house, as Gary made his excuses about having to retire to his studio to work on new material, she insisted they sit and watch TV together, something the workaholic Barlow rarely did. She did not enjoy the showbiz functions and parties they were invited to and soon refused to go. Nor was she content to live off his healthy bank balance. When Gary invited her on an all-expenses-paid trip to accompany him on a tour of Australia and the Far East, she turned him down because she had accepted a booking to appear as a backing dancer for Cher on *Top of the Pops*. When Gary eventually decided Take That should call it a day, part of his thinking was that he simply wanted to spend more time at home with his new girlfriend. Sensibly, as soon as she moved in with him, Dawn laid down some ground rules. She started by calling time on Gary's experiment of playing Bertie Wooster to his butler Maurice's Jeeves. 'Maurice can go,' she announced summarily. 'I'm not having him mincing around the place.'

But the relationship had its bumps too. In summer 1998, two years after they'd begun dating, the couple were reported to have split. Indeed, at that time, there was still something of the unreconstructed lad about Gary's behaviour when he was on the road. One visitor to his luxurious tour bus in 1998 describes Barlow and his band travelling back to their Amsterdam hotel, watching the infamous and resolutely triple-X home video made by Pamela Anderson and her rock-star husband, Tommy Lee, on their honeymoon. Gary, bouncing up and down in his seat in excitement, spilled his bowl of Honey Nut Loops cereal. 'That's fookin' beauty!' he howled in delight. Earlier during the show, girl fans had pelted the stage with his favourite chocolate bars, on which they had scrawled their names and phone numbers in felt tip.

Despite the brief hiatus, he and Dawn were soon settled back into comfortable, if cloistered, normality at Delamere. The house may have been grand, but Gary's taste in food, even when travelling the world with Take That, had perennially eschewed everything from the exotic to the even vaguely healthy. On the road in Take That, Rob was disgusted by the way Gary would bite both ends of a KitKat finger and suck his tea through it like a straw. All modern restaurants were written off as 'trendy rubbish' and he refused to eat anything green. Now, as depression set in, Gary began existing almost exclusively on a high-fat diet of Big Macs and fries.

He stayed at home watching Grand Prix races on TV and manically drawing ropy pictures with a Biro, which he had framed and hung next to his Italian Renaissance masterpieces. On his increasingly rare forays to London, Barlow began taking the train instead of flying in order to save money. At the same time, he took to using the hundreds of thousands of Air Miles he had earned flying back and forth to the US to pay for cheap holidays for him, Dawn and his parents. Even when he did venture out, he hated people looking at him and took to wearing a baseball cap to go incognito. Inevitably, when he was recognized in a shop or on the train, people would taunt him by asking him how Robbie was doing. He would ruminate on how despite, or because of, all his wealth, he had only made two friends since leaving school and one of them was Howard Donald, the only member of Take That he was still in touch with. Bleary-eyed, unshaven and smoking the latest in a day-long succession of cigarettes, Gary rang up his management company to complain about how he had come to the conclusion that 'solo' really meant 'so low'.

As Gary's confidence evaporated, he began running the songs he had written for his second album past his mother, Marjorie, for her approval. The writer of eight number ones and a winner of four Ivor Novello awards was now prepared to defer to a lab technician at the local high school if his mother pronounced the songs to be no good. He took to bringing out a chest that contained twenty-five home videos he and the others had shot during the Take That glory days. He would sit in front of the TV winding and rewinding, reliving the good times, but also watching Robbie closely, questioning the trademark grins through that tight jaw; the arched eyebrow, teasing and mocking; the quiet cockiness. Could Rob really have been so unhappy? Was this truly the time when he was drinking a bottle of vodka after lights-out in his hotel room and crying himself to sleep? Could he really have been so blind, Gary asked himself over and over, that never for one solitary second did he allow himself to consider that the boy laughing and waving at him through the lens of his video camera actually hated his guts the whole damn time?

Taking on the role of relationship counsellors, the BBC made a failed attempt to bring the two warring singers together for an unlikely duet for Children in Need in November 1999. In public, Gary was saying they wouldn't ever speak again, never mind work together. 'Robbie didn't despise his time in Take That like he claims,' Gary told the *Daily Mirror*. 'Robbie loves to be the victim, the outcast. It's a very sad way to be, one which I just can't appreciate. Most of the jibes come from his end. I was happy to end this thing two years ago, but he's got this problem. We'll never be friends again. That's just the way it is. This is a long race. He's up there now, but I've still got a lot to do. But since I'm not even thirty yet, I'm not going to start panicking.'

Privately, however, almost everyone who had anything to do with Barlow's career had begun panicking a long time ago. With no sign of a second album and with rumours abounding that he was about to be dumped from his record contract, BMG was forced to issue a statement denying the gossip. Unfortunately, the company's public backing of him only served to whip up the speculation further. Gary had effectively been given the sort of dreaded vote of confidence football chairmen give to their managers days before relieving them of first-team duties. Plus, unbeknown to Gary, a memo had been circulating round BMG that suggested the label was considering 'rebranding' him. The email, which was leaked to *Private Eye*, spoke of inventing a new, cooler and more laddish image, playing on his supposed love of dangerous sports and Grand Prix racing in a bid to make him seem more relevant to music buyers.

It was the ultimate kick in the teeth for someone who, just three years earlier, had been seen as the unrivalled star of the BMG firmament. When his second solo album finally appeared in October 1999, Gary gave a not-so-subtle hint at how long it had taken to make by giving it the title *Twelve Months, Eleven Days*. As well as the many delays before being released, it had gone over budget, costing £800,000 to complete. In the privacy of their offices, few at BMG, including Gary's new A&R man, Simon Cowell – who, as one of the company's artist and repertoire executives, was the liaison between the label and Barlow – thought it had been money well spent. Rob couldn't resist twisting the knife. On the album's release, he claimed he had gone out to buy the CD, but after hearing it, had gone back to the shop and demanded a refund.

Even before it hit the shelves, the record had led to disagreements and resignations within the promotion department of the company. As it was, *Twelve Months, Eleven Days* spent barely a week in the UK charts, reaching no higher than thirty-five and a tragic sixty-five in Germany. After the failure of 'Stronger', the second single from the album, 'For All That You Want', was virtually ignored by the major radio stations and limped into the chart at number twenty-four before disappearing without trace. By way of limiting the suffering, as much as refusing to throw good money after bad, BMG cancelled the scheduled release of a third single, 'Lie to Me'.

Still Williams refused to take his foot off his rival's throat. During an online question-and-answer session with fans, he mercilessly derided his old sparring partner. When Robbie was asked if he thought he could beat Gary in a fight, he replied: 'I don't know. He's a stocky fellow, low centre of gravity and low self-esteem – two things that make a powerful combination.'

For his part, Gary knew even before the record came out that it was a big dud, that it was going to bomb and make him look like a fool. Years later, he would muse on the disaster and say: 'Even if I had had ten "Angels" on that album, it would still have sunk without trace. My visibility was so low that I'd lost touch with my audience and they'd lost touch with me. Of course, Rob kicked me while I was down. In an interview, he said that he had bought my record but took it back because it was crap. Why would anyone as successful as Rob bother saying that? Why did he so want to make me unhappy?' To which the obvious answer appeared to be because he could.

Clearly, the battle between the two men had been over as a meaningful contest for some time. Williams had emerged victorious, his rival humbled, humiliated and a public laughing stock. It was cruel on Gary, who had simply, but perhaps naively, imagined at the start of his solo career that success would be defined by the music he was making rather than his ability to win control of the news agenda.

With the race won, EMI was already looking for new scalps on Robbie's behalf. Now that his domination of the UK and increasingly large chunks of Europe were in the bag, both the record company and Williams had started to eye greedily the immeasurable riches on offer if the boy wonder could transport his success across the Atlantic. *I've Been Expecting You* had been the biggest-selling import CD at Tower Records in Los Angeles, and Robbie accepted an invitation by some of the major players in the US record business to let them sample the phenomenon in the flesh at an invite-only gig at the Lucky Seven Club in Hollywood.

The assault on America would, however, bring his fragile state into sharp focus. The consensus at his US label, Capitol, was that Williams's astonishing success in the UK and Europe would readily translate into a similar domination of the American charts. By way of beginning the process of attempting to exploit his potential in the world's biggest pop market, in May 1999 the label had released *The Ego Has Landed*, a compilation of the best bits of Robbie's first two albums, but the stateside audience was not known to give in without a fight. In order to win it over, a tour of the US and Canada was commenced that would see him play twenty-three dates in six months.

Given his physical and mental state, Rob was in no shape for the fray. From the outset he had tried to give the impression to those around him that he could happily take or leave the prospect of securing the holy grail of cracking America. On other occasions, however, his natural competitiveness – and his black humour – came to the fore and he had been heard to say, 'Barlow will top himself when I crack the States, I just know it.' In reality, though, he was daunted and terrified by the prospect of trying his luck across the pond. The spectre of failure haunted him from the beginning, and for the first time in what had been, recently at least, a stellar trajectory, Williams began to show signs of nerves.

As the campaign to sell him kicked off in America, MTV aired an hour-long programme about him called *The Next Big Thing*. In terms of prestige TV, there was unbridled joy at Capitol when, in May 1999, the CBS producers of the massively influential *The Late Show With David Letterman* agreed not only to let him sing his debut US single, 'Millennium', but also be interviewed on the nightly chat show, recorded in New York. It was quite a coup given that their new star was, despite whatever success he had achieved elsewhere, still a complete unknown on the other side of the Atlantic. All that was needed was for Williams to work his easy charm on Letterman and, more importantly, the millions watching at home.

Surely, it was now simply a case of Robbie bagging the elephant. After all, this was the man who had effortlessly wooed Michael Parkinson on his first big chat-show outing in the UK, two years earlier, by going up behind his chair, beaming with childlike wonder into the camera and saying: 'Look, Mum – Parky!' But the Williams charm, like Robbie's Potteries accent, did not travel as well when it came to Indianapolis-born *Letterman* as it had with Barnsley boy Parky. In the event, Rob's appearance on Letterman was a disaster. Outside the Ed Sullivan Theater before the show, Williams looked stony-faced with nerves as he signed autographs for a few fans who were waiting for him. Once inside, his mood did not improve and he complained during rehearsal that the chill inside the studio, allegedly a ploy used by the host to keep his guests on their mettle, was making him even more disconcerted.

When it came time to perform 'Millennium', Rob insisted on wearing the coat he arrived in and was wide-eyed and shaky, fluffing the words at one point and embarrassingly sucking up to Letterman by inserting his name in the chorus. Worse was to come once he was seated at Letterman's desk. Suddenly, he was overawed and babbling. Beginning with a fawning monologue about how honoured he was to be in his host's presence, he went on to miss the mark with his gags as his famed charisma went AWOL. Meanwhile, it was clear that Letterman did not have a clue who his latest guest was. Throughout, he condescendingly insisted on calling the shaven-headed Williams, who was twenty-five at the time, 'the kid'. It was a humbling experience and one that would set the tone for the subsequent attempts Robbie would make to break the US.

During one of those several failed assaults, I was talking to a highly successful New York record-label head who had been informally asked by Robbie's people for his advice on how to solve the problem of the singer's inability to make any inroads in the States. He told me what he told them: that to Americans, Williams seemed 'hokey', meaning his act appeared contrived and corny, that he was trying too hard. Devastatingly, perhaps, for his hopes, the American audience was blissfully unaware of his backstory: he was the also-ran in Take That who confounded the odds and all logic to make it big in spite of himself, that his unashamedly self-referential lyrics could only be appreciated if you understood something of his chequered history. Not only was America in the dark about where he had come from, but it felt zero inclination, it seemed, to try to find out.

The gloom of the American experience was lifted by the fact that *I've Been Expecting You* was on its way to going ten times platinum in the UK, but even closer to home, Williams was finding the experience of appearing before his fans to be traumatic. In August 1999, he returned from the States to play a massive gig at Slane Castle, County Meath, but the experience – to employ an overused word in the Robbie Williams lexicon – made him feel 'sad'. His feelings of inadequacy and disconnection, and his pervading sense of dystopia crystallized as he stood in front of 80,000 adoring faces on stage at the outdoor event near Dublin. Later, he would describe the show as the moment when he became aware that he had stumbled upon paradise syndrome, when all his hopes and ambitions – everything he had ever wanted in his life – had come true but had not altered his fundamental self-hate. As far as he was concerned, he was as big as he was ever going to get. People loved him – worshipped him, even – yet it did not touch the inherent misery he carried around with him. The realization shook him. Before and after the show, he was in a state of near hysteria, panicky and short of breath. For a time, his miserable experience on stage in front of those 80,000 Irish fans would taint his relationship with his audience. What saps they must be, he was inclined to muse, to pay good money, face all the frustration of travelling to his gigs, parking, all the petty annoyances that go with it, just to watch him. Someone, he had long ago concluded, who was so talentless and already a parody of himself: a cheap Norman Wisdom impersonator who, God knows how, had found himself up there in front of them on stage, making a complete prat of himself and hating every minute of it.

By the end of the year, the grind of the constant trips back and forth across the Atlantic had taken its toll. In Atlanta, Williams walked on stage completely naked pretending to be lost. Still the much-predicted breakthrough did not come. 'Millennium' only managed to reach number seventy-two on the Billboard Hot 100 and *The Ego Has Landed* stalled at number sixty-three on the album chart. The disappointment led Capitol to issue their ace card, 'Angels', as a single, but even that peaked at forty-one in the US singles chart. The pressure of trying to turn things round, plus the stress of the constant promotion and touring, caused Rob to break out in a painful rash. He had also developed an embarrassing facial twitch, a telltale sign to everyone around him that he had taken coke. Meanwhile, his drinking had reached epic proportions. Rob began to take a perverse pride in being able to sink a full bottle of sambuca in ten minutes, and during his most reckless drinking sessions could down twenty-five pints of Guinness.

The balloon finally went up in Austin, Texas, at the beginning of November. Somehow, Robbie had managed to make it through the final date of the tour and was in the mood to celebrate. That night he went on a major bender. He could only remember snippets of the night's events – when he found himself surrounded by strangers – and the experience frightened him.

The next day, he needed to be physically carried through the airport. His team persuaded the airline to upgrade him to first class and he was loaded into his seat, where he slept off the excesses of the previous night all the way to Stockholm, where he was due to do a show thirty-six hours later. Once there, doctors were called to his hotel room, and with the clock ticking down to the show, he managed to make it to the venue. However, with hours to go before the gig, Rob announced he was pulling out, despite being informed by a panicking David Enthoven that it would cost him £500,000. To top it off, Rob told his manager he was also scrapping his planned European tour.

Meanwhile, his American label, busy devoting large sums of money to his promotion stateside, began getting nervy. The cancellation of the European tour was evidence, it seemed, that Robbie, who had on his first meeting with the senior executives from Capitol laughably tried to persuade them of his blameless lifestyle, did not have the stomach for the fight. Simplistic as it was, such an assessment was hard to argue with on the basis of the evidence at hand. In London, EMI and Rob's management attempted to launch a rearguard action to minimize the damage. The press was spun the line that he was suffering from a viral infection, and Williams went on Radio 1 to insist he had not touched booze for a month and to explain away the cancellation of the shows by claiming he had injured himself falling off a quad bike. Few of those with their ear to the ground were convinced, however.

Privately, too, Rob had for some months been saying he had had enough, that he could not handle the pressure, hated having to go on stage, was frightened and repulsed by his fans and would have a mental breakdown if he was forced to go back out on the road. David Enthoven, who increasingly was being expected to fulfil the role of emotional prop and father confessor as much as manager, was under no illusion that it was an idle threat. Enthoven was ideally suited to the task, having fought his own battles with addiction. After building a successful management business, which bought him a gilded lifestyle and a huge collection of motorbikes, he had contrived to lose the lot through an expensive cocaine habit and, later, a full-blown addiction to heroin. By the mid-seventies his marriage had imploded, he had lost touch with his children, and his business partners had cut him loose. Ten years later, he was living in his dead mother's dilapidated house and sharing her old bed with his two dogs. Like Rob, he had been close to killing himself, but got himself into rehab and clean before starting over his career in the music business.

For Enthoven, caring for his damaged charge was a full-time job. He regularly found himself in Rob's flat in Kensington Park Road, Notting Hill, putting him to bed or responding to an emergency call in the middle of the night with Rob demanding he come over to hold his hand. Even later, when Williams was clean and sober, the calls still came. David has lost count of the number of times he has taken calls at 4 a.m. from his high-maintenance client and had to get out of bed at his Surrey home and drive in his pyjamas to Rob's in West London on some new mission of mercy. Sometimes he would arrive bleary-eyed and Rob would want to tell him of some scary dream he had woken up from. On other occasions Rob was thinking about having a drink and needed to be talked out of it. Some drunk prankster may have gone past his house and pressed his buzzer or, most commonly, Rob would just say he was frightened and could not sleep on his own. Enthoven would bunk down on the floor or crash out on a chair and Robbie would at last get to sleep.

Cocaine-induced paranoia mixed now with Rob's naturally overactive imagination. He started to think he could hear spirits moving around in his flat and talking to him. He became convinced that a crazed fan was planning to assassinate him like John Lennon. Even more worryingly, he began talking openly to members of his entourage about the possibility that his body may have become possessed by a malevolent force. At other times he would speculate for hours on end about whether he should get his flat exorcized by a priest.

His father, Pete, once told me that Rob's belief in the paranormal had gone back to his childhood when they lived at the Red Lion in Burslem. Rob, whose mother, Jan, read tarot cards, was about three at the time, and he and Pete were in the pub alone before opening time. As they walked past the empty bar, Rob looked in and said there were two men sitting by the counter. Humouring his son, Pete told him he should wave to them. Rob told him they could not wave back because they didn't have any hands.

Since his relocation from Stoke to London, Williams had twice insisted on moving out of flats and into hotels after becoming convinced they were possessed by demons. He also began telling family and friends that he had become aware that he had lived at least three times in the past. He would ramble for hours about how he had been alive in France during the French Revolution, had been a pharaoh in Ancient Egypt and a starving farmer in Ireland.

The experience in America was the final straw. When he returned home exhausted and strung out, he had a full-blown nervous breakdown, crying constantly and begging pitifully for help from those around him. Jan was called for and travelled down from Stoke to stay with him. Now a drug and alcohol counsellor, his mother should have been the ideal person to talk him down from the emotional ledge, but even she was unable to get through to him. Unknown to her, he had tried heroin again. The first time had been two years earlier and he had been so terrified by the experience that he had vowed never to touch it again, but in desperation, after running out of cocaine, he had tried it a second time. Again it had made him sick and manic. Jan had become used to calls from her son's management team asking her to drop everything and come to his rescue. A year earlier, Rob had pleaded in vain with his mother to try cocaine so she would have some understanding of the hold it had over him.

Jan was often the only person who could talk Rob round. Their

A fresh faced Robbie and Gary pose together in the early days, but behind the scenes there were already tensions.

This page: the boys with their manager Nigel Martin-Smith (*above left*); Take That was originally aimed at a gay audience, so the early costumes contained a fair bit of leather and lycra . . .

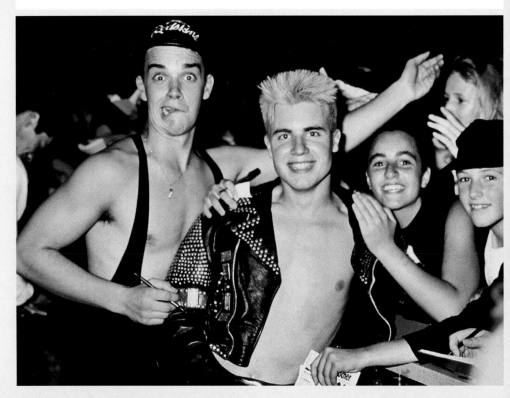

. . . until the huge appeal to teenage girls was realized and the wardrobe suitably adapted.

An early impromptu performance in an Anglesey car park in 1990.

The band gets the latest delivery of love letters from devoted Thatters.

Gary takes his place centre stage. Robbie, however, hated playing second fiddle to his nemesis and being what he termed 'Barlow's backing dancer'.

Opposite top: A mad for it Robbie with Liam Gallagher at Glastonbury in the summer of 1995. His appearance at the festival led to his split from the band who continued as a foursome (*middle*) for another few months, even going on tour (*bottom*).

Jason, Gary, Mark and Howard break many hearts at the February 1996 press conference to announce their split.

When both Gary and Robbie went solo the rivalry really kicked in. Their first public appearance together at the Concert for Hope in 1997 (presented by Denise Van Outen) was on the face of it amicable, but afterwards Robbie publicly laid into Gary.

As Robbie's career soared, Gary had to face the disappointment over his floundering solo career, which coincided with a disastrous acting debut with Bill Maynard in *Heartbeat* and the melting down of his Madame Tussauds waxwork to make way for Britney Spears.

relationship was, and is, based on mutual adoration. Perhaps because his father had left them, Jan compensated by spoiling and feting her only son. Likewise, his sister, Sally, who now ran his fan club, was always indulgent of her little brother. But despite Rob's fame, the very able Jan was at the time generally assumed by most people in his life to exert unrivalled influence over him. During his early solo career, record executives and members of his team would be amazed to find Jan, who had no formal role in his management, sitting in on meetings. It was notable too that in her company, Rob routinely reverted to little-boy mode, with Jan a slightly domineering presence. Nor was it always a harmonious relationship. Kevin Kinsella told me of furious rows Rob had with his mother and Sally, and how he would break off contact with one or both of them for weeks at a time.

Even so, Robbie's management was understandably keen to call on all the help they could get as they faced up, with mounting horror, to the prospect of seeing their major asset self-destruct – particularly after having put so much effort into breathing life into the once-washed-up boy-band reject. If only Robbie could be persuaded to hold it together, the rewards to those around him would be virtually limitless. Unfortunately, his drug use was making him ever more delusional. Williams began to believe that he was being targeted by Mafia gangsters and that Special Branch had entered his flat and sewn listening devices into his sofa. He also became terrified of going out in case he was abducted and gang-raped.

His cause for concern was not always drug-induced. In Jamaica on a writing trip with Guy, Rob left the safety of the hotel alone late one night in search of cocaine. At a nearby run-down bar, he was introduced to a drug dealer who sold him cocaine for $100, but when he got back to his room, Rob found out the coke was, in fact, nothing stronger than chalk dust. Unwisely, he returned to the bar in a fury, only to have to beat a humiliating retreat when the dealer marched him outside and held a machete to his throat.

Rob took to joking mirthlessly that he should not be left alone without a responsible adult, but was anyone out there suited to taking on the difficult job full-time?

CHAPTER FIVE

Dream Lovers

In early January 2000, Gary locked himself in a toilet cubicle in the clubhouse of a hotel on the Caribbean island of Nevis, changed out of his beachwear into a brand-new cream Savile Row suit and crisp white linen shirt, emerged a few minutes later with the suit carrier still draped over his arm and married his long-time girlfriend, Dawn Andrews, in a simple ceremony, watched by just their parents and brothers. Dawn wore her blonde hair in a simple elfin style, a plain white strappy dress designed by her brother and held a posy of cerise bougainvillea. That morning, Gary, who played a game of tennis to get over his pre-wedding jitters, had been warned that the press were making calls after being tipped off. Keen to ensure the occasion was not crashed by any unwanted guests leaping out of the undergrowth and brandishing 300-millimetre lenses, he cancelled their plans to get married on the beach and instead held the service inside. His desire to keep the paparazzi at bay was not to protect some megabucks deal with *Hello!* or *OK!* magazine, invited to 'share the couple's joy' over twenty-five glossy pages of soft-core fawnography; Barlow simply wanted to get married without having to offer it up for public consumption. After the short wedding ceremony, at which his father acted as best man, the bride and groom changed back out of their bridal outfits and went for a quiet family dinner.

By the time the press arrived, the couple were about to fly off to the tiny nearby island of Barbuda for their honeymoon. Originally, the plan had been for a big wedding in the grounds of Delamere Manor, with 150 guests, marquees and entertainment. Gary had sounded out Howard Donald, the only member of Take That he was still in regular contact with, about taking on the role of best man. In the end, though, Dawn, down to earth and unshowy, said she would prefer a minimum of fuss. They decided to get married on the beach with only those closest to them for company, the way Gary's brother had done when he married Lisa a few years earlier. The tiny and unspoilt Nevis, with its handful of hotels and reputation for respecting the privacy of its celebrity visitors, was eventually settled on by the couple, who had been living together at Delamere Manor for the past two years.

Previously, Gary had set his heart on a huge occasion on the lawn at the house. All the other members of Take That would be invited, he told an interviewer the previous summer, except one. 'Robbie's invitation will be lost in the post,' he growled, 'because I only want friends there. Robbie's comments about me have become part of life. Now I just want to move on. I've reached a new era in my life. I am very much in love and very content with my life, which is something people in music often fight against.' In an ill-concealed dig at his rival's messy personal life, he added: 'Some people have a great public image but their private life suffers. This time my personal life is outweighing my musical one. It feels good. I haven't had that before.'

When asked whether he would be selling his lavish wedding to the highest magazine bidder, Gary sniffed: 'That's for *EastEnders* actresses on £30,000 a year who need the money to pay for their weddings.' Certainly, despite his quickly sinking career, Gary did not have the added burden of being short of cash. Even in 2005, ten years after leaving Take That, the careful Barlow still had the £15-million nest egg he had exited the band with safely in his savings account. Meanwhile, Gary was talking excitedly about wanting at least four children, whom he would teach to play the viola, violin, cello and bass to create his own mid-Cheshire version of the von Trapps.

The low-key wedding was in keeping with their positively muted engagement. Gary had meant to take Dawn to New York to pop the question, but ended up proposing the previous February over a Chinese takeaway at the flat they kept in London.

With Dawn reluctant to be thrust into the corporate glad-handing, networking and the record-company dinners that had been so much a part of Gary's life until that point, he now found himself subconsciously disengaging from the business too. To some at his record company, however, his happiness in his idyll in the North was taken as increasing evidence that not only had Gary lost his way creatively, but that the one-time raw ambition and killer instinct that had served him so well on the way up had now deserted him. The gripe among some of those surrounding him was that domestic bliss and all the talk of his marriage had taken the edge off him, that he had become too comfortable, too middle class. It was not a criticism Barlow accepted at the time, though later he was to admit that by removing himself from the real world, he had effectively become his own jailer. By locking himself away on his rich man's country estate, he failed to tackle the creeping stagnation that for so long had dulled and eaten away at his once prodigious talent.

What neither of them knew on their wedding day was that Dawn was already a month pregnant with their first child. They headed off to Barbuda, away from the press, and into a £2,000-a-night ocean-side room at the opulent K Club. For Gary, the honeymoon was the chance to put the problems of his failing career and his ongoing fractious dispute with Williams to one side. For her part, the new Mrs Barlow was already confessing to her husband that she now regretted not celebrating their big day with their friends. In fact, unknown to her, the romantic Gary had spent the past couple of months secretly arranging a bash at Delamere for their return, and while the newly weds sunned themselves on honeymoon, their parents and friends were finalizing the guest list for the celebration.

When the couple arrived back at Heathrow, they jumped in a cab straight to their flat in London to rest and later that day caught a train to Manchester. Dawn was still in the dark about the party, and while she slept in her seat, Gary was in the smoking compartment on his phone, putting the finishing touches to things. When the car driving them from the station to the house turned up the drive at Delamere, instead of taking them to the front door it delivered them to a marquee in the grounds, where 200 guests were inside waiting to shout, 'Surprise!' Other than the presence of Howard, Mark and Jason, it was a showbiz-free event. Unsurprisingly, Gary had kept his promise of leaving Rob off the guest list and he was joined out in the cold by Nigel Martin-Smith. The guests were served hearty Northern fare of meat and potato pie followed by apple crumble, and Howard, in his new guise of celebrity DJ, manned the turntables.

A few weeks later, Gary posted a message to his fans on his official website announcing that Dawn was pregnant. Keen that the press, who had revealed the details of his wedding, would not scoop him this time, he wrote: 'Well, everyone, for once may I be the first to tell you some exciting and exclusive news. I AM GOING TO BE A DAD!!!!! As if getting married wasn't enough excitement for one year! I knew the year 2000 would bring great things and here's the proof.' However, an unlucky thirteen days later, on 7 March, Gary received word that he had been dropped by his record company, BMG.

The call breaking the news came as he was driving along Edgware Road in London on his way to an interview at Heart FM. He had half expected it, seen the writing on the wall and was ready after the unmitigated flop of *Twelve Months, Eleven Days*, which sold just 28,000 copies in the UK. But what was the first thing that came into his mind after hanging up the call from his manager? Was it how he was going to tell his new wife, Dawn? Was it his parents, who had stood squarely behind him during the recent tough months? No, his initial thought on hearing the bad news was the glee with which it would be greeted by his nemesis. 'I can imagine the chat they'll be having in Robbie-land tonight,' he wrote in his memoirs. 'The cheers, wolf whistles and belly laughs. There's no question now, mate, you're the winner, hands down, and it's not over yet.'

There was no point doing the interview. The survival instinct kicked in and Gary found himself heading to the motorway and home to Cheshire. On the journey back, he called BMG and was met with a brick wall. He was about to encounter a new and unwelcome experience: the realization that nobody wants to take your calls or return your messages, the feeling of being suddenly invisible.

A month before Gary and Dawn's wedding, as the millennium drew to a close, Robbie's own romantic escapades were providing a convenient distraction from the damaging stories circulating in the press about his boozing and drugging. Equally conveniently, Tania Strecker, his latest squeeze, also happened to be the step-daughter of his manager, David Enthoven. Strecker, a leggy blonde with a taste for publicity and famous men, was a very minor celebrity, noted more for being the ex-girlfriend of British film director Guy Ritchie than for her few TV presenting roles, principally on the Channel 4 show *Naked Elvis*. Unlike the new Mr and Mrs Barlow, who had done their best to ensure their wedding was a strictly private affair, Rob and his girlfriend of a few weeks were very keen, it seemed, on getting as much promotion for themselves as possible. Amid much publicity, Williams and the twenty-six-year-old Tania, a single mother with a prominent position on the London party circuit, saw in the new millennium on a high-profile holiday to the Swiss ski resort of St Moritz. A couple of months later, the couple caused a near scrum at the Brits when they posed for the cameras, with the six-foot-tall Tania sporting an impossibly short pink spangled dress as Rob arrived to collect two awards.

Having the photogenic Strecker on his arm distracted attention not only from Williams's very real substance-abuse problems, but also from the rumours that had been gaining increasing currency among his hard-partying set that he was gay. Those who had invested so much money in him were terrified, so the gossip went, that irreparable damage would be done to his stellar career if he were to be outed. Such talk was hardly new. The five members of Take That had been forced long ago to accept that the flamboyant early incarnation of the band, when they had played the gay clubs, had marked them down in the eyes of some as a bunch of closet queens. Not that much of the tittle-tattle was based on anything that could, even at a stretch, be described as credible evidence. Nonetheless, they had become used to occasionally having to run the gauntlet of homophobic catcalls from jealous males down the years.

That the gossip about Williams persisted several years after leaving Take That was harder to fathom, given that for virtually the whole of the intervening period he had been publicly in a relationship with one desirable woman after another. Yet still the nudge-nudging would not die down, and Robbie's sporadic attempts to kill the stories only resulted for the most part in stoking the fire. It must be said that, to the chagrin of some of the senior members of his team, Williams had developed the habit of publicly playing with the subject of his sexuality. As early as his first self-penned song, 'Old Before I Die', he set the ambiguous tone of things to come by including the line 'Am I straight or gay?' A couple of years later, on the track 'Kids', a duet with pop princess Kylie Minogue, Robbie taunts: 'Press be asking, do I care for sodomy? I don't know. Yeah, probably.'

At the same time, he insisted to a documentary film crew: 'I have never done anything with a man. The thought has passed my mind, but it always stops at his bits. You try everything once in life. I'm not discounting it, but it hasn't appealed enough for me to do it yet.' On another occasion, however, he admitted that he did once kiss a male friend in a nightclub, saying: 'I just walked in and there was a friend of mine and he came up and kissed me. I thought: Sod it. I'll kiss you, then, but in a manly way.' A few months later, he was at it again and hinting that his experimentation might have gone beyond merely a kiss. Asked for the umpteenth time about his sexuality by a Melbourne journalist, he snapped: 'Sorry, everyone, I tried being gay, but it just wasn't for me. If I could take a gay pill now, I would.'

Yet despite his denial, juicy tales of his private life were being passed round the best showbiz parties. Shortly after Kevin Kinsella took over the reins of Rob's early solo career, Jan Williams got a call from Kinsella's wife, with whom Rob had been staying for several weeks. She told Rob's mother they needed to speak urgently about her son. Once the two women were face to face, Mrs Kinsella came quickly to the point. 'You do know Rob's gay, don't you?' said his manager's wife.

A no doubt bemused Jan hit back: 'I know my son, and my son's not gay.'

According to Rob, Mrs Kinsella did not reply, but merely gave her a look that said: 'Well, if you don't believe me . . .'

It was, without doubt, a bizarre incident. Williams himself can only think that she had come to the wrong conclusion about him because of an occasion when he had been to a Manchester casino with Kinsella, his wife and a gay male friend of Mrs Kinsella who worked in television with Jeremy Beadle. Rob says he can only assume that because he did not crack any un-PC gags about the guy's sexuality, the Kinsellas somehow got the impression that he must be homosexual too.

Kinsella himself, however, tells a slightly different version of the same story. He told me that he was convinced by what Rob told him at the time that he was struggling with the possibility he might be gay. Kinsella says the culmination was the incident in the casino in autumn 1995. According to Williams's ex-manager, Rob was approached by an attractive girl who made it perfectly obvious to Robbie that she wanted to have sex with him. Kinsella says Rob broke down in tears, telling her, 'I can't shag you. You remind me of my sister.' Which doesn't exactly hold much water as evidence that Rob was gay, though it could have appeared that way to someone already convinced he might be.

In my conversations with Kinsella, he has always been of the opinion that he believed Robbie was gay when he knew him. In other interviews, he has been just as forthright. In April 2004, he repeated his claims in a Channel 4 documentary *The Truth About Take That*. The manager claimed he believed Williams could not come out because of fears that it would damage his career. 'I don't think he is bisexual. I think he is totally gay,' said Kinsella, 'but [he is] controlled by parameters which say you can't come out and say you are gay because it will affect your career and sales and people may not love you.'

Kinsella also claimed that during one conversation Rob told him he thought he might be gay. 'I said: "Well, it sounds to me like you are leaning towards gay, but do you enjoy it?" He said: "Well, yeah."'

Kinsella's comments appeared to be given extra weight because in the same programme Howard Donald also admitted he was unsure as to Williams's true sexual orientation. Howard said on air: 'Robbie just doesn't know what he is. It wouldn't surprise me if he was bisexual.'

Just what are we to make of Kevin Kinsella's comments? Well, to start with, it is important to put them into the context of his acrimonious parting of ways with Williams. Their split fired the starting gun on their long-running legal battle, with Kinsella claiming up to £400,000 in unpaid fees and expenses were owed to him by his former client. Rob's lawyers insisted there had never been a formal contract between the two men. As if to illustrate the depth of the falling-out, Williams penned a sarcastic dedication to the Kinsella family on the sleeve notes of his first album, *Life Thru a Lens*. 'You taught me so much about the business,' he wrote. 'I hope you get everything you want, but not from me!' The situation would later deteriorate to such an extent that Kinsella compiled a 164-page legal document outlining the details of his claim. Kinsella, who at one point was fighting the case without the help of lawyers, told me that sections of his statement were so controversial that in a pre-trial meeting the judge presiding in the case instructed him that they must be removed. Is it possible that the pugnacious Kinsella, a tough-talking former boxer, has had his opinion about Rob's sexuality clouded by the personal animosity between the two?

Nonetheless, Kinsella is not the only one of Rob's associates from that period who believes he was struggling with unresolved issues about his sexuality. Ray Heffernan, the friend who wrote an early version of 'Angels' with Rob, told me that when he met Williams at Christmas 1996, his angst over the subject was evident. The two men, who became friends when Rob celebrated the festive period on a drink- and drug-fuelled holiday in Dublin, spent time together talking about Rob's problems. The pair would go out drinking in the city and then go back to Heffernan's mother's house to crash out and recover from their night of partying. Heffernan is convinced that, when he knew him, Rob was unsure about whether he was straight or gay and suggests that he went for very attractive girls as if to prove a point. Heffernan adds: 'It was hard for him to find exactly who he was. Being in Take That had been a very hard time for him.'

As with Kinsella, however, Heffernan's relationship with Rob did not end well. Some years later, Williams claimed he had been freaked out almost immediately by Heffernan's odd behaviour. In Dublin, he said, Heffernan became increasingly clingy and began pestering him about whether they would see each other again. Rob says he gave him his favourite Stussy puffa jacket by way of reassurance that they would remain friends. When he returned home from Ireland, Rob was staying at his mother's new house in Stoke when the Dubliner arrived out of the blue on her doorstep one night. Rob had not given Heffernan his address and the experience shook him. 'What are you doing?' a shocked Rob asked him. According to Williams, it was clear that Heffernan had not been expecting such an unenthusiastic welcome. Rob says he gave him money for somewhere to stay and the fare for a ferry crossing back to Dublin.

Heffernan's version of events differs. He says Robbie had talked about him joining his band and invited him to England so they could hook up and write some more songs. Later, he says, Williams called him and told him to come to London, giving him a phone number to call when he arrived. When he landed in the capital, though, Rob was not there and Heffernan heard that he had gone back to Stoke to recover after a mammoth drinking binge. With nowhere to stay, he looked up a friend, who let him sleep on their floor for a few days. Still with no sign of Rob, and with the singer not answering his phone, Heffernan decided to hitchhike up to the Potteries. This, he says, would be nothing out of the ordinary in Ireland. Once there, he started asking around and was eventually pointed in the direction of Jan's house, which had her distinctive yellow Porsche on the driveway. As soon as the door was opened by a frightened-looking Rob, Heffernan immediately realized he was not happy to see him. Rob gave him a cup of tea and told him he was scaring him. The uninvited guest, who insists he thought Robbie would be pleased to see him, knew instantly that everything had gone horribly wrong and put his new friend's paranoia over his unscheduled arrival down to Rob's cocaine habit. Soon Jan appeared and took over the conversation, Heffernan told me, sending him on his way with £40 to stay at a local bed and break-fast.

It goes without saying, of course, that if Rob truly was in conflict over the issue, he would not have been the first person to suffer doubts before deciding it was his fate after all to be heterosexual. Nor must we discount the role his addiction might have played in his clearly messed-up emotional state. Whatever the case, it should not be used as a stick with which to beat him. Crucially, the effect that working in Take That had on him cannot be understated. Rob had been thrust into the gay scene at the tender age of sixteen. For all that Nigel Martin-Smith may have done his best to protect his young charges, it cannot be denied that during the band's early incarnation Take That was a product – a blatantly sexual product, with all its fetishist leather, studs and chains – aimed in part at least at gay men. What effect had being drooled over and ogled by older men as he danced for them on stage had on the teenage Rob? It is hard to argue that such an overtly sexual environment, be it gay or straight, is any place for an impressionable boy to be. If Rob had emerged conflicted, it would hardly be a surprise.

Kevin Kinsella says the situation was also a problem for the record companies. Given Williams's obvious appeal to the huge female audience they were aiming at, they were concerned, he says, that there would be a danger the Robbie brand would be damaged by any concrete evidence that he was not that into women.

Even Williams himself admits that a girl he was dating at the height of Take That's success accused him of being gay following a horribly cringe-worthy incident. It occurred when Rob returned from a Take That tour, during which the band had been supported by D:Ream, who'd had a number-one hit in 1994 with 'Things

Can Only Get Better'. While they were on the road together, Rob got to know the group's lead singer, Peter Cunnah, who had developed a large gay following. In 2003, Williams told US gay magazine the *Advocate* that he arrived back from the tour exhausted and had gone to bed with his girlfriend. Once in bed, he said, she began performing oral sex on him, but he was so tired he fell asleep as she carried on. Soon he was dreaming about Cunnah, imagining that they were talking about the show after one of their performances. Finally, Rob says, he suddenly said aloud in his sleep: 'Oh, Peter!' Understandably, it put something of a dampener on their lovemaking and his girlfriend later wrote him a letter telling him of her humiliation.

There also existed for a time a suspicion within the media that some of his other relationships with famous women had been dreamed up in the offices of the PR teams to whom Williams pays a fortune to keep him in the papers. Central to the thesis that he was pulling a fast one was Rob's relationship with Spice Girl Geri Halliwell. The two spent a highly publicized holiday together in the south of France during the summer of 2000, staying at a £10,000-a-week villa Geri was renting on the Côte d'Azur. Much of their time was spent offering various photo opportunities to the hordes of newsmen who had been, somewhat conveniently, tipped off about the trip. Back home, the press happily documented the supposed romantic progress of the lovebirds as Rob gave Ginger Spice a piggyback on the beach at St Tropez for the cameras. Williams even invited a *Radio Times* journalist to interview him in the starry confines of their 'Riviera love nest'. The media frenzy was certainly good publicity for Robbie's number-one single 'Rock DJ', which had been released the previous week.

Indeed, the reality, as Rob would concede some time later, was that the whole circus was a concoction, aimed at winning the couple the sort of career-building column inches that simply could not be bought. Despite the indiscretions of the couple's 'friends', who gave chapter and verse about the affair to the press, the twosome were actually ensconced in very separate rooms at the villa. The fabrication was all the more odd given that by 2000 Rob had developed a public loathing of the paparazzi, who had long since taken to following his every move. Not that the pair didn't make good use of the publicity while it lasted. When Geri presented Williams with the award for Best British Male Artist at the Brits the following February, she teased the crowd, saying: 'He is very male, he's very healthy, he is a talented artist, and he's got the biggest heart. According to the press, he is giving me one. Let me return the favour by giving him one – my dearest friend Robert Williams.' Geri, like her ersatz paramour, had a record for making the most of the column inches on offer when it came to her supposed famous admirers. The previous year, she had been accused of trying to drum up publicity for herself with another relationship, this time with the then Virgin Radio DJ Chris Evans.

Robbie himself was happy to resurrect the story during the promotional push for his 2001 album *Swing When You're Winning*. He made headlines by claiming he'd become scared of Geri when she started playing with dolls and speaking like a 'psychotic child'. Sleeping with the one-time Spice Girl 'wasn't really a sex thing', he added. It would be months before he finally came clean and admitted that not only had they never had sex, he had not dated a woman since his fling with Tania Strecker, two years earlier.

Likewise, he was happy to milk rumours that his relationship with Nicole Kidman, with whom he duetted on his number-one hit 'Somethin' Stupid' in 2001, had heated up once the crooning was over. Although his publicists did their best to talk up a romance with the Antipodean actress, who had recently split from Tom Cruise, nothing actually happened between them. Indeed, Williams later wrote the first track of his fifth album, *Escapology*, about his futile attempts to get her into bed. The crude and highly suggestive lyrics of 'How Peculiar', about an imagined sexual encounter with an unnamed Nicole at the Dorchester (her favourite London hotel), are not for the faint-hearted. But instead of being offended, when Nicole listened to the track – after being tipped off by mutual friends that she was the subject of Robbie's fantasies – she is said to have let out a 'squeal of excitement'.

Despite his attempt to deflect the gay tittle-tattle, it may have had some effect on Williams himself. That would have been one explanation for the supremely ill-advised stunt that Rob devised during his high-profile courtship of Rod Stewart's ex-wife Rachel Hunter in 2002. For several months the couple, who were first spotted together at a LA Lakers basketball game, became the subject of almost constant attention from the paparazzi in Los Angeles, where Williams had relocated from Britain earlier that year, in part at least to escape his hated photographer pursuers. Finally, in what appeared to be a major tabloid scoop, the *News of the World* in London ran a series of 'snatched' photographs of the two lovers frolicking on a sunlounger in the grounds of a Los Angeles hotel. Rob was naked and the shapely Kiwi model was topless in the pictures, which looked for all the world as if they had been taken by a sneaky long-lens camera, but in reality the shots turned out to be a set-up, staged by Rob and Miss Hunter, and sold via a photographic agency for £120,000 to the unsuspecting paper, although Williams gave his share to charity.

Given his utter contempt for the freelance snappers who trail him around and the papers they sell their pictures to, it was a very strange thing for Williams to do. Within days of the pictures appearing, rival newspapers were openly questioning their authenticity, and after the ruse was eventually exposed, Williams was forced to come clean. He shamefacedly admitted that the whole shoot, which actually took place at the house near Mulholland Drive that he was renting from Hollywood actor Dan Aykroyd, was a stunt, dreamed up and choreographed by himself.

Once his plan was rumbled, he sought to defend himself by explaining he'd contrived to invade his own privacy because he believed that if he flooded the market with sensational pictures of himself, the currency in pap pictures would be severely devalued. If that was the case, it was as naive as it was foolhardy. In fact, the hoax, into which his managers were reluctantly drawn, served only to intensify the press's interest in what might really be going on in his private life.

There is an even more bizarre postscript to the story. Later, Rob claimed that the photos had been the first of a set of three that he was going to offer to the tabloids he so despises. In another publicity stunt, he planned to have himself and Rachel photographed in the midst of what would appear to be a blazing row in the street, and him kissing Miss Hunter's sister. A third set, which he actually went so far as to pose for, consisted, he admits, of him being photographed coming out of a Gay-Mart store in LA hand in hand with a male friend. After the debacle of the first pictures, however, he says he had the 'gay' pictures destroyed.

For the most part, Williams has been prepared to accept that the gossip goes with the territory. The exception came in late 2005, when he took legal action against the *People* newspaper over untrue and sordid allegations that he had sex with a male stranger in the toilets of a Manchester nightclub. Robbie sued the paper, which reportedly paid him £200,000 in damages.

Since leaving Take That, Williams had been publicly linked to a carousel of women, but relationships with the likes of the Honourable Jacqui Hamilton-Smith, actresses Anna Friel and Joely Richardson, and another Spice Girl, Melanie Chisholm, were notable in the main for their brevity. His longest relationship to date had been with singer Nicole Appleton, of nineties girl band All Saints.

They met in 1997 backstage at a TV show, and at the end of the year were both on the bill of the Princess Diana Concert of Hope at Battersea Power Station, after which the blonde singer invited Rob to a party in London for her twenty-third birthday. They posed for a picture, taken on the Polaroid camera Nicole had received as a birthday present, and the following day, she asked her manager to get her Rob's phone number. At the time, Rob was publicly linked to Denise Van Outen, the presenter of Channel 4's *The Big Breakfast*. When Nicole eventually called him, Rob, who was recording at a studio in Buckinghamshire, invited her to meet him in the country for dinner.

From the very outset, however, the relationship was governed by Williams's addictions and all-round flakiness. Their next date was typical of the course their early romance would take. Rob was at a pre-New Year's Eve house party in North London and rang Nicole, asking her to join him. By the time she arrived, though, the party was over, a few stragglers were tidying the place up, and Appleton's new boyfriend was in a drug-induced coma, flat out on a sofa. Realizing he couldn't be left, she ordered a taxi, had him carried into it and escorted him back to his flat. A couple of days later, she was photographed leaving his place and news of their relationship was out. As far as the media were concerned, Nicole was viewed pretty much as a female version of Williams himself: a voracious party animal with a taste for drunkenness and falling out of the Met Bar and the Atlantic Bar and Grill at all hours of the night. They were also to a large extent after the same audience. Shortly after they got together, Robbie released his make-or-break single 'Angels'. The couple were in bed one morning when Williams's manager rang with the new chart positions, and to inform a deflated Rob that All Saints' single 'Never Ever' had beaten his to number one.

The couple were soon a fixture on the party and club circuit of the West End, turning up at the Brits together in February 1998. Once again, though, the competition between them was in evidence. Williams was vying for four awards but ended up winning none, while his girlfriend's band scooped two awards for Best British Video and Best British Single. Meanwhile, the relationship quickly came under strain because of their mutual work schedules and Nicole's unhappiness due to tensions within her own band. In her memoirs, *Together*, Appleton wrote: 'Rob was kind and sympathetic – he had been there himself. But ironically that is what made it so difficult. I would start off talking about All Saints and end up helping Rob out with the horrors of his own past in Take That. One night, we sat on the roof terrace in his flat in Notting Hill and he burst into tears talking about Take That. Bad management, the power of band members – he had seen it all before. I knew Rob's problems went a lot deeper, but it was hard for him to go that deep. He didn't want to be with his pain.'

In March, while Nicole was in Vancouver on a promotional tour, she discovered she was pregnant with Rob's baby. She calculated that she must have conceived on Valentine's Day, the previous month. Coincidentally, she found out she was expecting on the same day as her All Saints band mate Melanie Blatt. Nicole rang Rob in London. The conversation was stilted. Rob said he was tired. 'I have some news, something to tell you,' she said. He was silent, waiting for her to speak again. 'Mel and I both did a pregnancy test a few hours ago and I'm pregnant.'

'That's great, babe,' Rob instantly replied. 'I'm really happy about it. It's what I want.' His positive reaction was a relief to Nicole, who had allowed herself to doubt if her lover of three months would be as thrilled with the news as she had been, given that they had already split up temporarily a couple of weeks earlier. Plus the sad reality was that Rob at the time was not exactly father material. Aside from the obvious disadvantages that serial addictions present to fulfilling the most basic paternal duties, even keeping hold of a baby would have proved a potentially hazardous exercise for the infant because of the pronounced twitches and muscle spasms caused by the father-to-be's cocaine habit. Rob was twenty-four and his girlfriend a year his junior, but they gave the impression of being much younger. They would spend their nights alone, like a couple of schoolkids, in the playroom on the top floor of Robbie's house, playing computer games and pretending to be DJs. At the same time, they were prone to petty bickering, brought on by their prodigious capacity for drinking, and would embarrass their friends by flying off the handle with each other over such trivialities as what music to listen to, or what food to eat.

Once Nicole was back in the country, Rob, suddenly smitten with the idea of fatherhood, took her to see his grandmother Betty Williams in Stoke. He also showed her the new flat he was planning to buy. Standing outside on the pavement, he pointed at an upstairs window and announced that it would be their baby's room. They decided that if the baby was a girl, they would name her Grace. And Rob, who put his hands on his girlfriend's stomach and said that the baby was going to save his life, wrote a song called 'Grace' for his unborn child that would eventually feature on *I've Been Expecting You*.

Soon, though, outside forces were making themselves felt. Nicole says her management and record company began putting her under pressure, claiming a baby would damage her career and cajoling her into having the baby aborted. She says the record company even phoned her mother, saying she was making a mistake and that Williams was trouble. They tried the same tactics on Melanie Blatt, says Appleton, but while she dug in her heels and refused to contemplate giving up her child, Nicole began to be worn down by the corporate coercion she found herself faced with.

Nor was her relationship with Rob built on solid footings. The couple had to cope with spending weeks apart pursuing their respective careers. Williams was promoting his new single, 'Let Me Entertain You', and getting ready for a sell-out national tour, which was due to start in May 1998. For her part, Nicole was with All Saints in the US as they began a coast-to-coast PR campaign. The news of her pregnancy had, in truth, been little more than a transfusion given to a dying patient. Privately, they had both been telling friends they were unable to cope with the difficulties of trying to conduct a relationship that was taking place, in the main, over the phone. Nicole had also become weary of Rob's neediness, how the conversation would sooner rather than later come back round to his problems, his hang-ups, his career. Unlike some of his other girlfriends, notably the high-born Jacqui Hamilton-Smith, Rob's parents liked Nicole, and despite the fact that much of his drinking was done in her company, they felt she was a good influence on him.

A month later, with All Saints in New York for a tribute concert to Burt Bacharach, Nicole was close to breaking point. She rang Rob from her room in Trump Tower and in tears told him she had decided to have an abortion. He did not try to talk her out of it. He asked if she was sure it was what she wanted and told her he would support whatever decision she took. He said he was going to take the first Concorde flight out of London and would be with her the next morning. In Manhattan, the couple sat up all night talking, with Nicole crying as she wrestled with the decision. The following morning, they went together to a private abortion clinic. Rob waited outside the room while she had the procedure. The couple took the record-company limousine back to her hotel and the next day caught the Concorde flight home.

That summer of 1998, they got engaged, with Williams making his proposal on one knee and presenting her with an antique emerald-cut diamond ring. They immediately went on holiday to St Tropez to celebrate their upcoming nuptials, but already London was buzzing with unconfirmed rumours that Rob was seeing other people. A lap dancer with the comedy name of Sandy Palermo told a newspaper she had put on a show just for him at his flat. And the showbiz lovebirds were soon separated again when the girl band headed off on a tour of Brazil, Mexico and Argentina. Within two months Rob had had enough of the long-distance romance. His girlfriend checked her voicemail in Rio and heard her husband-to-be telling her the marriage was off. When she eventually managed to get him on the phone, the conversation was a one-sided affair. Rob wanted out. He was sick of not seeing her and had made up his mind.

Somehow, by the time the press got wind of the story, it was Nicole who had been the one doing the dumping, with Williams telling the *Sun* he had been left in tears by the split and was hoping they could patch up their problems. It didn't seem like Rob was having too much trouble getting over his heartbreak; off he went again to the south of France and was photographed on the beach with a bunch of beautiful girls. Then he was seen on the Costa del Sol enjoying all-night drinking sessions with a couple of blondes. Meanwhile, back home in London, a barmaid claimed she'd had sex with him at his house after serving him booze at the club DTPM. In spite of this, he still told a journalist at the time that he was 'the loneliest man in the world'.

Given his capriciousness, however, it wasn't a surprise to anyone around him when he suddenly announced to his friends that he wanted Nicole back. They went out for sushi at Nobu on Park Lane and emerged drunk, with Rob giving Nicky a piggyback ride for the waiting snappers. Within days the marriage plans were back on.

Their turbulent relationship also served as inspiration for several of the songs on Robbie's second album, *I've Been Expecting You*. One track, 'Win Some, Lose Some', features Appleton purring: 'I love you, baby.' As well as 'Grace', 'Heaven From Here' was written about their romance. A year into the relationship, however, it was increasingly obvious that it was on its last legs. Rob's drinking only complicated a situation that, even without the addition of stimulants, was riven by petty jealousies, competing egos and childish arguments. In a gesture typical of Rob, he sent a thousand red roses to the hotel room where she was staying on tour, but a few days later, he was drunk and belligerent. On Christmas Eve 1998, he went out again and got wrecked. The next day, he and Nicole had

been invited to her parents' house in North-West London for
Christmas lunch, but Rob was hung-over and unable to eat.
Embarrassed, she tried to eat some of his food, so her parents would
not notice how bad a state he was in. Later, Rob went to a nearby
pub in Belsize Park and spent the rest of the day drinking. Once
back at Nicole's flat that night, he had a panic attack and went
wild. She told him that he was scaring her and he said: 'All right,
I'll leave.'

Appleton replied: 'If you go out the door, don't come back.'

Rob made off into the Christmas-night snow. Out of his tree and
needing somewhere to bed down, he somehow managed to find his
way to a faceless London hotel, but the corporate surroundings of
the Stakis Hotel in Edgware was no place for anyone on Christmas
night. Rob, smashed out of his head, propped up the bar, telling
anyone who would listen about his row with Nicole. Later, he
invited four men to his room and then disappeared. He made it
only as far as a sofa in a corridor and passed out. As he lay there,
wasted, passing guests decided it would be a fun idea to smear him
with toothpaste and shaving foam and flog the resulting photos to
the *Sun*.

Four years later, in autumn 2002, Rob debuted a new song from
his album *Escapology* on stage. To much cheering from the audience, he dedicated the track 'Sexed Up' to his ex-fiancée, who was
now living with his old sparring partner Liam Gallagher. One
doubts it is a song Nicole likes to play at dinner parties. Time had
clearly not been a healer. In public, Rob had wished his ex well
and spoken philosophically about how the relationship simply had
not been meant to be. On record, it was a different matter entirely.
This was payback on a compact disc, a nasty, get-even piece of

vitriol in the key of C. No punches were pulled, no hostages taken. It was full of white-hot antipathy and resentment.

Despite, or possibly because of, the way his high-profile relationships with a succession of beautiful and famous women were played out for public consumption, the gay gossip – privately so vexatious to those responsible for Brand Robbie – would endure for some time to come.

CHAPTER SIX

Back for Pud

At what point does the realization finally kick in? When does the moment come that it all crystallizes, when you know it's finally over? In the case of Gary Barlow, the particular instant when the lightning bolt struck came as he stood in front of the mirror at home in Delamere Manor one day in early 2001 and looked failure full in the face. Not surprisingly, he did not much like what he saw. It was late afternoon and he was still in the grubby-looking dressing gown that had pretty much constituted his entire wardrobe for as long as he cared to remember. He was unshaven, with the burned-down butt of a Marlborough Light fixed between gritted teeth. His face was puffy, grey and old. He pulled down the red-rimmed lid of one watery eye with a nicotine-stained finger. When, he wondered, as he regarded himself incredulously, had he got so fat? He had not weighed himself for months, but he knew he must be well over fifteen stone. He tugged at the sides of his gaping robe, drawing them together over white man boobs and a pale pink paunch, and let out a rattling, wheezy shudder.

The previous day, Gary had been called in to see Celia McCamley, the Sony publishing executive who had drawn the short straw and was now responsible for what was left of Barlow's career. He brought her in a few months earlier after calling time on his long association with Virgin Music Publishing. The conversation, however, had not gone well. Even during the usual pleasantries McCamley sounded grave. She skirted around the subject for a bit, embarrassed about what she was about to tell him. She had, she said at last, been sending out tapes of his new songs to every record label she could think of, but they had been coming straight back. People were not even bothering to listen to them. In desperation, she admitted sheepishly, she had even begun to leave his name off the tapes in the hope that someone – anyone – would at least give them a hearing. Summoning up all her courage, she said finally: 'Gary, the only thing you can do is leave the country.'

Barlow was incredulous. 'Leave the country? What do you mean?'

'I think it would make sense,' McCamley replied, 'for you to get away and work somewhere else for a bit. Britain needs to forget about you.'

It must have been pretty tempting for Gary to explain that from where he was standing, it seemed fairly obvious that the country was well on the way to doing just that without him going to all the trouble of relocating abroad. Nonetheless, he was forced to agree that she had a point. By the start of 2001 Gary had slipped from being merely pop's perennial joke figure to a twenty-four-carat musical leper. If he was seeking evidence of the full extent of his startling demise, he needed to look no further than the humiliation of his recent collaboration with the now ex-Spice Girl Victoria Beckham. He had been working on and off with Victoria at his studio in Delamere Manor on new material for her ill-fated solo career. After their writing sessions, David Beckham, who at the time was still a Manchester United player, would drive out and collect her. When a newspaper got wind of the collaboration, however, it reported that she had denied it. Which begs the question: just how bad do things need to be before even Posh Spice is embarrassed to admit to working with you?

She was not the only one. Gary had also been writing some songs for bubblegum teeny-boppers Steps – until, that is, he was rung by their manager. The manager, says Gary, told him he had received a phone call from one of the newspapers to the effect that if Steps used any of Gary Barlow's songs on their new album, the paper would refuse to write about the band. At the same time, Gary got a call to say that with regret Madame Tussauds were having to melt down his waxwork dummy because they needed it to make Britney Spears.

The intervening months had gone by in a haze. Lounging around in his studio, he tried to work while Dawn was out, but days would go by without a chord or lyric being recorded. He found himself slumped over the console at four or five in the morning, still hoping that the well was not completely dry, that somehow he could lead himself through the overgrown maze in his head and back to the door marked 'Hits'. More often than not, he would skulk off to bed and find that by the time he felt able to get up again, it was already past noon. In recent times, he had taken to writing out songs faintly in pencil so he could easily rub them out when he realized how bad they were. The awe-inspiring creativity he once had was long gone.

Matters weren't helped by the fact that along with the three or four packs of fags he was getting through a day, he was also smoking up to fifteen spliffs. His new routine involved ending the evening by smoking only half of his last joint so that when he eventually woke up the next day, he could get his next cannabis fix without having to skin up. The only joy in his life was the ultra-loyal Dawn and their firstborn, Dan, who arrived in August 2000. Dawn spent a horrible twenty-four hours in labour before their son appeared, weighing a substantial 9 pounds 1.5 ounces. His arrival was to prove correct a prediction that Gary had made early in the couple's courtship. Two weeks after they'd got together, Gary had told his new girlfriend they would one day have a son called Daniel. Now Gary would spend hours playing with the baby by way of putting off having to face sitting once again at his keyboard.

He would study his old songs, desperately trying to work out how he had lost his once prodigious talent. 'I can't stop crying,' he wrote in his memoirs. 'Just when I think I've finished, I start again . . . How can something go from being so easy to virtually fucking impossible?' Few would have blamed Gary if he had begun to suspect he was the victim of a big practical joke dreamed up by some piss-taking higher power. What he knew for sure and what those around him who loved him also knew was that having his gift removed unequivocally and without warning was the cruellest of blows.

Nevertheless, Robbie was still in no mood to show the compassion the defeated Gary now surely deserved. In summer 2000, Williams had named his third album *Sing When You're Winning* in a transparent dig at his vanquished adversary. In another blatant jibe, he also called one of the tracks 'Knutsford City Limits' after the town Barlow had moved to during his early Take That years. The artwork on the CD consisted of five images of Rob dressed in a football strip, bearing his initials on the badge. Four of the beaming Robbies held up the fifth, who brandished an FA Cup-style trophy. As symbolism goes, it was hardly subtle, but clearly Rob liked the gag. So much, in fact, that he used it again the following year for his *Swing When You're Winning* interpretation of the Rat Pack standards of Frank Sinatra and Sammy Davis Junior. He was not the only one to dish it out. At the same time, Simon Cowell unkindly went on record to say that in the early days he had turned down the chance to sign Take That because Gary was too fat and he did not think he had what it took to be a star.

But whereas Gary's drug of choice generally came deep-fried, Rob's was more of the high-octane variety. In any event, Williams's bravado was little more than a fig leaf covering his own myriad problems. For some time he had been telling anyone who would listen that he had no wish ever to perform again; the task for his handlers now was to try to ensure that despite his evident self-loathing and apparent hatred of the experience of going on stage, the highly profitable bandwagon remained on the road. When, in summer 2000, the dates for Robbie's forthcoming UK tour went on sale, an unprecedented £6.7 million in tickets were sold in fewer than six hours. More than 44,000 seats for his shows at the NEC in Birmingham were gone before lunchtime on the first day of their sale. Meanwhile, phone lines crashed as the race began by fans to get their hands on 75,000 tickets for his appearances at Manchester's MEN Arena.

Unfortunately, just getting him on stage was proving a major obstacle to his team. Of course, the constant cajoling needed to get him to perform is an illustration of the basic deceit that lies at the heart of the relationship between artists and their record companies and management. For all that Rob has always called the people who

surround him twenty-four hours a day his 'friends', in reality the
bodyguards, managers and PAs are, when all is said and done, paid
to be there. They need Robbie Williams to go out and sell records
and get up on stage. It has sometimes been their job to put him out
in front of a crowd when he has been in no kind of shape for the
task. At other times, he has simply wanted people there to talk him
into facing an audience. The complicated relationship between
Robbie and his entourage can on occasion undoubtedly be warm
and caring, but it is not friendship in the true sense of the word.
Essentially, it is one of employer and employee, and another example
of the unreal orbit in which Williams found himself at the time. Like
most stars, he had surrounded himself – either out of preference or
by chance – with a support network whose sycophancy was
rewarded in their pay packets. They laughed at his jokes, indulged
his moods – the long, rambling accounts of last night's dream, the
self-pity and occasional tantrums – because, for the most part, their
livelihoods depended on it.

However, given the role that addictions had played in damaging
his own personal life, David Enthoven took an almost fatherly
interest in supporting Rob's efforts to face up to his drinking and
drug-taking. Ever since Robbie's visit to rehab three years earlier,
his manager had accompanied him to the Alcoholics Anonymous
meetings the singer visited on an ad-hoc basis. Even so, Williams's
continued assertions to interviewers that he was off the booze or
had kicked coke into touch were not fooling anyone. At the same
time, even Rob was becoming as scared by his own increasingly
volatile behaviour as those around him were. *Sing When You're
Winning*, which was released in August 2000, had been achieved
in spite of Williams, rather than because of him. As if to acknowledge that his input had rated no higher than the bare minimum,

on the sleeve notes of the album Rob dedicated the record to Guy Chambers, who, he wrote, 'is as much Robbie as I am'.

The pragmatic Chambers had developed a simple strategy for dealing with the recording process. If Rob found performing live, which was and is the one aspect at which he truly excels, to be a strain, then the laborious business of laying down his songs in the studio was akin to torture for him. The efficient and rigorous Chambers, however, quickly became adept at coaxing partial performances from the often-unwilling singer and cutting and pasting them into finished backing tracks that he and Steve Power would spend days and weeks crafting without Rob needing to be present. In many ways, the system worked perfectly. Williams didn't, for the most part, relish the thought of being within a hundred miles of a mixing desk or condenser microphone, and Chambers was content to turn out massive-selling pop records without the annoying distraction of the guy whose picture just happened to be slapped all over the front of it venturing his drunken opinions.

The realization on Rob's part that action needed to be taken to deal with his twin props of booze and drugs was, at this point, still some months away, but there seemed to those around him to be an inevitable progression towards him reaching some sort of full stop. It was impossible to predict, however, whether that would be his decision to stop taking drugs for ever, to get himself clean and begin a new sober phase, or if something altogether uglier was approaching,

Despite his condition, *Sing When You're Winning* was another blockbuster. In July, the single 'Rock DJ' went straight to number one, selling 250,000 copies in its first week alone. To put his sales into some sort of perspective, it was perfectly possible at the time to reach the top of the charts by shifting no more than about 75,000 units. Meanwhile, the album was another number one, going eight times platinum in the UK and topping the charts in Germany, Ireland and New Zealand. However, during the making of the video for the third single off the album, 'Supreme', in November, Rob was stoned and ill, and filming had to be abandoned. There were also rumours he had got into a fight at the MTV Awards in Stockholm. His Sermon on the Mount Tour had kicked off that October, but by Christmas Rob's management and record company were desperate about his state of mind and sent him to Barbados, where Guy Chambers was given the poisoned chalice of trying his best to straighten Williams out while also attempting to cajole him into writing songs for their next album.

Meanwhile, locked away in Cheshire and unable to face the world, Gary took to refusing to venture out of Delamere – once for four months. As depression took hold, he only felt comfortable in the company of Dawn and baby Dan, his parents, his brother, Ian, and Ian's wife, Lisa. Friends no longer called. Now pretty much the only time the phone rang was with dreaded offers from reality-TV producers. There were also offers to appear in pantomime in Liverpool, and a part in *Joseph and the Amazing Technicolor Dreamcoat* – only not the lead role, just playing one of Joseph's brothers. Gary turned them all down. He had already had his fingers burned when, in March 2000, as he struggled to reconnect with a public that was stubbornly refusing to buy his records, he rashly agreed to appear in an episode of ITV's sixties-set drama *Heartbeat*.

His first professional acting role had Barlow playing the unlikely part of a hitchhiking soldier who recounts his various army experiences, then ends up getting arrested as the credits roll. It was a harsh comedown having to accept a cameo role on a Sunday-night drama, so it was all the more sadistic of the scriptwriters to ask Gary to deliver the immortal first line 'Onwards and upwards' to a lorry driver who stops on the road and asks him where he is going. Later, his character is seen describing how his best friend died in his arms in the war, with Barlow summoning up all the emotional intensity of a Monday-night bingo caller in an assisted-living common room.

As Gary was wheeled out by the makers of the series to talk to the press prior to his appearance on screen, it was clear the experience had not been an altogether positive one. 'When I was on the set, I just turned to jelly,' he admitted candidly. Nor, he revealed worryingly, did the show's budget stretch to supplying even international celebrities with their own stunt doubles. When the lorry in which he was travelling with actor Bill Maynard was required to slam into a tree at 50 miles per hour, Gary was simply strapped into a harness inside the cab and sent careering in the vehicle as the cameras rolled. Even given his genuine terror, though, on screen the novice thespian somehow contrived in the final analysis to convey what looked like only mild irritation at the prospect of the impending carnage. Rather optimistically perhaps, given that his performance was unlikely to trouble the BAFTA panel, Gary added: 'I don't think I'd do it again, even if *Coronation Street* asked me. But I might just be persuaded if I got a call from Robert De Niro to star in some big Hollywood blockbuster.' Suffice to say, the call never did come. Hardly surprisingly, the TV reviewers could not resist giving him a pasting, and the following day, he received the message that he had been binned by BMG. In retrospect, it is tempting to conclude that the two events were not unrelated.

Gary was not the only one coming a cropper in his attempts to forge a new career in acting. Jason Orange, who had spent most of his time since the demise of Take That travelling around the world on a journey of self-discovery, had made his on-screen debut in May 1998, playing a DJ in the Channel 4 thriller *Killer Net*, written by Lynda La Plante. Likewise, he was subjected to an almost universal mauling by the critics.

For his part, Howard Donald, in his new guise as a club DJ, was making ends meet by doing £1,000-a-show sessions behind the turntables at Butlin's in Skegness, while Mark Owen had been pursuing a solo career.

Reluctantly, Gary decided to heed his manager's advice and break for the border. He and Dawn decided to relocate to Los Angeles with Dan. The three moved into a swish rented ocean-view apartment in Santa Monica in early 2001. Despite the area's large contingent of expats, Barlow was to find a new anonymity and freedom away from the stares and sniggers that invariably stalked him back home. Crucially, it was also a massive relief to put 5,500 miles between himself and Robbie, and pray that the tentacles of Rob's enmity were unable to span oceans.

Gary revelled in the obscurity California offered. On their arrival, Dawn told him she was going to the supermarket, fully expecting as usual to make the trip on her own, but for the first time he could remember, Gary decided to tag along, amazed that he could push his trolley around incognito without the risk of being accosted as he ran the rule over the cake aisle. After the misery of showing his face in public back home, shopping and dining in Tinseltown's eateries became an unexpected treat. Even during the good times in Britain, he had always hated the experience of walking into a restaurant and having all eyes on him. In London, he would sit praying that someone more famous than him would come in and divert the attention of the gawping diners.

His newfound liberation was, however, as much a curse as a

blessing. After several months of working his way through the menus of LA's finest establishments, he ballooned to more than sixteen and a half stone. By way of completing the disguise, he decided to opt for a remarkably unflattering shaven-headed look. In truth, the barely there barnet was merely gilding the lily. Even with his old hairstyle, Gary would have been almost completely unrecognizable to his one-time fans. He took to wearing XXXL tracksuits and soon stairs were only attempted if there was the inducement of something to eat at the top of them. But at least he had given up his cigarette habit on the flight over from the UK.

Nominally, the plan was that Gary would hook up with the LA office of Sony Publishing, who would, in turn, put him in touch with other writers in the hope that the old magic would come flooding back. While in America, Barlow attended writing workshops and renewed his acquaintance with fellow British songwriter Eliot Kennedy, who had worked with Take That on their second album, *Everything Changes*, and had also written songs for the Spice Girls. The collaboration with Kennedy was instantly comfortable for Gary and within weeks the two were offered a production contract by Sony to form a writer-producer partnership. Barlow and the Sheffield-based Kennedy set up True North Productions and Barlow's agent, Martin Barter, told the *Daily Mail* at the time: 'Gary has absolutely no plans to be an artist again.' By way of heralding his transformation from performer to backroom boy, a song he wrote for boy band Blue, called 'Girl I'll Never Understand', eventually appeared on the group's debut album in November 2001.

Barlow returned from his sojourn in America at the end of that summer fat, but with his shattered confidence having been given a minor boost. Now the issue of his weight needed to be addressed.

The tipping point came when he was papped by photographers from the *Daily Mirror* coming out of his local pub in Cheshire. At the same time, Dawn told him that she had been agonizing over the subject for a while now but felt she had to tell him for his own good that he needed to see a doctor. The physician's scales told him he was nudging seventeen stone and Gary heard the doctor saying the words 'clinically obese'.

His arrival back on home shores also coincided with him getting back in touch with his ex-Take That band mates. After months of radio silence, Gary contacted Mark, Jason, Howard and Nigel Martin-Smith to propose their first get-together in more than five years. On Barlow's part, it was an act of contrition and forgiveness. For one, he had been feeling guilty about the way he had sacked Nigel three years earlier. As with Robbie, the situation between Gary and Martin-Smith had quickly descended into a legal squabble that resulted in considerable bad blood between the two men. Now Gary was prepared to let bygones be bygones. He was also keen to make amends with Jason. The two were not on speaking terms after Jason's brother, Simon Orange, went close to being forced out of business following a legal spat with Barlow.

Gary had insisted on signing over all his financial affairs to Simon Orange's company, but in 1996, the firm was inadvertently drawn into an investigation by the Fraud Squad over the purchase of a building in Manchester that had been resold to Barlow as an investment. Without waiting for an explanation from Simon Orange, Gary, assuming wrongly that he had been ripped off, called in his lawyers and ordered accountants to freeze all his financial dealings with Orange. Meanwhile, he ordered his legal team to remove every penny he had invested with him. As the once friendly relationship with Simon was forgotten overnight, Gary refused to take any of the phone calls Jason tried to make on his brother's behalf and issued a writ against Simon Orange's company. It was not until later, when his accountants were finally able to report back to him, that Gary discovered that not only was Simon Orange innocent of any wrongdoing, but he had actually done an excellent job of caring for Barlow's finances. Orange's business would later recover, but Gary naturally felt guilty over the way he had behaved, and the episode had created a tension with Jason that Gary was keen to resolve.

Barlow's new desire for harmony was one of the more obvious side effects of his sojourn in California. During his stay there, he had become infected – like so many before him – with the New Age contagion prevalent on America's West Coast. Of all the themes he had been exposed to out there, the one that resonated most was the theory known as the Law of Attraction. Soon Gary was a card-carrying devotee. The school of thinking was a principal part of the teachings of the New Thought Movement of the early years of the twentieth century, which essentially held that an individual could achieve what he or she wanted through positive thought. Likewise, the Law of Attraction ascribed metaphysical powers to thought processes. In a nutshell, disciples of the theory believe that 'like attracts like' and that positive and negative thinking bring positive and negative physical results. As with most things, its American aficionados have found a way of bringing the hypothesis to bear on the subject of making money. Hence the man wanting more money is taught not to say: 'I wish I had more money.' Instead, he is advised to focus his mind on achieving the goal by saying: 'I will find a job that makes me more money.'

For his part, Gary decided the lessons he had learned in LA could be put to good use back home when it came to making amends to those he had stepped on during the previous traumatic few years. Inspired by this new way of thinking, he drew up a list while in Tinseltown of all the people to whom he wanted to say sorry. Once purged of the negativity he had been carrying around with him, he would be free to focus his attention on achieving his exciting new goals. If it all sounded vaguely hippyish, it was, but Gary approached this new religion with all the unselfconsciousness and unquestioning zeal of the recent convert.

Astonishingly, his mood of conciliation even extended, admittedly somewhat reluctantly, to the hated Williams. After arranging to meet Nigel and the others boys at Martin-Smith's house, Barlow agreed that Jason should make contact with Robbie's agent to invite him to what, despite Gary's best intentions, promised to be a somewhat tense affair. Unsurprisingly, Williams was a no-show, but the occasion proved to be pleasantly harmonious, with the four former Take That members falling relatively easily back into their old bantering ways. Only Martin-Smith, keen to put his ex-protégés to work again, spoilt the mood by trying to persuade them to agree to appear in a documentary about the band and its break-up. Gary was unequivocal. To embarrassed silence he stood up and shouted that he would not be taking part. He was adamant, he told them, that he would never again be in the public eye.

Rob, too, was announcing a significant change in his professional status. Earlier in 2001, at the London Arena in Docklands, where he was starting rehearsals for a vast European stage of his latest tour, Rob stood before his assembled band and crew to make an announcement. He was, he declared, now officially clean. He had stopped drinking and taking drugs, he told them. Yes, he knew that many of them had seen him quit before only to start again, but this time he was committed to making his new period of abstinence last. He had accepted he was an alcoholic and drug addict, and knew that if he had to watch those around him getting drunk or high, there was a huge danger he would relapse. Therefore, he decreed, the tour was going to be dry, not just for him, but for all of them.

Once again David Enthoven accepted the job of part-time hand-holder and full-time nursemaid and found the locations of AA meetings in every city of the European tour so he and Rob could head off together before shows. There, the continent's biggest pop star would sit before a room full of strangers and announce: 'My name's Robert and I'm an alcoholic.' Where once his nights were spent doing his best to avoid the possibility of making even the briefest re-entry into the realms of reality, now the bottles of sambuca and chopped-out lines of coke on his hotel coffee tables were replaced by a pile of playing cards as Rob, Enthoven, Rob's bodyguard, Duncan 'Pompey' Wilkinson, and various select members of the crew were invited to join him in a hand of the children's game Uno. Sitting around drinking Evian and coffee, the group would also play round after round of the Hat Game, in which players put the names of famous people in a hat and have to do an impersonation of them while everyone else tries to guess their identity.

His newfound sobriety bore instant fruit. Where so recently the prospect of touring had been enough to evoke a feeling of gnawing dread and his attitude to playing live had been one of visceral revulsion, Rob now simply didn't like them. But at least it was a start. In fact, as the tour progressed, the situation improved to such an extent that when it neared its conclusion, his feelings towards the whole process of being on the road could actually be described as ambivalent.

Even a disturbing and potentially dangerous incident during the tour could not throw him off track. In February 2001, on the German leg of his European tour, Rob was attacked on stage by a deranged fan. The frightening episode took place at Stuttgart's Schleyerhalle as he was singing the first verse of 'Supreme'. A man somehow managed to dodge the security team placed at all corners of the stage, run up behind Williams and push him off the front of the stage. Rob fell six feet into the orchestra pit, followed by his attacker. Rob's guitarist Fil Eisler jumped down to help Rob, followed by the security team, who dragged the attacker away. Williams escaped with no more than a bruised knee and, to his credit, got back up on stage and carried on with the show, but the incident only added to the sense that he was under siege, particularly when it transpired from his interview with the Stuttgart Police that the stage invader was not just some drunk or prankster who had done it for a dare, but a bona-fide nut who was convinced the man he had attacked was not the real Robbie Williams but an impostor. From that moment on Williams ordered that instead of simply having his minders with him when he was on tour or working, he now wanted round-the-clock protection whether he was out for dinner, walking his dogs or simply sitting at home watching TV.

But there were, Rob was prepared to admit, even moments when he actually enjoyed being up there in front of his screaming acolytes, when getting paid a fortune every night to strut his stuff on stage and have every word that came out of his mouth cheered to the rafters felt like something approaching pleasurable.

Even so, he remained unsure about whether he wanted to carry on going to work as Robbie Williams. In spring 2001, Rob went to Los Angeles to record a video for the reworking of 'We Are the

Champions', the song he performed with the remaining members of Queen for the forthcoming film *A Knight's Tale*. During the recording of the song, Brian May and Roger Taylor of the band had invited him to take over the role of the dearly departed Freddie Mercury and go on the road with them on a major world tour. Rob thought about it long and hard and was very close to giving up his solo career to become a member of a band again before finally turning down the offer.

Nevertheless, such is the make-up of the Williams psyche that even the happy revelation that he was once again partly able to enjoy being on stage was, perversely, the trigger for further angst. Why, he took to asking – both publicly and privately – had he wasted so much time hating what he was doing? This was his gift, after all. It would not last for ever. There would be times in the future, in the near future likely as not, when he would be washed up, ignored and laughed at, when he would become another pop postscript like that sad sack Gary Barlow, rejected and despised. What wouldn't Barlow do, Rob mused, to swap places with him now? Just how much would Gary give to stare, like he did every night, into the eyes of 15,000 or 20,000 people and see nothing but love and adulation reflected back at him?

Indeed, down the years it has become something of a private joke among those closest to Williams that Barlow's name has a habit of cropping up in Robbie's conversation at either the happiest or saddest of times. One associate tells the story of an occasion shortly before his decision to get clean when Rob had been brought close to his lowest ebb by his addictions. Various discussions had taken place without Robbie's knowledge by management, his family and friends in a bid to come to some definite agreement about how best he should be treated. During one of the many heart-to-hearts with him that were attempted by various members of his then inner circle, some friends were attempting to persuade Rob, for the umpteenth time, that he was in danger of throwing away everything that he'd worked so hard for. Throughout the pep talk Rob, who was coming down after a particularly heavy night, had been listless and unresponsive. Then, all of sudden, his eyes widened in a look of outrage. 'Throw it all away?' he spat back. 'And see that fat cunt Barlow dance on my grave? No fucking way!'

As Gary knew only too well, the Robbie Williams approach to interpersonal conflict invariably resulted in him deploying the nuclear option. Rob seemed to revel in combat, opening up new fronts all the time to add to his perennial bêtes noires of Barlow and Nigel Martin-Smith. Others who have felt the white heat of his ire include singer Sophie Ellis-Bextor, who made the mistake of turning down the chance to support Robbie on tour and then criticized his single 'Millennium' on TV in 1998. Unbeknown to Ellis-Bextor, her comments were aired the night before the funeral of Williams's beloved grandmother. The next day at the service, he was appalled to find paparazzi hanging around taking pictures at the church. Somehow in Rob's mind the two events – Ellis-Bextor's comments and the death of his grandmother and her funeral – would become conflated. As a result, he bore a massive grudge against the daughter of ex-*Blue Peter* presenter Janet Ellis. Even years later, the fervour of his loathing had not abated. According to Williams, Ellis-Bextor was a 'poisonous witch', was 'malicious' and had a 'face like a satellite dish'.

Likewise, he has never forgiven World Party front man Karl Wallinger, who wrote one of Williams's biggest hits, 'She's the One', after he allegedly made some unflattering comments about him.

Rob has wasted no opportunity to exact payback. During rehearsals for a sell-out show at Edinburgh's Murrayfield Stadium, he launched into a diatribe against Wallinger from the stage as he introduced 'She's the One'. 'Robbie Williams records it and makes it hugely popular,' he spat. 'Karl Wallinger – is he happy? Is he fuck. The ungrateful bastard. Ungrateful fat bastard, eh? I bet he was fucking happy when the royalty cheque came in. Every fucking time I sing that song now I'm thinking of that cunt. Who's the bigger cunt, then? Him! The answer's him!'

Then there was the bizarre case of a paparazzo called Jason Fraser, who made the mistake of trying to talk to Williams in the VIP area of a nightclub in the south of France. Rob gave him short shrift, but that was not enough. Later, he told his entourage he wanted to kick the photographer's face through a window, that he wanted to glass him and make him blind, then take razor blades and cut his feet open and pour Tabasco sauce on to the wounds. Warming to his theme, he carried on, saying he would make the hapless snapper take acid and hire a helicopter, blindfold him and have it take off so Fraser thought it was a mile up, when in fact it was only two feet off the ground. Then, he continued, he would chuck him out and watch him shit himself.

Another to feel the full force of his opprobrium was Louis Walsh. Williams and the *X Factor* judge had once been friendly acquaintances, and Walsh had arranged a studio for Rob to use when he wanted to record a demo of 'Angels' in Dublin. The Irishman burned his bridges with Robbie, though, by calling him a 'useless karaoke singer' and saying he would have been nothing without Guy Chambers. The remarks later led Rob to buttonhole Walsh outside the Conrad Hotel in London and launch a tirade against the squirming Boyzone manager.

Even relatively minor infringements are rarely forgotten. Shortly after he moved to Los Angeles, some years later, Rob became besotted with Cameron Diaz and sent her a DVD of his appearance at the Royal Albert Hall in the hope of impressing the actress enough to go on a date with him. Eventually, after much negotiation, she agreed to visit a go-karting track with him and a group of their friends. The flirtation, however, was over before it had begun and the beautiful Miss Diaz politely gave him the brush-off. Safe to say the rejection did not go down well with Williams, who thereafter took to calling her 'Zippy' after the wide-mouthed felt character from seventies kids' TV show *Rainbow*.

Grievances are allowed to smoulder and fester, each new perceived slight composted down for reuse at some future date. Creatively, however, these feuds and petty fallings-out have been fertile ground. When it comes to revenge, Robbie can serve it hot or cold. One of those to feel his ire on record was his father, Pete. The height of Rob's addictions in 2000 saw the beginning of a two-year estrangement in their relationship that had its origins in a growing resentment he felt over Pete's long absences during his childhood as he followed his own showbiz dream, and his belief that his father had never expected him to amount to much. Rob's sense of abandonment simmered; how could his father have walked out and abandoned him as a three-year-old to go schlepping over Britain and stay in two-bit dives, doing what he loved? There would be recriminations. Robbie had already laid into his father on a track from his *I've Been Expecting You* album, called 'These Dreams'. In the song, Rob metes out a musical kicking to Pete over the heartache his abandonment caused Jan. During the hiatus in their relationship, Rob's seething anger at Pete once again came spewing out in the lyrics of single 'My Culture', recorded with

1 Giant Leap in 2002. In an excoriating rap he taunts his father for underestimating him and writing off his chances of making it as a pop star.

The words could just as easily have been written for Gary. Perhaps it was simply a case of the artist in Williams feeling the overwhelming compulsion to put down on paper and on record his true sentiments. Or was it Rob's utter refusal to accept what he perceived as his role as victim in his relationship with both Barlow and his father, his belief that his only recourse is to go on the attack, to pour out the bile and venom by way of taking back the power? Pete, like Gary, would just have to take his medicine, but he must surely have been forgiven for asking himself if it was really necessary for his son to set out to berate and belittle him so publicly.

Gary, of course, knew the feeling, as did Nigel Martin-Smith, who in the years to come would find himself on the end of yet another musical Williams broadside. So too would ex-girlfriends like Nicole Appleton as we have seen. More than love, loss and longing, it has been hate that so often has been the propellant he has employed to fire his creativity – running counter to his public mantra of 'Let Love Be Your Energy'.

Conversely, such negative emotions have never sat well with Barlow. His default position has always been to find conflict of any sort emotionally draining and artistically stifling. It is no coincidence that the bitterness and rejection he felt at being dropped by BMG coincided with a period of creative paralysis. Robbie's reaction at such an impugning of his talents, such monumental impertinence, would doubtless have quickly involved thoughts of how he could get even on record. Barlow, however, simply went into his shell. So it is no real surprise, then, that where discord has existed, Gary has sought, not always for purely altruistic reasons, to neutralize it sooner rather than later.

For now at least, Rob's feud with Gary was far from over, despite Barlow's tentative proffering of an olive branch.

CHAPTER SEVEN

My Way ... or the Highway

At its most basic level, the concept of Robbie's *Swing When You're Winning* album and his performance of the record's Rat Pack standards at the Albert Hall in October 2001 was a classic case of celebrity conceit. Williams insisted on taking on the joint projects for the simple reason that he could, safe in the knowledge that he was now undisputedly the biggest pop star in the country. The album and the companion DVD, *Robbie Williams: Live at the Albert*, was a huge ego trip, a chance for a kid from Stoke to dress up sharp and play at being his heroes, Frank Sinatra, Sammy Davis Junior and Dean Martin, for the night. That, at least, was the way his record company, EMI, viewed the vanity project when Rob first mooted it. In fact, so unenthusiastic was the label, initially its executives refused to agree that the album would be counted as the fourth and final record of the singer's deal with them.

They need not have been concerned. *Swing When You're Winning* became an instant mammoth money-spinner, going straight to number one in the UK and staying there for six weeks. In all it stayed a record fifty-seven weeks in the charts, selling more than two million copies and going seven times platinum. It also went to number one in Germany, Austria, Ireland and Switzerland. In Germany, where Williams was now loved as much as at home, the record remained at number one for nine straight weeks, spending close to two years in the charts and becoming the biggest hit of his career. So far it has sold somewhere north of seven million copies around the world.

The *Swing When You're Winning* experiment moved Williams up another level. By celebrating his love of the cool classics of the fifties and sixties, he displayed a credible musical hinterland that few could have guessed at. The live show, recorded at the Albert Hall on 10 October and released in time for Christmas, also helped establish him an audience beyond pop fans. Now his skills as the consummate stage performer were suddenly apparent to people who had previously written him off as simply a bit of pop fluff.

The night of the show itself was highly charged and emotional for Williams, a true culmination of a dream, and Rob was keen to milk it for all it was worth. There were his initials, fifty feet high in lights, at the back of the stage, even a cheeky and cheesy duet with Ol' Blue Eyes himself, as the disembodied voice of Sinatra shared verses from beyond the grave on 'It Was a Very Good Year'. Then there were the guest appearances by his lifelong friend from Stoke Jonathan Wilkes, actress Jane Horrocks and American comedian Jon Lovitz.

For the finale, Robbie belted out 'My Way', receiving a standing ovation from the assembled dinner-jacketed men and women dolled up to the nines. On the verge of tears, Williams laid down his microphone halfway up a vast staircase on the stage and soaked up the adulation from his adoring audience. Then, as he ascended the staircase to exit, he could not resist going back to retrieve it. With a beaming smile, he announced to his mother, Jan, standing cheering at one of the stage-side tables: 'Mum, this is your son singing. I love you.' It was classic Robbie, undoing the previous five minutes of cool crooning with a moment of jejune schmaltz, but the crowd loved him all the more for it.

It is tempting, watching that tumultuous moment back now, to think that his valedictory parting shot would have been more fitting if it had been aimed instead at two men who were not in the audience that night, Gary and Rob's father, Pete Conway. Neither, of course, was on the guest list, but how Williams must have longed, as he looked down from the top of those mirrored stairs, to pick them out in the sea of faces below. Not least because they had both been, for very similar reasons, the inspiration for the entire extravaganza.

How eaten up with envy Barlow, the musician-pop singer, would have been to see Robbie – the jester and the musical nonentity from Take That – being backed by a fifty-eight-piece orchestra of the finest musicians in the country. Just what would it do to him to know that his old 'backing dancer' was now so highly respected that Sinatra's legendary producer and engineer Al Schmitt and the players who supported Ol' Blue Eyes wanted to work with him on the record at the legendary Capitol Studios in LA where Robbie had relocated to make the album? How would it rip Gary's insides out to hear his nemesis making those old songs, like 'Have You Met Miss Jones?' and 'Mack the Knife', his own. After all, they were the very same tunes that Gary had to learn by heart for the open-mic nights at a dozen indistinguishable British Legions around the North-West, when drunken punters would stagger up and murder the greats. And, anyway, wasn't the Albert Hall Gary's natural territory, a grown-up theatre for a grown-up artist, the one who was supposed to go on to win over the older, more sophisticated audience once he walked away from the bubblegum of Take That? Shouldn't it have been Barlow up there striding the stage as a host of braless dancing girls, dressed in Christian Dior, flitted around him?

In fact, the same week Robbie's swing album was released, in November 2001, Gary Barlow left a short message on the premium-rate phone line he had set up to keep his fans abreast of developments in his career. 'It's my very sad duty to inform you we are closing down the Gary Barlow Fan Club,' he said. The phone line would also be disconnected, he added.

And what a buzz Pete would have got out of seeing his boy nailing the numbers that had been his own stock-in-trade for all those years in the nightclubs, cabarets and holiday camps. Pete loved the swing classics, had played Rob his old Sinatra and Ella Fitzgerald records, and instilled in his boy a reverence for them. Nobody would have blamed Pete, the showbiz trooper, if his pride at seeing his lad's crowning glory was tinged with just a touch of envy. This was the sort of night Pete must have dreamed of as a young entertainer, giving up his factory job at English Electric and hoping that one day he'd be roaring out the songs of his heroes on that very stage, hearing the applause of that audience for himself, feeling its love. The closest Pete got was watching the event when it was aired on the BBC. Instead of the Albert Hall, he had to make do with Thorseby Hall, the Warner Holidays adults-only camp in Nottinghamshire, where he worked as compere and host, telling a few gags and singing a few oldies, backed by a bloke on a Yamaha keyboard and a couple of girl dancers doing their best to inject a touch of pizzazz into a damp Wednesday night. Pete's primary function for the evening had been to tell the predominantly geriatric punters what they had just missed on *Coronation Street* while they'd been having their dinner.

The swing show was a massive kick in the teeth for Pete. If only subconsciously, it was Rob's way of telling his father that the pissing contest was officially won. It was Williams junior who had the power now. He had bettered his father on his own territory, and how he relished the control it gave him. Now it was Pete who was excluded, the way Rob had been from his father's life when Pete had walked out without even saying goodbye. It didn't take a Jungian analyst to work out that Rob bore resentment against the man he had once worshipped for abandoning him and his beloved mother; and for what? The lure of a half-cut bunch of caravanners at Perran Sands, or the prospect of chasing the dolly-bird dancers to whom ladies' man Pete had always been partial? Pete's idea of paternal nurturing had been to teach his son the things he did not need to learn from a father: how to open your eyes and let the audience in, how to time a gag and how to place a bet in Ladbrokes on a Saturday morning when all Rob wanted to do was play a game of football in the park with the dad he did not see enough of.

For Rob, all the men he had looked up to and idolized – his father, Gary and Nigel Martin-Smith – had let him down by withholding the love he so craved. Now it was payback time. The Albert Hall show marked the midpoint of the near two-year hiatus in his relationship with his father. Even before Rob cut off all contact, however, Pete had been expected to get used to his place as junior partner. Pete told me at the time how he would phone his son for a chat, only to find he had to deal with the phone-answerers and minions the star now employed to screen his calls. Pete, with his comic's cheery front and natural distaste for anything 'emotional', would make jokes at how he'd ring his boy and Rob would tell him he was busy and that he'd call him back. He would often wait weeks – and sometimes months – before Rob would bother to pick up the phone and announce blithely: 'See, I told you I'd call back.' Pete related the story with a smile, but it was clear it hurt him nonetheless. By the time his enforced exile from Rob's life was complete, he found he could not get further than Rob's protective PA, Josie Cliff. A proud man who shares a little of his son's stubbornness, Pete's reaction was simply to stop calling.

Even Rob's newfound sobriety didn't temper his bitterness towards his father. And Gary, too, who knew the disastrous consequences of falling out of favour with Williams, was finding that a clean and sober Robbie was no less capable of vindictiveness than the shit-faced variety. During encores, Robbie introduced a new tune to his live pop sets, a punk version of the Barlow-penned Take That hit 'Back for Good'. It was not so much a reverential reworking of the instant classic as an unvarnished piss-take. Publicly, Williams conceded it was a cheap trick, but admitted he couldn't stop himself. 'I wish all the lads the best of luck,' he said at the time, 'but when Take That's brought up, I still take the piss out of them. I don't mean it, but I can't help it. It's just a knee-jerk reaction. When Gary Barlow's name is mentioned, I just say something rude or nasty. There's no need for it.'

The recording of the Swing album coincided with Rob beginning a peripatetic existence between Britain and the US. Rob decided that he wanted to rent a house in Los Angeles to see if he could escape the daily problems that came with living in London – the constant attention of fans and the paparazzi – and relocate full-time to the States. His management team was instructed to find a suitable home and within weeks Williams signed a three-month lease on a house with a pool on Woodrow Wilson Drive in the Hollywood Hills.

The house had a showbiz pedigree and was owned at the time by *Ghostbusters* actor Dan Aykroyd, having previously been home to Ringo Starr and Mama Cass. As soon as he moved in, though, Rob began telling his friends he was convinced he was sharing the house with ghosts. His paranoia was not helped by the fact that Aykroyd had a similar obsession with the paranormal and had left behind a library of books and films about spooks and extraterrestrials. Having already signed the contract and with no way of getting out of the deal, Williams sat down on the bed in the master bedroom and began a one-way conversation with the house's supernatural residents. 'Hi. My name's Rob,' he began nervously, 'and I'm from England. I'm here for three months, and I know you're there, but I want you to know that I'm a bit scared of you and I'm here just trying to get my life together and I hope you don't mind, but I'll be in your space and I know you'll be in mine, but if you just don't come through, because it'll scare me. Thank you.'

Later, he says he arrived back at the house to discover all of the doors and windows wide open. Too scared to go inside, he got his bodyguards to search the place, but no sign of a forced entry was found. On another occasion, he says his new pet wolf, Sid, was left terrified and shaking after the ghosts made the creature teleport through a closed door. The situation was not helped when Williams met Zak Starkey, the son of Ringo, one day in LA and Starkey told him that there were the ghosts of two children in the garden and an old woman in the house. Aykroyd himself, in an indictment of the actor's skills as an estate agent, also wrote that the house was haunted by the spirit of the Mama and the Papas singer Mama Cass, and that she had got into his bed with him there one night.

Suffice to say, the ghost stories only further exercised Rob's already overactive mind. When he was first in LA, he took to inviting his friend and fellow expat the British actor Max Beesley to stay over for company and protection.

Despite things going bump in the night, the experience of living, if only part-time, in a city where he was virtually unknown was a liberating one.

Meanwhile, despite his insistence that it would be a cold day in hell before he ever considered going back on stage, Gary was beginning to have second thoughts. In May 2002, he and Dawn had a daughter, Emily. Her arrival had been a surprise, insomuch as Gary had fully expected they would have another boy – he himself was one of two boys, and his brother and his wife had two sons, Liam and Lewis. In the maternity suite, as Gary wept with happiness at having a daughter, Dawn gently pointed out that she was the one who had just gone through childbirth. Compared to the nightmare of her protracted labour with Dan, though, Emily's birth had been relatively straightforward, with the baby girl being delivered in no more than two hours.

Shortly afterwards, Barlow was working with American singer Donny Osmond, who had hired him to write songs for two albums in Salt Lake City. Gary and his songwriting partner, Eliot Kennedy, decided on the spur of the moment to take a trip to Las Vegas for some light relief and Donny persuaded them they should check out the Cirque du Soleil show entitled O. The Canadian theatre troupe's extravaganza at the Bellagio was a dazzling combination of synchronized swimming and feats of acrobatics, all of which took place in and around a 1.5-million-gallon tank of water. To add to the razzmatazz, the theatre itself was designed to look like a fourteenth-century European opera house.

Gary went along out of duty to Donny and because the tooth-some Osmond paid for the tickets, but the effect of the show on him was to prove unexpectedly visceral. Barlow sat rapt in his seat, stunned and moved by the staging, the music and the sheer skill of the show's eighty-five acrobats. At the end, as the cast walked forward en masse and sank into the water, Gary was already jumping up and down, clapping and crying. Out of nowhere memories of his time in Take That, and the unvarnished joy of performing, came back to him, as well as the thrill of the audience's emotional outpouring. He had been sincere when he said he never wanted to perform again. Now he wondered if he had simply been in denial. But the dreaded fear of failure remained. His confidence had been pretty much shattered and he was scared that he would not be able to deal with rejection again.

Subconsciously, however, Gary was already laying the groundwork for his eventual return to public life. Quietly, he began to deal with the problem of his weight. It was a slow, laborious and at times frustrating process. He tried the Atkins Diet, Weight Watchers and every fad going, but eventually, with the help of a nutritionist, and by taking up running and simply eating less, he began to shed the pounds he had put on during his days of melancholy. He set himself the target of reaching what, for him, seemed like a positively anorexic thirteen stone, but for several months – despite his best intentions – he found himself stuck at fourteen. Nonetheless, he was at least going in the right direction, and the improvement in the way he looked made him significantly more open to the idea that Howard Donald came to him with in autumn 2002.

After the fruitless outcome of the band's last meeting at Nigel Martin-Smith's house, Howard had been back in touch with their ex-manager and was keen to resurrect Take That. The proposal was that they would do a short tour of six shows to test the water, and if the omens were good, they could consider going into the studio to record some new material. Gary was surprised that his instant reaction to the plan was not the vehement opposition he had felt only a year earlier. Within a couple of weeks plans were laid to begin a UK tour the following year, and by October Howard was happily telling the press about Take That's upcoming reunion. 'I got in touch with everyone and we agreed to give it a shot,' he said. 'It is nerve-racking, but very exciting at the same time.' Meanwhile, Mark was talking fondly about how the four of them had met up again and found that the old camaraderie was still there.

Behind the scenes, Mark had also set to work trying to persuade Robbie to consider re-joining them. A line of communication between the two men, best friends during the early days of Take That, had been open for some time. Mark told Howard at the outset that he would only be interested in resurrecting the band if Williams was also on board. However, even by agreeing to allow Mark to make contact with Robbie about the proposed project, Gary was forced into the deeply humiliating position of having to agree that – in the unlikely event that Williams was amenable to coming back on board – he, Barlow, would have no choice but to sup with the devil. If the band was to re-form, however, there was no real alternative. From the early soundings that Howard had taken, there was scant interest from the larger promoters in the prospect of a reunion that did not include Robbie. The consensus at the time was that there was little public appetite for Take That as a foursome, given the huge success of Williams's career and the fact that Barlow's failure as a solo artist was still fresh in the memory.

The addition of Williams would have been viewed very differently by the moneymen being lined up to back the project. Gary

found himself in a catch-22 situation: either bite
come to an accommodation with Robbie, or kiss goꞇ
re-emerging desire to get in front of a crowd once again. ꞇ
for time to think about it. When eventually he returned Hꞇ
call, he announced that they should count him in; the others ꞇould
contact Rob and Gary would swallow his pride and not stand in
the way of the five of them giving Take That another shot. Mark
was despatched to make contact with Rob, and, like the others,
Gary waited for his reply.

As they held their breath, however, Williams released his fifth
solo album, the much-vaunted *Escapology*, in November 2002.
Among the hits, such as 'Feel' and 'Come Undone', was a so-called
'hidden track' that was to become the subject of much hilarity. After
more than six minutes of dead air at the end of the album, Robbie's
voice suddenly reappeared, singing a rambling and seemingly spontaneous ditty accompanied by a single acoustic guitar. For a little
over three and a half minutes Williams warbles nonsensically about
some imponderables such as why do Biros have holes, and is the
Richard Gere gerbil story true? Later, he muses: 'Does God ever
get it wrong? Where has Gary Barlow gone?' It seemed Rob had
given Gary his reply.

It goes without saying that the making of an album is, particularly in these days of corporate naval-gazing, a long, arduous and
often laborious process. Thanks to the emergence of editing software
like Pro Tools in the early nineties, tracks can now be endlessly
tweaked, altered and reworked before a final edit is deemed ready
for public consumption. Williams had had months since recording
the hidden track to tire of its lame gags, to decide on the mature
approach, dump it from the album and call time on the feud that
for so long now had been, publicly at least, all one-way traffic. That

he could not bring himself to do any of the above is testament to the conflicting elements in the Williams psyche.

During the recording of a BBC television special *The Robbie Williams Show*, which was filmed in November 2002 to coincide with the release of *Escapology*, he was yet again announcing that it was time for him officially to bring a halt to the hostilities. 'I want to apologize, because when I left, I said some really bad things about the band,' he told the audience of 400 fans at Pinewood Studios, Buckinghamshire. 'And it's the truth about some people in the band. They didn't love me. But I just want to say I'm really, sincerely sorry – we're only young once.' The mood of reconciliation didn't last long. Within minutes he was taking the piss again. 'I heard Take That are getting back together. Who's going to do this, then?' he announced as he began doing naff boy-band dancing. Next he was laughing at Jason Orange's singing, saying he would not be up to taking over Robbie's own lead vocal on 'Could It Be Magic'.

As a result of the snub, Gary and the others quietly shelved the reunion plans. But what neither Gary nor Robbie knew was that the seeds of their eventual reconciliation had already been sown, as Williams's relationship with Guy Chambers was quickly deteriorating. At some point in the dim and distant future, Rob would be looking for another musical mentor and facilitator – and Gary would be waiting.

Rob's parting of the ways with Chambers would mirror almost exactly the animosity and bitterness that accompanied his split with Barlow and Take That. Like Gary, Guy would soon discover what it was like to be on the receiving end of a Williams blitzkrieg. Ironically, it was Rob's newfound sobriety that had begun to test his once close relationship with Guy. For the first time Williams was a fully functioning member of the team, no longer the bit-part player his addictions had dictated he must be. That presented a challenge to the organized and in-control Guy, who previously had been given carte blanche by Rob to make Robbie Williams records in his own way. Now Rob wanted a much bigger say in the way his music sounded, about production, the musicians they used and the songs that would appear on future albums.

The tensions between the two men were visible during the recording of *Escapology*. Rob had been unimpressed with their last pop album, *Sing When You're Winning*, most particularly its failure to make a dent in the elusive American market. His suddenly heightened sense of reality had also revealed to him the flaws, as he saw them, in his writing partner's make-up. The strain had been evident during the recording of the swing album the previous year. Rob found himself increasingly annoyed by what he saw as Guy's off-hand nature and almost Tourette's-like compulsion not to pull any punches when evaluating others' work – Robbie's included. It also got Rob's back up that he thought Chambers had been rude to Frank Sinatra's one-time producer, Al Schmitt, and had not showed the old-timer enough respect. Certainly, those who know Guy well admit that he can be the model of tactlessness, often too preoccupied with producing his best possible work to care about treading on the egos of those around him. In truth, their relationship had been prone to a few incendiary moments even during Rob's 'lost years'. Once, after a row, Williams responded by chucking Guy's beloved twelve-string guitar into Lake Como.

It would be no surprise if Rob's sudden urge to stick his oar into the recording process, which had been the exclusive preserve of Guy and Steve Power, raised Chambers's hackles. Not only that, Robbie summarily announced during the recording of *Escapology* that he wanted a producer's credit to fulfil his ambition of seeing his name in *Music Week*. In the end, however, Rob simply had to settle for his usual writing credits, which did nothing to improve relations between the two men.

Furthermore, Guy was no longer inclined to indulge the long, wallowing monologues that Rob launched into at regular intervals, in which he would describe his feelings of misery, resentment or occasional happiness in mind-numbing detail. In this respect, at least, Chambers was utterly unsuited to playing the game that was vital to long-term survival in the Court of Robbie and at which some were more adept than others.

An additional problem was that being sober for the first time in years did not make Robbie immune to the bouts of self-loathing that frequently extended to almost everything he had done musically. That Guy was officially one half of Robbie Williams also made him 50 per cent culpable in the star's eyes. Indeed, for months Robbie had been saying to some in his circle that it was time to 'break Robbie Williams up'. Guy's days were officially numbered.

Early in 2002, as was usually the case at the beginning of albums, Rob and Guy had taken a holiday together in a bid to come up with some songs for the record. This time they headed to the Bahamas, but Rob was singularly unimpressed with what the collaboration produced. They returned home and immediately planned a second writing trip to Los Angeles, but at the last minute, Rob cancelled.

Unofficially, Rob had come up with a plan to launch a rock band with a few musician friends he had met in LA, including Jane's Addiction guitarist Dave Navarro. All the members of his new group would write the music, thereby taking the pressure to come up with new material off him. By way of testing the water, while he was recording *Escapology* with Guy, Rob was already getting together with new songwriters in the hope of coming up with songs that were not so obviously Robbie Williams numbers. He travelled to New York from LA where he had found another house, this time in a gated community close to Mulholland Drive, and began hanging out with a Norwegian songwriter called Boots Ottestad. The pair, along with two other writers, Ashley Hamilton, the son of actor George Hamilton, and another musician called Daniel Pierre, came up with 'Come Undone'.

The demo of the song had the raw, undiluted lyrics and sound that Rob had been searching for, but when he returned and played the song to Chambers, he was less than thrilled with his reaction. As far as Williams was concerned, Guy made it perfectly clear that he did not like the track. Moreover, Guy told Rob that he was 'shocked' by the lyrics of the song, which famously end with Robbie virtually howling: 'I am scum.' Likewise, Guy was equally cool about 'Nan's Song', the admittedly toe-curling tribute to Rob's now dearly departed grandmother, Betty Williams. Unsurprisingly, given its subject matter, Rob was touchy about Guy's criticism – not least because it was the first song on which he had written both the lyrics and the music, figuring out the chords on the acoustic guitar he was learning to play.

With a fast-developing bad atmosphere between them, Chambers could scarcely be blamed if, after reading the runes, he decided to seek alternative employment. If Rob's decision to write with other people had gone down badly with Chambers, then Guy's announcement that he too planned to work with other artists only intensified the froideur. Suddenly, Guy was being linked in the music press with big-selling American stars like Britney Spears. He also launched his own record label, Orgasmatron, to which he signed all-girl band the Licks. Just to add to Rob's displeasure over Guy calling time on their exclusive partnership, close to the end of recording the album he also discovered from Josie Cliff that Guy was planning to use what should have been a Sunday off to go back into the studio to work on a song with the Australian singer and former soap actress Natalie Imbruglia. The subsequent row led to a slanging match that saw Rob tear into Guy's brother and manager, Dylan.

Guy also incurred Williams's wrath by changing some of the chords to 'Come Undone'. Later, when Guy threw a playback party for the album in London, which Rob did not attend, he was furious to discover that Guy had played the album but had pointedly omitted to air publicly either 'Come Undone' or 'Nan's Song'.

The dynamics of the relationship were also changing, given that the pair – who once regularly used to share drunken nights out – were separated by Rob's recent relocation to Los Angeles and Guy's decision to get married and settle down. Without the universal adhesive of alcohol, they found that not only did they not have much in common, they actually found each other mildly irritating. Rob became increasingly annoyed that Guy would, with some justification, refer to Robbie Williams as 'we' in conversation. For his part, Guy had come to tire of Williams's constant pranks and larking about in an attempt to liven up proceedings in the studio: setting fire to tablecloths in the vocal booth, loudly breaking wind or letting out high-pitched, high-decibel shrieks into his microphone when Guy was listening to him through headphones.

But if Williams was showing signs of stress, he could be forgiven. With his contract with EMI now at an end, he had undertaken to finance the expensive process of recording the album out of his own pocket. It was an unusual move to say the least and, despite Robbie's undoubted pulling power, something of a calculated gamble. The plan, agreed by Rob, David Enthoven and fellow joint manager Tim Clark, was to finish *Escapology*, then take it to a select group of leading record companies; the best offer would secure not only the album but Robbie as well, on a long-term deal. The stakes were incredibly high. In the unlikely event that none of the big fish was to bite, Tim Clark had been hard at work setting up Rob's own independent record label, which would put out the album if all else failed. London-based media consultants Equinox were hired to advise on strategy, while Clark had serious negotiations with CD manufacturers and retailers. Even so, it was not their preferred option by a long chalk and it added considerably to Rob's stress levels during the making of *Escapology*.

It was originally planned that once the record was completed, Williams and Chambers would begin working on a greatest-hits album, which would include several new tracks, but the singer shelved the project because he felt Guy was overly critical of the new songs Rob had written by himself. Guy was still slated to reprise his role as musical director on Williams's upcoming tour, but now Rob wanted Guy gone. He arranged to go over to the bungalow where Guy was staying at the Sunset Marquis. Chambers knew it must be something serious if Rob was coming to see him, but in the event Williams made him sweat by turning up two hours late, saying he'd been held up because he was watching the Oscars on TV. It was no way to treat a man who had been pivotal in his success over the last four years.

Rob wasn't about to pull any punches. He was aggressive and cold, telling Guy he did not want to work with him any more. He was sick of being Robbie Williams, he said, and sick of the band of musicians that Guy had built around him. He was not happy with the music they were making and wanted to be in a band where the other members were his 'mates'. For Guy, who considered Rob to be a friend as well as a business partner, it was the ultimate kick in the teeth. Privately, he thought Williams had gone completely and utterly mad. Perhaps he equally suspected that Rob had fallen victim to the culture of sycophancy and synthetic positivity that pervades Tinseltown.

Soon, however, Robbie had second thoughts and Guy was reinstated, but the relationship took another dip immediately after *Escapology* was finished and Guy met Tim Clark in London to tell him he wanted an improved royalty deal. Rob also says that Guy refused to promote 'Come Undone' if it was released as a single because he hated the track. When Williams, who was in Calgary, Canada, filming the cowboy-themed video to the album's debut single, 'Feel', in September 2002, found out about this, he hit the roof and demanded Chambers be fired. Clark was given the task, but failed to track Chambers down over the weekend. Guy was not told he had got the sack until he arrived at a London studio the following Monday morning to begin rehearsing the Robbie Williams band for the upcoming tour.

Meanwhile, negotiations over a new record deal were coming down to the wire. Although EMI were favourites to renew their deal with Williams, several other leading labels, including Universal and Richard Branson's V2, were vying for his signature. Eventually, Branson would blink first and pull out when the bidding reached £25 million. In October 2002, a press conference was called at IE Music, Robbie's management team's office in Shepherd's Bush, West London, where Rob – sporting a Mötley Crüe singlet – famously bellowed, 'I'm rich beyond my wildest dreams,' to the waiting press. EMI had succeeded in luring him back to the label with an

£80-million offer – more than twice that paid to Elton John, until then the UK's highest record deal.

The full terms of the deal were complex, but in effect EMI secured Williams for four studio albums and set up a business – called the In Good Company – to handle the proceeds from his merchandise, publishing and concert tours, in which the label would own a 25 per cent stake. If he wasn't already, Williams was now very seriously wealthy.

The deal had not been without its hiccups, however. As the final details were being ironed out, Williams claims the then chairman of EMI, Tony Wadsworth, received a phone call from Guy Chambers to inform him that he had been sacked by Robbie and they would no longer be working together. Chambers said he felt that the company should know. As EMI panicked, Tim Clark was pressed into action to reassure Wadsworth that with or without Guy, his company was buying into a winner.

For Williams, with his preternatural disinclination to let bygones be bygones, what he saw as Guy's treachery would not be forgotten. To make matters worse, he felt his generosity in giving Guy a large cash gift a couple of years earlier to buy a house in London had been thrown back in his face. Soon Chambers was in danger of taking over from Gary Barlow as his preferred public scapegoat. To begin with, the singer had appeared uncharacteristically reluctant to set free the attack dogs. 'My partnership with Guy, unfortunately, for the foreseeable future, has come to an end. I don't want to get into it. It would embarrass him and it would embarrass myself. But I can categorically say I never once asked for an exclusivity deal with Guy,' he was quoted as saying when news of the split was leaked.

Before long, however, he couldn't keep up the diplomatic face.

Less than a month later, at his comeback gig at Pinewood Studios, he let it be known that Guy had been given the chop. 'We have had a redundancy in the band,' he announced to the audience. Later, when he was again asked by a journalist about his songwriting partner's exit, Rob raised his glass to cover his mouth, put on a comedy voice and announced in a stage whisper: 'He's a man who wanted too much money.' By the time his book *Feel* was released, less than two years later, the gloves were well and truly off. Now, according to Williams, Chambers was a 'stupid fucking cunt' and a 'dickhead' for asking for so much money. Guy, he said, was irked by how much money he, Robbie, had made. Guy had been broke with a leaking roof when they had met. 'And now he's in a multi-million-pound house and he's got a lovely lifestyle, and it's Robbie Williams that sells the records,' he added. 'It's not Guy Chambers that gets up in front of all those thousands of people and entertains them. And that's the fellow that can't go out because the paparazzi are outside the house.'

The departure of the influential Chambers would lead to a vacancy, one it would not prove easy for Robbie to fill.

CHAPTER EIGHT

Prey

There are certain people who just don't readily come to mind when you conjure up a mental image of a deranged, vengeance-fixated hit man. It is safe to say Gary Barlow would come fairly near the top of that list. In early November 2002, Rob was back in London preparing for the release of *Escapology*. One late morning at the house in Notting Hill he'd purchased earlier that year as his UK base, Rob came downstairs after a night of fitful sleep and discovered two bullet holes in one of the front windows. Pandemonium must have ensued in the household, with staff questioned by Williams's security detail, and the police quietly contacted so that the incident would not leak out to the press. Apparently, when asked if he could think of anyone who might have a grudge against him, anyone who would want to scare him, after various other names were mentioned and quickly discounted, Williams paused for a moment, thinking, and announced with a seemingly straight face: 'Barlow?'

I include this previously untold story, which does indeed sound utterly preposterous in the retelling, if only to illustrate the depth of paranoia that can infect the lives of those who have come to feel hunted, watched and hounded. For Robbie, sobriety and the removal of cocaine from his daily life had done little to alleviate the affliction. In public, he presented an image of a new, clean-living incarnation, free from the addictions that had so coloured his mental outlook in the previous dark years, but he was far from cured of his reliance on chemicals to get him through the day. In the absence of booze and coke, his perennial addiction to cigarettes and coffee was quickly supplemented by a growing reliance on prescription medicine. He had recently begun taking the antidepressant Effexor and had found the drug improved his mood, but it had only exacerbated Rob's insomnia. To counteract the problem, he had been prescribed the controversial sleeping drug Ambien, the side effects of which can include nausea, hallucinations and impaired judgement and reasoning. In the case of Williams, he began suffering terrifying nightmares; he dreamed that his toes were afflicted by leprosy and were dropping off, and that gypsies had stolen his pet dogs and were demanding a ransom and threatening to chop them up.

A few months earlier in Los Angeles, a doctor had recommended that he start seeing a high-profile female therapist whose Rolodex included some of the biggest names in showbusiness. But those around him remained at times fearful about his strange emotional state. For some time the situation when he was back in London had been untenable. For long periods Rob was too afraid to go out – and certainly never without his minder, Pompey, or one of the other ex-SAS bodyguards. Even the success of *Escapology* could not lift his anxiety. The album went to number one in Britain, Germany, Sweden, Ireland, Switzerland, Austria and Finland, and would rack up seven platinum discs in the UK alone. Meanwhile, three singles – 'Feel', 'Come Undone' and 'Something Beautiful' – would all make the top ten.

But with huge record sales came even greater attention. Rob's West London house was now surrounded by a virtual twenty-four-hour cordon of fans and paparazzi. His loathing for both groups of tormenters was equally extreme. He would emerge from the house and bark abuse at the fans, which included a particularly dedicated hard core of girls who had upped sticks from Italy and arrived en masse to live in West London so they could make their daily pilgrimage to his front door. Meanwhile, the Williams hatred for the growing band of photographers who swarmed around the fashionable street where he lived frequently bordered on the violent. The relationship between celebrities and the breed of freelance cameramen whose livings are made by the quasi-stalking of their famous prey is invariably a complex one. Many of those Rob would ritually abuse as he emerged from his house in the morning were the same snappers he could just as easily be beaming at from the red carpet that night if he was on the publicity circuit or had an album to sell. In Williams's mind, though, there is a distinct line between on duty and off duty, with no acceptance that he should not be able to pick and choose when and how he sups with the devil.

Just to highlight his mercurial attitude towards the media, he was still privately and publicly gauging his popularity by how much coverage he was getting in the papers, and had been telling fans at his comeback gig that autumn that he was scared he had been forgotten because other pop stars were getting more press than him. At the same time, he took to emerging from the house in a mask of himself, made for the film *Rob by Nature*. His theory was simply that the first time he wore it, the photographers would get their shot and the resulting pictures would be splashed all over the papers, but the next time, the pictures would look exactly like the previous ones and the papers would very quickly get bored of using photos of him. The result, he reasoned, would be that after a short time, the photographers who hung around him every day would have their source of income cut off and would slope off to make some other celeb's life a misery. In practice, however, the scheme only intensified the press's interest in him, thanks to his bizarre decision to wear the thing in the first place.

He also began to suspect that someone close to him was leaking information to the press and began giving out fake information to his friends to see if it would end up in the papers and enable him to identify the culprit. At the same time, he became obsessed with the thought that his calls were being listened to and ordered his British phones to be checked by a firm of security experts to make sure they were not being tapped. Such was the level of his mistrust and suspicion, however, that he was soon fretting that the people he'd hired for the job may have planted their own bugs on the line and demanded another firm begin the process all over again. In the end, his removal from London became inevitable. The incident with the bullet holes in his window – still not explained to this day – was the final straw, reigniting his paranoia that a crazy with a gun was set on assassinating him.

Rob began suffering panic attacks once more and developed agoraphobia, so that even a stroll in Hyde Park could bring on an episode of shaking and sweating. With his public profile approaching its zenith, he started to fixate on being gunned down on his doorstep like the TV presenter Jill Dando three years earlier.

Even during his extended stays in California, he was not always alone and the chance of being followed by expat British photographers and the American paparazzi, who supply the UK press, was still a risk. In LA Rob took to getting the driver of his SUV to perform regular U-turns once they had left the safety of the private streets around his home to establish whether or not they were being followed.

Despite the occasional hassles, Williams adapted quickly to the Californian lifestyle and the relative freedom it afforded him. Like Gary before him, he readily bought into the quirkiness of the city's seemingly endless procession of self-help gurus and road-to-enlightenment charlatans. Soon he was buying every kind of vitamin and health-giving herb and embarking on any number of quack diets that were the new fad du jour in Tinseltown. He also took to God, praying on his knees by his bed every night and telling friends that he would occasionally wake in the morning and find that God had written a song for him and implanted it in his mind while he slept. At the same time, he began to surround himself with a new circle of American friends, collected virtually en masse soon after his arrival in Hollywood. They were of a type that will be familiar to anyone who has spent any significant time in LA. They consisted largely of a group of young, well-off slackers, many with parents who were prepared to indulge their rather aimless lifestyles. What they had most in common, however, was an unrivalled familiarity with the couches of some of the most expensive shrinks and analysts on the West Coast.

They were largely an emotionally damaged breed, many of whom, like Rob himself, had in the past channelled their misery into a taste for drugs and booze. What they had learned during their recovery was a new and virtually unintelligible language of psychobabble and twenty-four-carat therapy speak, which they spent evenings spouting at each other during long, 'meaningful' conversations. A friend of Rob's, who was an early visitor to his house after his arrival in California, told me of one fairly classic exchange at an impromptu party at Rob's new place. 'I got talking to a Valley-girl type, blonde and pretty, who within two minutes of us meeting was running through a list of every substance she had been addicted to since she'd started taking drugs at the age of thirteen,' says his friend. 'It went on and on like she was reading out her Sainsbury's shopping list. Then she starts saying that she owes her life to some Indian guru who had drawn her a map of the energy fields he could see inside her body and told her to rub together a couple of stones he gave her above her head twice a day. She was away with the fairies.'

But although Rob was not admitting it publicly, the relocation to America was likely to have been driven as much by a commercial imperative as by his genuine desire to escape the madness of his existence on this side of the pond. After the disaster of his tour of the States three years earlier and the disappointing sales of *The Ego Has Landed*, recording *Swing When You're Winning* in LA had reignited Robbie's interest in all things American. The fact that he worked with respected American musicians on the record, who were fulsome in their praise of him during recording sessions at Capitol Studios, gave him the confidence to think it was worth giving the States another shot. Although the swing album was not given a formal US release, Williams was already planning that *Escapology* would be the one to break him across the Atlantic. Plus now there was a crucial difference: this time he was clean and sober and ready for the fray.

Robbie wasn't alone in his assessment that now was the time for the US market to roll over for him and stick four paws in the air. Factored into his mega-money new contract with EMI was the calculated gamble by its executives that if the singer was going to earn them back the fortune they had invested in him, then cracking the North American market was vital.

As with the swing album, Rob's decision to locate himself in Hollywood while he recorded *Escapology* during 2002 was, in part at least, because he wanted to immerse himself in US popular culture in the hope that a greater understanding of what made the American public tick would help him make records they would, at long last, want to go out and buy. The strategy that had been agreed on by a cabal of Robbie himself, the now departed Guy Chambers, Tim Clark and his American label, Virgin, was that *Escapology* would see him subtly shift his focus from the more whimsically English flourishes of his earlier albums towards a resolutely AOR sound that would make it radio-friendly from Sarasota to Spokane. Robbie virtually hyperventilated as he trumpeted his newfound devotion to his adopted home city by screaming, 'Gotta love LA. California, USA! USA! USA!' on 'Song 3', which was deemed rather too fawning even for American audiences and was dropped from the US version of the album, along with another homage to Los Angeles, 'Hot Fudge', and a third song, 'Cursed'.

The resulting collection of songs, including the commercial standout track – the anthemic 'Feel' – was indeed the sort of mid-tempo, middle-of-the-road offering that would be expected to appeal to the US record-buying public. When *Escapology* was finally released in America on April Fool's Day 2003, Williams began a marathon round of publicity that saw him appear on *Good Morning America*, *The Tonight Show* – on which he gave guest host Katie Couric and fellow interviewee Simon Cowell slapstick lap dances – and on a late-night talk show hosted by Carson Daly. Earlier, he had endured a freezing and snowbound New York to perform at the Rock the Vote gig, which acted as a prelude to the Grammys.

With the response from the US music critics muted, but generally positive for the album, hopes were high in Robbie's camp that the record would easily outstrip the meagre 126,000 sales of his latest album to be released there, *Sing When You're Winning*. Once again, however, America stubbornly refused to bite. 'Feel', for which Hollywood actress Daryl Hannah had been hired at huge expense to appear in the video in a bid to make US audiences sit up and take notice, did not make the Billboard Hot 100. Meanwhile, the album itself only managed to reach a disappointing number forty-three. Five weeks later, after selling just 31,000 copies, it had slipped to number 156. Once again, the fortune the label had spent on a huge marketing drive, plus Robbie's own attempts to woo the country, had been for nothing.

Five months earlier, when *Escapology* had come out in the UK, Gary Barlow chose the day of its release to make a rare foray into the public arena, launching an attack in the *Daily Mirror* on the state of popular music. 'I'm fed up with all the rubbish in the pop charts now and I want to do something about it,' he said. As digs at his old sparring partner, Robbie, went, it was pretty transparent, but Barlow's catcalls could not divert the inexorable skyward trajectory of Williams's career at home, if not across the pond. Gary's only consolation was that American executives at Robbie's US label had decided that, along with the three tracks they were dropping from the album, the hidden track lambasting him would be removed too – but only because not one of them had heard of Gary Barlow.

Nor was it, in truth, the ideal time for Gary once again to be raising the subject of re-forming Take That. After being snubbed by Williams, he was trying to talk up the prospect of the group making a comeback as a foursome. 'I've spoken to the other lads from Take That, other than Rob, and they are all interested,' Barlow told an Irish journalist. 'I feel like we split up before our time, but we're still young and have a lot to offer. I have written new songs and I think people will like them.'

One happy side effect of Robbie's recent use of antidepressants was that he was at last ready to pick up the pieces of his fractured relationship with his father. As Rob began his failed assault on the US in spring 2003, he started seeing Pete again. The spur for their gradual rapprochement came a few months earlier, thanks in part to a Channel 5 documentary that the station was making about Williams senior. While Pete, proud to the last, blustered when he was questioned on screen about whether he felt hurt by the two-year estrangement between them, his friends were more than willing to go before the cameras to describe Pete's sorrow at being cut off by his only son. Halfway through filming, Rob got to hear about the programme. After Pete's two years in purdah, Rob now rang to invite his father to meet him in New York. A ticket on Concorde was arranged, and Pete was told that he wouldn't need any luggage because Rob was going to take him on a shopping spree once they had hooked up in Manhattan. Nevertheless, his father was told in no uncertain terms that the Channel 5 crew who had been following Pete around for the documentary were not welcome. Pete was instructed not to breathe a word about the reunion and told me he was flabbergasted when all the details – Concorde and all – appeared in the *Sun* a few days later. Worried that Rob would think he had blabbed, Pete had to call him to say he'd had nothing to do with it.

Before long, Pete was being invited to Rob's new house in Beverly Hills, where he would forgo his favourite white-wine spritzers and join his son in abstaining from anything stronger than endless cups of coffee. But his happiness at being let back in from the cold was obvious. Pete, who likes a night out, even managed a contented smile when he talked to me about the very un-rock-'n'-roll lifestyle chez Robbie. Evenings would invariably consist of popping out for yet more coffee at Starbucks, before having dinner somewhere and heading home. Invariably, with Rob having disappeared for an early night, Pete would find himself alone downstairs with nothing to do by 9.30 p.m. The father and son took to playing golf together during his stays and would pair up for highly competitive games of table tennis at the house.

Later, Williams would claim that he had purposely distanced himself from his father as he sought to overcome his alcoholism. In his 2004 book, *Feel*, he says: 'The problem is, I needed a dad and I didn't need a friend. That's it. And I got a friend, a drinking buddy, which is great, but I did need a dad.' He would add that being prescribed antidepressants had helped him build bridges with his father. Certainly, the relationship between the two men has healed since its painful fracturing and the nadir of Rob's vindictive rap on 'My Culture'. But to those who have watched them closely, it is clear that the dynamics of their relationship are still undeniably more like a friendship than anything classically father and son. It has revolved for the most part in recent years around a constant stream of joke-telling and games of ping-pong or pool whenever Pete is a visitor to his son's Beverly Hills hacienda, with both men still displaying the same barely concealed will to win.

A few years ago, when Pete was the resident compere, comic and crooner at the Warner Holidays hotel Thoresby Hall in Nottinghamshire, I asked him if he ever considered singing any of Robbie's songs during his nightly act. Pete thought for a moment. 'The problem with that is,' he replied, 'if I was to do "Angels" and it wasn't much good, people would say: "Oh look, he's rubbish." But if I was to sing "Angels" and it was better than Rob's version . . .' He tailed off, modesty preventing him from saying what he was clearly thinking. 'So you see,' he began again, 'I just couldn't win.'

In the months following their reunion, relations improved to such an extent that for the release of 'Something Beautiful' in summer 2003, Rob made his fifty-nine-year-old father the star of the single's video, with Pete playing the role of a celebrity judge in an *X Factor* spoof. At the same time, Robbie also invited his father up on stage with him when he returned to Britain to record *Top of the Pops*, hugging Pete in front of the studio audience between takes. But with Pete having by then given up his £350-a-week job at Thoresby Hall – and the tiny staff flat that went with it – his living arrangements back home were a far cry from the spacious lodgings in the guest annexe of Rob's mansion. After being put up for a while by a friend in Stoke, then taking a room in a cheap hotel, Pete moved into a rented flat above a hairdresser's in the Potteries.

Meanwhile, Gary was planning a partial relocation to sunnier climes. In early 2003, he and Dawn bought their first home together, a three-bedroom house in the south of France with views across the Mediterranean to Cap Ferrat. Although the house was not on the scale of his friend Elton John's pink palace along the Riviera coast, it still boasted a swimming pool and a studio for Barlow to work. The couple set about decorating it with simple, if expensive, contemporary furniture by David Linley, rather than the fusty antiques of Delamere Manor. Gary, Dawn and their two children, Dan and Emily, began disappearing to Nice for the summer, where they quickly hooked up with a well-off set of boat-owning British couples who spend the holidays flitting around between St Tropez, Cannes and Monaco.

Unfortunately, Gary was to become the butt of a thousand jokes by Rob who believed that the parsimonious Barlow – who at the time had roughly £15 million in the bank – had bought the house only after establishing that he and his family could make use of a budget airline operating out of Liverpool's John Lennon Airport.

Meanwhile, Barlow continued to pursue his role as backroom boy. He and Eliot Kennedy, who met daily at Gary's studio at Delamere Manor to write songs, renewed their links with Blue, co-writing the single 'Guilty', which was a number-two hit for the boy band in autumn 2003. They also worked with Lara Fabian, the Belgian-born soprano, who is highly successful in the Euro zone. At the same time, Gary was responsible for co-writing six songs on teenage Australian soap star Delta Goodrem's 2003 debut album, *Innocent Eyes*, and began writing for Charlotte Church, for whom he penned the track 'Easy Way Out', which eventually appeared on the former child prodigy's pop album, *Tissues and Issues*, in 2005. His collaboration with Donny Osmond resulted in the single 'Breeze on By', which would go on to give the Mormon heart-throb an unlikely British top-ten hit in October 2004. Meanwhile, Barlow and Kennedy helped with tunes for German girl group Monrose, Atomic Kitten and former *Pop Idol* winner Michelle McManus.

Gary was also contacted by Island Records to try to breathe life into Mark Owen's flatlining solo career. Barlow and Kennedy co-wrote the single 'Four-Minute Warning' for Owen's second solo album in summer 2003. The song was a moderate hit, reaching number four in the charts. But the album, *In Your Own Time*, was a flop and within a year Owen was dropped by Island. Like Barlow, he had previously been let go from BMG following poor sales of his debut solo album.

Despite his not inconsiderable success as a writer for other people, however, Gary soon tired of writing songs to order, often working by committee with artists and their company A&R men to come up with yet another formulaic and instantly forgettable song designed to placate the corporate powers that be. While he was making decent money, he found himself longing for the days when he had simply been able to sit at his keyboard and write yet another Take That hit. He yearned for the creative autonomy he had enjoyed in those early days and pined for the time when records were made in weeks rather than months and did not have to pass through myriad levels of quality control before being spewed out as indistinguishable retreads of the same old ideas.

The joy of having children and a wife who loved him was, at this worst of times, the only thing that stopped Gary from sinking into melancholy over the loss of his performing career. Working from home, and during breaks from recording with the likes of girl band Atomic Kitten, he could spend hours drawing and colouring with his kids and sit down to dinner with them. He found he was a naturally tactile father, kissing his offspring constantly in a way he had never experienced with his own loving but emotionally reserved parents. And with a new house in France, Gary, who had never enjoyed the English winter, could also take time for himself by vanishing there for a few days when the weather got unbearable in February. Gary would jump into a hire car at the airport, drive to the house and quickly melt into anonymity. He would take a book and sit in a restaurant and read, or simply sit looking out to sea.

With Rob's partnership with Guy Chambers having come to

a messy end, the word from the top of EMI was that its executives must begin the task of finding someone with whom their £80-million signing could begin writing his next album. A string of producers and writing teams were contacted to see if they would be available to hook up with the world's most successful male pop star. There was no shortage of takers. One of those who passed up the offer was Cheshire-based True North Music. The company was approached by a naive young executive who did not realize until it was too late that one half of True North's writing team was a certain Mr Gary Barlow. Ironically, Gary would soon be able to add to his CV the one achievement that had so far eluded Williams – a US hit. His track 'Love Won't Wait', from *Open Road*, was remixed in early 2003 and credited to Disco Box featuring G.B.

At what point do fame, money and power begin to exempt one from the normal conventions to which mere mortals are expected to conform? It is highly likely, you would think, that if Michael Jackson had not been the King of Pop, taking a chimp as his primary travelling companion, dangling his children from the balconies of Berlin hotel rooms and ordering the construction of his own funfair in his back garden might have resulted in him being led away for psychological assessment in relatively short order. Likewise, when publishing magnate William Randolph Hearst built his 165-room personal Xanadu in California and obsessively proceeded to stuff it to the gunwales with priceless international artefacts, he probably wouldn't have appreciated someone pointing out to him that he was in danger of overdoing it just a tad with the home-improvements thing.

In the end, of course, it is incumbent on somebody in your orbit to break it to you that a) you are in grave danger of going completely off your trolley and b) it might be time to think about getting a grip. As we have seen, though, when those people around you are almost exclusively on your payroll, there is a temptation on their part simply to keep schtum.

In summer 2003, despite – or possibly because of – the success of *Escapology*, Robbie was, perversely, giving every impression of wanting to disappear into the sort of anonymity from which Gary and the others were hoping to re-emerge. Bizarrely, he was also secretly formulating a plan to retire Robbie Williams and replace him with a new character of his own invention. The strange idea germinated during the recording of his follow-up album to *Escapology*. Robbie decided that he wanted to make and promote the record not as Robbie but as a singer called Pure Francis, who would, he declared privately, become his new public persona. In order fully to get into character, he would don a disguise consisting of a wig and fake nose whenever appearing in public as his new incarnation. Not only that, he would also eat, dress and live like him in order to inhabit the role.

Earlier that year, as he wrote songs for the album that he was quietly insisting would be a huge change of direction and sound nothing like his previous work, Rob was also coming up with a highly detailed backstory for his new creation. Pure Francis, he decided, was an American singer in the middle-of-the-road mould of Neil Diamond. Originally from the Orange County area of Southern California, he had moved to West Hollywood to try to make it in the music business but was now down on his luck and an alcoholic. He had been a session singer and had been through a lot of personal pain but was now trying to give his floundering career one last go. The album, which would be sung in the voice of the fictional character, would chart the story of his professional and personal failures, and would be called *Diamond*.

To the dismay and concern of those around him, the plan was not some flight of fancy, a good joke dreamed up out of boredom one day in the studio and quickly forgotten. The scheme soon took on a life of its own. For months he talked animatedly about what his new character would look like, how his hair would be styled, how he would speak and the types of food he would enjoy. He also began making trips to the tacky novelty shops of Hollywood Boulevard in search of just the right prosthetic nose that would help turn him from Robbie Williams into Pure Francis. During rehearsals for his upcoming tour, he took to regaling his band and members of the crew with his plans, including how he was planning to invest in a pair of coloured contact lenses to make the transformation. Initially, he had resolved – wisely perhaps – to keep his Pure Francis idea secret from Tim Clark and David Enthoven, but gradually, as he became more and more enthused by the scheme, he started telling members of his management team that creating a new American persona for himself could ultimately help him break the elusive US market. He also became convinced that because he was in the process of planning to release a greatest-hits album, the only way he could consider bringing out a record at the same time was if he released it as someone else.

It says something, perhaps, about how the normal checks and balances break down when one is as famous as Robbie Williams. Instead of those close to you saying, 'You know what, you're beginning to scare me with this stuff,' they smile and tell you what a great, thoroughly avant-garde idea you have come up with, how you are a true genius and that the public will go simply wild for the groundbreaking concept. So for Rob, the Pure Francis idea became all the more exciting. He announced to his circle that he wanted him to sound like a cross between the aforementioned Neil Diamond, German industrial band Kraftwerk and Depeche Mode, and discussed with Enthoven the possibility that he might even consider doing interviews in the guise of his new alter ego.

Fair to say, it is the sort of behaviour that might have a record company, who not so long ago had invested £80 million in Williams, examining the fine detail of their insurance policy. Nor was this the full extent of his eccentricity at the time. As he prepared for a gig at Edinburgh's Murrayfield Stadium at the end of June 2003, Rob invested several thousand pounds in an Austrian-made Vacunaut suit that was supposed to help him lose weight. Every day he had to be helped into the rubber body suit, which, the makers claim, helps the patient lose weight through 'vacuum therapy', increasing circulation around the stomach and getting rid of love handles. The downside is that the wearer resembles a vaguely anorexic Michelin Man. In Williams's case, the suit's internal vacuum pump also contrived to make his left testicle swell worryingly and turn purple.

Shortly afterwards, while in bed in a suite at the Hotel d'Angleterre in Copenhagen, Rob became convinced that he could hear two ghosts walking around in his living room and banging on the door of his bedroom to be let in. He immediately phoned Gary Marshall, the bodyguard detailed to protect him that night, but unable to raise him in his room, fled his suite. Members of staff found the singer wandering around the hotel lobby at 5 a.m. looking for his minder. Williams then refused to return to his suite and instead asked for the smallest room in the hotel, stipulating that its bed must be pushed hard up against the wall.

In the absence of Guy Chambers, Rob brought in Stephen 'Tin Tin' Duffy to help him write and produce the Pure Francis album.

Duffy was the antithesis of Chambers. Mild-mannered and modest, his approach was laid-back and collegiate. Crucially, he also had unimpeachable eighties credentials. Briefly a member of Duran Duran, he had had a one-hit wonder in the eighties with 'Kiss Me', then formed his own group, the Lilac Time. From the off Robbie was insistent that the new album should eschew the slick production and AOR feel of *Escapology* and instead flirt with the more stripped-down and raw electro sounds he remembered from his youth.

It was a symbol, perhaps, of how Rob was subconsciously attempting to withdraw from the madness of the world in which he found himself into the comfort blanket of his youth, when he had listened for hours at a time to the Human League, the Pet Shop Boys and Prefab Sprout. At the same time, he became virtually fixated with looking up his old friends from St Margaret Ward High School in Stoke, joking in a message he posted to his fellow ex-pupils about his one-time ambition to be a holiday-camp entertainer. 'It's turned out well for me so far – got the interview at Butlin's and haven't looked back,' he wrote. 'If you need an entertainer for your children's party, I do magic tricks and everything!'

But while he longed for less stressful times, he was to learn to his cost that his attempts to turn back the clock would only lead to further heartbreak. An episode from the time that illustrates the cleft stick in which he found himself involved a former childhood sweetheart called Rachel Gilson, whom he had described as his 'one and only true love'. The couple dated at school and had been in touch on and off in the intervening years. As Rob became increasingly nostalgic for a life long gone, he decided to look up the girl he described to friends as 'the one that got away'. Finally, he rang Rachel out of the blue at her home in Bury, Lancashire. He was keen to get to the point. He had been thinking a lot about wanting a more normal life, of settling down and maybe starting a family like his old friends from school, and neither of them was getting any younger, he told her. Rachel was entitled to feel more than a little perplexed, given that their relationship had been scarcely more than a playground crush in the final year of school and had ended when Robbie left and joined Take That and Rachel was spotted by a local model agency. Nevertheless, Rob was not in the mood to let reality spoil his romantic flight of fancy. He told Rachel to pack a bag and said his PA would arrange for a ticket to fly her out to Los Angeles a couple of days later. What girl would not be swept off her feet by a multimillionaire pop star's declaration of undying affection? So Rachel flew to LA and into Robbie's arms. Before the week was out, however, she was flying tearfully back to Britain. Initially, Rob had been delighted to see her and mooned over her for a couple of days like a love-struck teenager, but after a petty row, he had suddenly asked her to leave and arranged for his staff to book her on a flight back to the UK.

Sometime later, he would describe the angst of becoming so quickly dislocated from his early life by fame. 'The only thing that mattered to me as a sixteen-year-old was having a white Porsche Carrera, being able to buy my friends new trainers and being on *Top of the Pops*,' he told an interviewer. 'That was the extent of it. The school doors shut, the pub doors open. There's an audition for a boy band. You get in. You make your first video, you're sixteen and naked, and there's jelly on your arse. Sixteen? You wouldn't get away with that now. And then you're quickly introduced to the world of gay clubs. The next minute, you're on a plane to Japan. Eating sushi. Then you come back to Stoke-on-Trent, you walk into the pub, and your friends see an alien.'

Like Robbie's management, Stephen Duffy played along with the Pure Francis hokum until, to the relief of everyone involved, Williams eventually tired of the idea after several genuinely worrying months for his jittery handlers. Rob, who was a big fan of the Lilac Time, found the experience of working with the easygoing Duffy a welcome relief from the tension that came to infect his relationship with Chambers on the previous album. The pair would sit around playing guitars together in Duffy's tiny North London studio or in the studio Rob installed in the bedroom of his Beverly Hills home as he was preparing for the biggest shows of his career. They would be the exultant pinnacle of the Williams phenomenon, but significantly would also mark the beginning of a new era of professionally troubling times.

CHAPTER NINE

Hubris

When it comes to the hubris stakes, seeing the man you belittled, stifled and wrote off as a gurning nonentity stand on stage in front of a combined total of 375,000 ecstatic fans to milk their collective outpouring of awe and love has pretty much got to take the biscuit. Robbie played a record-breaking three consecutive nights at Knebworth House in Hertfordshire at the beginning of August 2003, beating the previous record held by Oasis, who did two shows at the giant open-air venue in 1996. On the second night, Channel 4 screened the gig live. First, there were the obligatory aerial shots of the multitude who had come to worship at the Williams altar, then a helicopter, emblazoned with a blue-and-white RW logo, landed and the star of the show emerged like the pontiff himself, ready to be greeted by his flock. Cut to the close-ups: pretty blonde girls screaming, others already beside themselves, mouthing the word 'Robbie', mantra-like, over and over. A little kid is perched on his father's shoulders, his face painted in the black-and-white devil make-up from Rob's Kiss-spoof video for 'Let Me Entertain You'. Now comes the first F chord of a piano-heavy intro, and huge red-and-black curtains are parted to reveal the stage. There is Robbie, dressed in black and hanging upside down, suspended by his ankles from a rope fastened to a crane. Some more shots of the crowd going mad and now Williams is standing centre stage, cool in black bug-eye shades, black shirt and white tie. 'Heaven's gone and hell is here,' he begins.

Watching at home, Gary Barlow saw Rob's show-stopping performance. How quickly he was reaching for the 'off' button on his remote we can only speculate.

While events away from the stage suggested all was far from well, Knebworth was the zenith of the Robbie Williams phenomenon. It was the moment when he transcended the boundaries of musician, pop singer and celebrity. Knebworth was an event. For three days it became part of the fabric of the nation. It dominated news bulletins and even had its own dedicated travel reports, as fans making what should have been the forty-five-minute drive from Surrey or Middlesex sat in nine-hour jams between two junctions on the A1. Even people who didn't actually like Williams were going to the gigs. It was one of those 'I was there' things, something to tell the grandkids one day. Williams did not disappoint. Even those who had remained stubbornly resistant to the whole Robbie hoopla had to concede that – like him or loathe him – he had set a new standard by which all future super-gigs would be judged. Robbie managed to make the sprawling set of the stately home seem intimate, introducing his mum, Jan, to the crowd and daring a couple in the audience to snog for the TV cameras. At the end of the show, as he was given a deafening final ovation, he declared: 'I'm a singer; I'm a songwriter; I'm a natural-born entertainer.'

His celebratory sign-off was not quite the off-the-cuff proclamation it first appeared. This was Williams acknowledging what even he assumed would always be seen as the high-water mark of his career. And standing on such an elevated platform gave him the perfect vantage point from which to take pot shots at his enemies in their foxholes below. This was a metaphorical two-finger salute to the likes of Barlow and Guy Chambers; this was Robbie ramming it home that he alone was the author of his idolatry. He was reliant on no one but himself, no sidekick writer or boy-band back-up team. This he had achieved by himself and he would carry on the same way, answering only to himself and the fans who adored him.

Even after two years the 'Back for Good' joke hadn't paled enough for Robbie to drop the piss-taking version of Gary's song from his shows. When Williams performed the song at Knebworth, he brought his ex-Take That cohort Mark Owen on stage to help him perform it. No doubt the plan was conceived with the best of intentions, but there was something about the whole thing that left an uneasy feeling. This was Williams bestowing his largesse on little Mark, whose solo pop career had been stuttering since being dumped by BMG in 1997, and who only a few months earlier had broken down in tears after winning *Celebrity Big Brother* because he did not think he had any fans left. Now for the privilege of sharing a stage again with Rob, he was expected to join in the trashing of one of the band's biggest hits, while Williams placed a patronizing arm round his shoulder and eventually cut him off mid-verse.

Owen could hardly be blamed for grabbing the opportunity to bask in Robbie's reflected glory, no matter how briefly. Like the rest of the band, he had almost forgotten what it was like to feel the elemental power, the adrenalin buzz of a big audience.

The Knebworth shows made Williams somewhere in the region of £12 million, while *Live at Knebworth*, released a month later, became the fastest-selling live album in UK chart history, beating *The Beatles at the Hollywood Bowl*. An astonishing 117,000 copies were sold in the first week alone. A live DVD, *What We Did Last Summer*, was released in November and went to the top of almost every Christmas list. In the UK, more than 48,000 flew off the shelves in the first week, and in Germany, 18,000 copies were sold on the day of its release. Thanks to his continued success, the Sunday Times Rich List estimated Williams's earnings had peaked at £26 million, putting him at number four in the hierarchy of music and media celebrities in the country.

Within EMI there was suddenly increased optimism that *Escapology*'s failure to dent the US charts was not proof that the company had massively overpaid when they had ceded to the singer's demands and signed the £80-million deal the previous November. A week after Knebworth, *Escapology*, which had last topped the album chart eight months earlier, went straight back to the top spot after thirty-eight weeks in the chart.

The three Hertfordshire shows were not the only highlight of a tour that had begun in Edinburgh in June with Robbie playing to 63,000 in the city's Murrayfield Stadium. By the time it ended, the tour had taken in most of Europe. In Germany, Rob played seven gigs, and the level of hysteria proved, if it were at all possible, that he was even more adored by his Teutonic fans than in his own backyard. When the dust eventually settled, with him playing three final nights in Australia at the end of 2003, Williams had played to nearly 1.25 million fans.

Perhaps more importantly, Rob seemed to be enjoying himself

once more on stage. The long, mournful after-show post-mortems had, for the most part, been ditched as the natural euphoria of his achievements evened out his mood. Once the exhilaration died away, however, he was still bemoaning his everyday life. Interviewers were let into his personal miseries; he was rich but lonely. He wanted love, to meet someone and settle down, but he knew he would not be able to cope with such grown-up concepts as relationships and marriage. Most of all, he was depressed. Privately, too, Rob had come to a worrying conclusion. For years, ever since he first got drunk at school or took his first Ecstasy tab at a gay club with Take That in Spain, he had assumed that eventually having the resolve to deal with his addictions would offer the panacea for all his problems. Now he had been clean and sober for the best part of two years and the happiness he had expected would come like magic, along with his AA card, had failed to materialize. From here on in he would have to accept that he drank and took drugs because he was a depressed person whose family history included more than its fair share of relatives who had had to deal with similar demons. The realization shook him.

If Knebworth had been the zenith for Williams, it could be seen as the nadir for Barlow, the moment, beyond even the failure of his solo career and his axing by BMG, in which all his myriad humiliations would crystallize. Yes, Gary had gone about a revival of sorts in his work as a backroom boy, writing and producing for others, but his enemy's mammoth achievement by staging the gigs was definitive evidence of the gap between their respective careers. As far as the contest went, Gary was flat out on the canvas. But with his humbling finally complete, at least he knew he had hit the bottom. In his hour of desperation, he found a sudden clarity of thought. And let's face it, there was now only one way for Barlow's fortunes to go – and that was up. In the coming months Gary's thoughts would inexorably turn to the possibility that he might allow himself to emerge at long last from his self-imposed exile and contemplate performing once more.

At the beginning of 2004, Gary was in the process of moving into a new flat he and Dawn had bought as a base for their semi-regular trips to London when he received a phone call from Jason Orange. Jason said he was in the capital as well, and did he want to meet for lunch? Gary accepted readily, excited at the thought of meeting his old Take That cohort for the first time in ages, to have a few laughs and relive some of the old times. Once the preliminary hugs and mutual backslapping were over, however, it quickly became clear that Jason was not in the mood for a happy jaunt down memory lane. What, Orange asked him, did Gary think about when he remembered their time together in the band? Gary said something about how he did think about it now and then, and admitted he still missed it more than a little. Why, Gary asked, did he want to know? His question was the cue for the floodgates to open. 'Well,' Orange replied, 'it was bloody difficult working for you and Nigel. You were a nightmare.'

Unsurprisingly, perhaps, Barlow was unprepared for such a brutally frank assessment of his behaviour during the Take That years – particularly after all this time – and spent the rest of lunch praying for the moment the bill would arrive so he could get out of there. Over the coming weeks and months he would replay the conversation in his head. It was not so much the shock of Jason's sudden assault on him that shook him, but more the recognition that he had gone all this time without ever realizing the way he was viewed by Jason, Mark, Howard and, yes, Rob. Most thought-provoking of all was that Jason had used the words 'working for you' rather than 'working with you'. The difference, he concluded, was nowhere near subtle. How could he have been so myopic, he asked himself, that he never for one moment considered that rather than the friend he had always thought of himself being to the others, he had been nothing of the sort? Now he knew how he was viewed by Jason and the others – as Nigel Martin-Smith's lieutenant and part-time henchman. Not as one of the boys, but as Nigel's chosen one, apart and aloof.

Certainly, Gary was far from naive about the way things had been in Take That. He knew he was the leader. It was a role he had not so much grasped for himself as had bestowed upon him by Nigel. Martin-Smith made no bones about the fact that, as far as he was concerned, Barlow was the one with the real talent and the obvious choice as front man for the group. And Gary had, consciously or otherwise, taken the burden of making Take That a success onto his own shoulders. He had always felt it was his preordained role to be the one who did the thinking for the rest of them, who did the worrying, who made the tough choices. To a large extent, it was his single-mindedness, his drive and focus that had – often by sheer force of will – propelled them from nowhere to somewhere. It says much about the nature of the Barlow psyche during that early period that he had never considered, until Jason finally and belatedly gave it to him straight, that any of the others might have had a problem with the way he had simply assumed control.

Now, for the first time, he was forced to put himself in their shoes, required to imagine how he would have felt if it had been Mark, Jason, Howard or – worst of all – Robbie who had been the one calling the shots, writing the songs, standing out front. How would he have felt if he had been the one going home at night feeling that his contribution was ignored, devalued and stifled so that one of the others could take all the plaudits? Was there any way he would have stood for it? And if he had, just how resentful would he have been about the whole thing?

Later, in reflective mood, Gary would write in his autobiography, *My Take*: 'Throughout our life as a band I was driven, pig-headed, single-minded, selfish, domineering, devious and extremely ambitious. I can see all of those things now; I couldn't then. The other four lived, worked and travelled with me; they experienced and shared things with me and were on the receiving end of me. Back then, although I was a friend to everyone in the band, for me it was all about *my* career and *my* experience.'

Furthermore, it was not just the creative stranglehold he had over the band that, he realized, had forced a wedge between him and the others. He saw now that his elevated financial position must have been hard to swallow, particularly given his habit of parading his vastly superior wealth in front of them. He had left Take That seven times wealthier than Orange, Donald, Owen and Williams. He had taken, as of right, all the writing credits for the songs and jealously guarded his sovereign territory as the musical director. Would it have hurt him to have been just a little more giving, he now asked himself, to have brought the others into the songwriting process to nurture the talent for writing that was clearly there in Robbie and Mark in particular? A wiser man, he decided, would have shared the financial spoils more evenly, if only to instil the sort of harmony on which long careers are built. Crucially, he was aware for the first time that for the others, the experience of being in Take That had been nothing like his own. Suddenly, he was obliged to ditch the rose-tinted spectacles, to question every happy memory, to replay it all, and this time he was required to view it uneasily without the prism of his insensitivity, thoughtlessness and self-obsession.

Soon after the sobering experience of his lunch with Jason, Gary received a phone call from someone else from his past when Nigel Martin-Smith contacted him out of the blue.

There was a growing nostalgia for all things Nineties, Nigel told him, and BMG were keen not to be left behind. The record company wanted to issue a Take That greatest-hits album and had told him they thought there was a good chance they could sell about 60,000 CDs if they could get them into the supermarkets. What were the chances, Martin-Smith asked, of the lads being up for promoting it? Gary was lukewarm. If BMG wanted to put the record out, that was fine, he said, but he would not be getting involved. Martin-Smith, however, had other ideas. He wanted to have a band meeting to discuss the project and expected Gary and the others to make the time to pitch up for it.

So, almost a year and a half since they had last been in a room together, Barlow, Donald, Owen and Orange reluctantly sat down in the living room of Martin-Smith's sister's house while Nigel held court. For Gary, it was not a meeting he was relishing. Since his conversation with Jason he was suddenly aware of how much the others must hate him. He purposely decided to stay quiet for once and let them have their say. In the event, none of them got the chance. From the off Nigel reverted to type, handing out sheaves of papers on the front of which was written 'NMS Management'. As they sat in silence, Martin-Smith talked excitedly about the deal he was going to secure with BMG and how much money they could all expect to make from the greatest-hits package. Watching him in operation, Gary noticed for the first time the effect that just being in the same room as Nigel had on the others. Jason looked ill and worried, Howard was silent and Mark reverted to type, deferring to his ex-manager and not complaining when he tried to speak and Nigel rudely talked over him.

Nigel was oblivious to the Pavlovian response he engendered in the others. He was domineering and controlling, as though time had stood still since the five nervous youngsters met for the first time at his office in Manchester fourteen years earlier. The only difference, at least as far as Gary was concerned, was that now the blinkers were off. Unlike then, there was no appetite for the project among the ex-members of the band, something Martin-Smith had clearly not been expecting. Most unenthusiastic was Mark, who said he would need time to consider what he wanted to do. Like Gary, he now had his own manager and, unlike the rest of the group, had been pursuing his solo career virtually non-stop since the break-up of Take That. He was not sure he wanted to throw himself back into the band and, more importantly, whether he wanted to put himself under Nigel's control again.

For his part, Gary, who had been non-committal about the whole thing during the meeting, was up for doing some promotion to give the record a lift. His antipathy towards the idea of performing again had lifted and he realized that there was substantially more money in the deal for him because of the royalties he would make from being the writer of many of the songs that would appear on any Take That greatest-hits record. Nevertheless, the sense of déjà vu really hit home when, with the plans for the album still up in the air, within minutes of Gary leaving the meeting Nigel was on the phone, criticizing Jason for asking what Gary thought was a perfectly reasonable question about how much promotion the record company was prepared to give them. 'Can you believe it?

He's just a painter and decorator,' Gary heard Martin-Smith saying, disparagingly referring to Orange's former profession.

Given the band's reservations about the album, the project dragged on through the summer of 2004. Martin-Smith was also keen for them to make a TV documentary that could be released to coincide with the record. In fact, both Nigel and Howard had already appeared in a Channel 4 documentary, *The Truth About Take That*, which had been broadcast that April, but Martin-Smith was not happy with the result and was keen to put together his own retrospective.

By late spring of that year news had leaked out about Take That re-forming to promote the record. In April, Gary attended a party thrown by Simon Fuller's 19 Management at the Albert Hall and told the *Daily Mirror*: 'We're all getting back together this Christmas for something really special. It's not strictly speaking a concert, but we're doing something in time for Christmas and Robbie has definitely signed up to do it.' The *Sun* went further by announcing the group would appear on stage at Christmas to perform a one-off show to promote a compilation DVD. When Robbie's PR team was contacted by the paper and asked if he would be taking part, his spokesman told them: 'I'm afraid there's more chance of hell freezing over.'

It might have been helpful, however, if Williams's people had actually bothered to contact the singer himself before shooting the idea down in flames. Indeed, there were reasons why Rob might have been receptive to the idea. He had returned to Britain after suddenly announcing to friends that he had become bored with his Californian idyll and was currently at a loose end as he struggled to finish his new album. In March 2004, he moved into a rented £7-million, twenty-two-bedroom castle called Whithurst Park, in

Kirdford, West Sussex. The huge house, complete with swimming pool and gym, was chosen for its unrivalled privacy and was to be his base for the six months Rob had decided he wanted to spend in Britain. Returning to Notting Hill, where he would be expected to resume running the daily gauntlet of fans and paparazzi, was no longer an option. Instead, Rob decided he would experience the seclusion of the English countryside and live the role of lord of the manor for a while. Certainly, a rather regal approach was in evidence when he discussed with his father his plans to move into the house. Pete, delighted that his boy would be based in Britain again, asked him where the house was. Rob had to admit he did not know because he had only ever visited it by helicopter. He quickly had the main drawing room on the first floor converted into a studio to accommodate a grand piano and more than twenty guitars.

Literally within days of moving in, however, Williams was admitting that the experiment was a mistake. Instead of revelling in playing the country squire, the walls of the mock fortress quickly became his prison. Lonely and miserable, he tearfully phoned friends to tell them he was in the grip of a bout of depression so severe he feared it might never subside. Perhaps even worse, Rob was soon confiding to his friends that his return to the UK was driving him back to thoughts of drinking again after three years on the wagon because he felt he was being watched wherever he went.

Unwisely, given his precarious emotional state, he also began allowing himself to be put in the way of temptation. On one evening, he visited a local pub when returning from having dinner with friends in a wine bar in Billingshurst. He was confronted by a scene of wall-to-wall drunkenness. He accepted the offer of a game of pool with a lesbian couple, but before long some of the regulars were trying to persuade him to trade his orange juice for tequila. He then became freaked out when he was followed into the Gents by an old guy who wanted to know what it was like to be Robbie Williams. Later, he told friends he had to escape the pub because he was convinced those inside were staring and leering at him. In the days that followed, he relived the scene over and over in his mind, only in his imagination he had accepted the offer of the drink. According to some of those close to him, he became so terrified of being plagued by the public that he took to walking his dogs in the middle of the night to avoid being hassled.

In an attempt to resolve his many personal issues, while in Sussex he turned to ever more bizarre therapies, some of which seemed from the outside to involve an almost morbid preoccupation with his past. He became fascinated by a book called *The Toltec Path of Recapitulation* by Mexican New Age writer Victor Sanchez. The premise of the self-help book involves 'healing your past to free your soul'. To resolve one's problems, Sanchez argues controversially that it is necessary to relive earlier traumatic events by 'gearing healing towards the energetic body'. Using a ten-step programme, Sanchez shows readers how they can enter a trance to relive the pain of their past and start the process of 'energetic restoration'. Oddly, the whole process, known as 'recapitulation', must take place alone inside a hinged wooden box. Keen to try out the technique, Williams had a box built for him in which, for a time, he would lie in a trance-like state. He also took to sitting in bed at night watching old Take That videos at high volume into the early hours.

Perhaps as a result of this latest fad, when Robbie received a call from Mark Owen about the tentative discussions to re-form Take That, he was – to the astonishment of all concerned – surprisingly open to the idea. In the recent past, it had been Mark who, out of

Take That's final line-up, had been the most resistant to working together again, but now he was without a record deal. He first called Williams early on the morning the *Sun*'s story was published. Owen told Rob that yes, the idea had been discussed, but he had told the others he would only commit to doing it if Robbie was also part of the proposed reunion. Williams, who had just got out of bed, told Mark he would ring him back when he was fully compos mentis. In the meantime, Rob rang his PA, Josie Cliff, and told her: 'I'm quite interested in doing something . . . completely for fun, no ulterior motives other than there was something beautiful there and I'd like to celebrate that.' Later, he called Mark back and said roughly the same thing and that he felt it was time to make amends for mercilessly deriding Take That over the years.

It says something for his state of mind at the time that for several days he convinced himself he would be able to work with Gary again, despite his continued private tirades against his sparring partner. Even more strangely, he was also saying that even the involvement of his bête noire Nigel Martin-Smith in the project might not necessarily be a bar to him participating. It is fair to say that his change of heart did not go down well with his own team. As would become something of a pattern whenever the subject of Take That was brought up in the months and years that followed, a jittery David Enthoven gave Williams a lecture about how it was a bad idea, that going back was never an option, that he should remember how hard the experience had been on him the first time and, crucially, how it could do serious damage to the solo career he had spent so long building. Indeed, given Enthoven's uncool reaction the first time the subject of a reunion had come up, Rob would deliberately return to it from time to time just for the fun of watching his manager squirm. On this occasion, however, as is so often the case with the capricious Williams, his initial enthusiasm quickly waned and within a week he had told Mark to count him out. In the meantime, Robbie, who was now heading back to California after his unsuccessful sojourn in Sussex, released the first single of his collaboration with Stephen Duffy, and in October 2004, the partnership produced a number-one single, 'Radio'.

By late 2004 the initial optimism that a Take That reunion of some sort was still on the agenda had been dealt a significant blow by the publication of *Feel*, a book written by Williams and co-writer Chris Heath that covered the making of *Escapology* and Robbie's follow-up album, which would be called *Intensive Care*. Once again Rob, who had been publicly making conciliatory noises about the long-running feud with Barlow, could not resist the opportunity of baiting Gary in print. Throughout its pages Barlow was ridiculed for everything from his meanness with money to his dancing. Indeed, at the time, one of Rob's favourite party pieces was to do an impersonation of Gary dancing while on Ecstasy but still not fully able to let himself go. In the book, he mused about the possibility of telling Barlow his feelings about him in a letter, before coming to the conclusion: 'I'd feel better if I kicked his fucking head in.' Meanwhile, he wrote that he did not believe that confronting his enemy about his behaviour towards him would actually achieve anything. 'He's one of those people that hasn't got a fucking clue what you're on about when you call him on stuff,' Robbie wrote. 'He probably feels really hurt by everything I've said.'

Just to up the ante, when Williams appeared at the Brits in February 2005 to collect a retrospective award for 'Angels', he was introduced by Matt Lucas and David Walliams playing cruel caricatures of Gary Barlow and Howard Donald. As he accepted his gong, Robbie said: 'Sorry, Gary, but I was always the talented member of the band.'

BMG, which was in the process of merging with Sony, had been keen to release the Take That greatest-hits album for the previous Christmas, but deadlines came and went as negotiations over the form any documentary might take drifted. It was not until early 2005 that Nigel Martin-Smith and the four ex-members of Take That finally sat down with the label to thrash out a deal. The company's marketing department was now predicting they could sell 100,000 copies of the album, which to all intents and purposes was the same compilation that BMG had released when the band split nine years earlier. Meanwhile, Nigel was in negotiations with Fremantle Media to make the documentary, while Sony/BMG wanted to put the production into the hands of Simon Cowell's Syco TV. According to Gary, however, Nigel was – once again – putting in an overbearing performance, embarrassing the others by going on about how it was all about the money as far as the boys were concerned.

Now, after keeping his counsel for so long, Barlow acted. He suggested the four of them meet again at his house to discuss the project further, but crucially Martin-Smith would not be invited. Gary, now slimmed down and feeling more confident than he had in a long time, found he was actually looking forward to making the show and being back on television, but now the dynamics of the group had to change. They were all in their mid-thirties, yet they were still deferring to a manager who had not appeared to notice that the boys he moulded for stardom had become grown men, some of them with their own families. If they were ever to be able to work together again, Gary concluded, every decision needed to be made jointly by the quartet of principal characters, not simply because nobody was prepared to stand up to Martin-Smith.

In Robbieland, meanwhile, he had begun seeking to fill his hours of loneliness and isolation by poring over the outlandish musings of former BBC presenter turned international conspiracy theorist and all-round crackpot David Icke. In particular, he became fixated on Icke's theory that many of the people in positions of power in the world are genetically descended from an extraterrestrial race of reptiles from a star constellation called Draco and are capable of changing their shape to take on human form. Icke, a former Coventry City goalkeeper who once infamously claimed to be the Son of God, claims the reptiles then use their positions of power to indulge in paedophilia. Two of the most famous shape-shifting reptilian child abusers, Icke hilariously claims in his 1999 book *The Biggest Secret*, were former prime minister Ted Heath and country singer Boxcar Willie. So wrapped up in Icke's theories was Williams that he incorporated the reptilian theme into the pop video made to accompany the paranoid-sounding lyrics of 'Radio'. In the video, Robbie gradually transforms into a lizard-like creature with a scale-covered tail, fangs and white eyes.

One acquaintance recalls being buttonholed at a dinner party in Los Angeles in early 2005 by Williams, who was keen to discuss his thoughts on the reptile conspiracy. 'I don't know how it happened,' says the guest, 'but the conversation turned to the Queen. I said something about the fact that I supposed he must have met her and Robbie sort of brushed it off in a shy sort of self-effacing way, which I thought was quite sweet. Then from nowhere he started going on about some stuff he'd heard that there were a bunch of reptiles who had taken over the world and were running everything – governments, the CIA. He said he'd also heard one of them lived quite close to him and ran some sort of cookie-making conglomerate. It was clear he wasn't joking. He opened his eyes really wide and was talking really fast like he couldn't get his words out quick enough. Then he said, "Well, you know the Queen's one of them, don't you." I must have laughed because he started saying that he wasn't accusing anyone personally of being a reptilian, it was just a theory he'd been exploring and hadn't made up his mind either way.

'But it was obvious it wasn't just a passing interest because he was going on about how George W. Bush was supposed to be one of them. Then he started saying something to do with how these reptilians got their superpowers from the negative energy in the world and created things like wars, sexual abuse and mental distress to feed off the negative energy all this bad stuff created. He sounded particularly worried that someone might be feeding off his negative thoughts. I didn't say that I thought it all sounded gaga, and because I suppose I was indulging him, he just kept talking. The funny thing is that there were obviously occasions when he could hear how wacko the whole thing sounded and he would say, "Well, that's the theory anyway." I didn't know if he had come up with it all himself, and I don't remember him mentioning this Icke guy, but when I got home, I checked it out on the Internet and there was all this craziness about how the Queen and her three sons are supposed to be these shape-shifting reptilians. I have to be honest and say I've been dining out on the story ever since.'

At the same time, Rob also made contact with strange comic-book writer Grant Morrison, who would later help design the sleeve of Robbie's sixth studio album, *Intensive Care*. Williams set up a meeting with Scots-born Morrison, who claims he was abducted by aliens on a trip to Kathmandu in 1994, after seeing him speak on a DVD made by a conspiracy-theory website. Williams invited the bald-headed Morrison to his house in Los Angeles and the meeting sparked Rob's interest in a branch of witchcraft called Sigil Magic. The technique involves the practitioner creating a symbol, or sigil, to represent something they want from their lives. Morrison, who admits to experimenting with hallucinogenic drugs to practise the form of witchcraft, taught Robbie to write a sentence explaining what it was he most wanted, then remove all the vowels. So, for example, if he had stated, 'I want a hit in America,' he would be left with WNTHTNMRC. Then Morrison showed him how to lie the letters on top of each other. Once certain parts of each letter are removed, what is left looks to the untrained eye like a meaningless hieroglyphic. This sigil must then be memorized by the practitioner and concentrated on at what Morrison calls 'a moment of intense concentration and clarity'.

Friends of Rob say that Morrison explained to Williams how he must undergo a strange initiation ceremony in order to make the transition to fully fledged magician. This involved clearing the mind of all other thoughts and was best achieved, so Morrison told him, at the point of orgasm. He advised him to draw his personal sigil symbol on the back of his hand or – if his partner was willing – on her forehead so it would be readily available to be focused on at the moment of climax. He advised his most famous convert to Sigil Magic that he should also indulge in masturbation several times a day to 'get into practice'. That way, he claimed, the magic spell Williams cast would always come true. Morrison, who says he has been using Sigil Magic for thirty years, claims that in the late nineties he incited more than 6,000 followers to masturbate en masse to save a comic strip he'd written, called *The Invisibles*, from being axed by publishers DC Comics. The experiment was not a complete success, however, as *The Invisibles* was dropped the following year. In 2003, Morrison also claimed in an interview that if enough people became involved, it would be possible to depose US president George Bush in a process called 'wanking Dubya out of office'.

At the same time, Rob began frequenting occult bookshops and collecting the works of Aleister Crowley, the nineteenth- and twentieth-century English occultist, renowned drug-taker and bisexual who founded a religious movement called Thelema and claimed to be the prophet of a new age called Aeon of Horus. Nor would it be the end of Williams's preoccupation with all things otherworldly.

Despite the reservations within Take That about Martin-Smith, his undoubted talent as a manager still had its uses. As talks about the album dragged on into the summer of 2005, the band agreed it should feature at least one previously unreleased track. Eventually, it was decided that they would include a song called 'Today I've Lost Love', which was a favourite of the band, but for one reason and another had never made it onto a Take That CD. Sony/BMG were quibbling over the £20,000 it would cost to remix the track and demanding to be allowed to hear the song before committing to putting it on the album. Martin-Smith called the label's bluff by saying he would pay for the track himself and then license it to rivals EMI. If the single was a hit when it was released at Christmas, then Sony/BMG would be in the commercially unenviable situation of not having it on their greatest-hits package. In the event, the label backed down and it was agreed Robbie's vocal would be left off the final mix.

While Williams had put the kibosh on joining the band to

promote the record, he had been persuaded to cooperate with the Take That documentary, which – after much negotiation – was to be made by Cowell's Syco TV, where Nigel Hall was the director of television. Hall and Martin-Smith would be executive producers of the show, which had already been commissioned by ITV to air in November. As part of the deal, Martin-Smith had an arrangement that he could remove any parts of the film he was unhappy with. In turn, he had offered to give Barlow, Owen, Orange and Donald a written sub-agreement that they would have the right to edit out any sections they didn't like. According to Gary, once the deal was signed, the image-conscious Martin-Smith booked himself in for a facelift in preparation for his appearance on screen.

An agreement with Williams and his management team stated that Robbie would be interviewed first by the film crew, and separately from the rest of the band. However, prior to the airing of the documentary, to be called *Take That: For The Record*, he was resurrecting old grievances by telling the press he had turned down £5 million to get back together with the rest of the boys and that it was Martin-Smith's presence that was standing in the way of him doing it. 'I can say something nice about every single member of the band,' he said, 'but when it comes to Nigel Martin-Smith, I want to rip his uterus out.'

It was also clear that the tension between Gary and Rob was far from easing. As the publicity drive in the build-up to the show began, Gary revealed he had not spoken to Williams in nearly ten years. 'When he started the war of words, at first I wanted to retaliate,' Barlow said, 'but I never called. My deal was, I have had the same mobile-phone number for fifteen years. I'm not hard to get hold of. If he really wanted to reach out to me, he could do. I know the day will come, and I'm here when it does arrive.' At the same time, he was denying he was still jealous of his rival's stellar career. 'Robbie's career got so big I'd never want to be him,' Gary added.

Barlow wasn't the only one in the band who had issues with their ex-band mate. Jason publicly accused Williams of being a liar over his claims that the others had left him alone to cry his eyes out in hotel rooms on tour. 'I'm not saying that he hasn't got emotional issues, but I think Rob is very clever and knows what he should say, how to be a drama queen and to exaggerate things,' he said.

By the time the documentary's director, David Notman-Watt, recorded his interview with Gary at Delamere Manor, it was late September 2005. Gary had already worked out what he wanted his agenda to be: it was crucial, he decided, that the public warm to his personality. He needed to be less guarded, open up and say what he was really thinking. In short, be more like Robbie. Gary was filmed showing the camera crew round his over-the-top country pile with its yellow flock wallpaper, ancestral portraits and brocade curtains. On camera, Gary, sitting at his grand piano, was in conciliatory mood and saying of Robbie: 'I feel guilty for not noticing a lot of the things that I'm now told that Rob went through. I never noticed him drinking. I remember the drugs starting, but I don't remember the drinking. I think the biggest problem of Robbie–Gary was that we were both trying to do the same things. We both wanted solo careers, and when you get that, you get the press and the whole media wanting a competition. There's nothing more exciting than a duel, there just isn't – it goes back in history, that. Everybody loves a fight-out. And at that point, I know for certain that I was probably at my worst personally, the biggest my ego has ever been, and I reckon Robbie was probably in a similar place. Coming out of a band, you think the world owes you everything. When you have been at that height, you just think that everything you touch, everything that moves turns to triple platinum.'

Later, in mid-October, Gary, Mark, Howard and Jason convened at Cliveden, the former stately home of the Astors, in Taplow, Buckinghamshire, now a luxury hotel. As well as the setting for some misty-eyed reminiscences around a roaring log fire, the reunion was a suitable excuse for the film-makers to inject the pathos and dramatic tension that every great production needs. As the boys sat around chewing the fat, they were also waiting to see if Robbie would accept their invitation to join them, to turn four into five once more, to bury the hatchet and offer up a happy tale of redemption to close the show. Cue the four, in pensive mode, watching every car as it drove up the gravel driveway, desperate to see if Rob had finally found it in his heart to let bygones be bygones. Then Gary being filmed talking about seeking Rob's forgiveness as he admits: 'I still feel bad about that day when Rob left because I think we all did gang up on him on one side of the table. We were just trying to protect Take That.'

For the denouement, a male voice from off camera tells the boys what the viewing public had long since worked out: Rob was not going to grace the event with his presence. 'We asked Robbie to come tonight,' he says. Then, after a theatrical pause: 'But he's declined.' Later, Gary would say he hated being filmed as they were given the news that Williams was not coming and that he had been left feeling exposed and vulnerable.

However, with or without Robbie, Take That was a band again – at least for the purposes of promoting their new greatest-hits album, *Never Forget: the Ultimate Collection*, which was due for release in the middle of November to coincide with the documentary. Privately, they began discussing the idea of doing a one-off tour in the New Year, depending on the success of the album and the reaction to the TV show. Two weeks before it aired, Mark's manager, Jonathan Wild, took a call from a tour promoter called Simon Moran, who was convinced there would be a market for them performing as a band again on the road. Better still, he was offering each of the four members £1 million to get involved. At the beginning of the month, Gary, Mark and Howard met in a bar in Kensington to discuss the offer. Between them they agreed that Nigel Martin-Smith should be given the task of establishing if Moran's offer was as good as they were likely to get. Nigel made contact with international tour promoters Clear Channel, but was told bluntly that without Robbie, Take That would not be able to sell tickets. Suffice to say, it would not go down as one of the company's most astute business decisions.

CHAPTER TEN

Retake

On a dark late autumn evening, a limousine edged its way carefully through the West London rush hour. Outside, there was the dull growl of bumper-to-bumper traffic broken by the occasional high-pitched squeal of a car horn. Inside, there was silence. Sitting in the back, Gary Barlow, Mark Owen, Howard Donald and Jason Orange fidgeted uneasily in their seats. As Gary and Mark exchanged anxious glances, Howard stared unseeing out of the window while Jason, pale and ill-looking, steadfastly refused to make eye contact with the others. Finally, as the car neared its destination, Mark broke the spell. 'Shall we just go to the pub and give it a miss?' he announced to a few half-hearted sniggers.

In the run-up to the premiere of their documentary, an air of foreboding had quickly descended on the Take That camp. Suddenly, the fear kicked in that this was going to be yet another humiliation in a long line of reverses since they had called it a day. For Gary, in particular, his natural optimism soon gave way to a gnawing dread about what he was letting himself in for. The one consolation of his latter years in the wilderness had been that slowly but surely the gags had pretty much dried up. He no longer felt the need – as he had done when the mere mention of his name was invariably met with a stifled cackle from complete strangers – to ask his bank if he could change the name on his credit card so people didn't take the mick when he rang up to order something. He had built up a healthy, steady business writing and producing for others. More than that, he genuinely enjoyed the role of mentor and guide to up-and-coming artists. Why, he asked himself, was he risking everything he had worked for on the promise of – what? A few lousy moments back in the spotlight with all the dangers that held. What if the album flopped and no one watched the show? What if he was about to become the butt of the same old jokes again? What if he was just giving Robbie the opportunity to twist the knife, to gloat once more at his failure and humiliation?

A cursory reading of the runes did not suggest that Take That would be welcomed back with open arms by a public longing for a second helping of their particular brand of nineties pop. Embarrassingly, Simon Cowell's production company had not even managed to secure a West End cinema to screen what – inauspiciously – was being referred to as the documentary's 'mini-premiere'. After much discussion about whether the event even warranted an official press night, it was eventually decided that the small Coronet Cinema in Notting Hill Gate would serve as the venue for the first screening.

Gary was not the only one regretting the idea. Jason – who had left show business, travelled, then gone back to college to study literature, psychology and sociology, but now candidly admitted to doing 'absolutely nowt' – was nearly sick with worry. On the day of the premiere, as they met to discuss their outfits for the evening, he was beside himself with anxiety and angry that he had talked himself into venturing once more into the lion's den. As the clock ticked down, he told the others: 'I just can't do this.' It took Gary and Mark to talk him into going through with the event. Mark, too, expected nothing more positive of the evening than being given the chance to say thank you to the people who had helped the band in the early days. Later, he would say: 'It felt like an end for me, not a beginning.' Only Howard, the one band member who had been resolutely against them splitting up in the first place, was grateful for the chance to do it all again, even on such a small scale.

So, as the limousine pulled up outside the cinema, they were amazed to see arc lights beaming into the night sky and policemen in the road guiding their car towards the entrance. More astonishing still, there were fans. Not many – maybe fifty or a hundred – but enough, and what's more they were cheering and begging for kisses. And to their utter relief, the press was there too. The boys emerged from the car blinking into a battery of popping flashguns. Suddenly, the feeling of dread lifted and Gary would later say it felt like the clock had been turned back.

The previous week, Gary, who could not remember buying a new outfit in four years, had made the trip down to London to find something to wear for the big night. Oddly, he found himself reluctant to ask Mark, whom he had usually relied on to give him fashion advice in the old days, to go shopping with him. Now, he was forced to admit to himself, he simply did not really know Mark that well. In the end, he asked his friend Patrick Cox, the shoemaker, to take him to Selfridges to choose some suitable stuff. When they met up on the afternoon of the screening, Gary was dismayed by how much they didn't look like a band – just four blokes who in reality were little more than strangers. Their reception at the Coronet, however, changed everything. Now, as they worked the crowd and posed for photographers, they were Take That once more. Somewhere inside them, a switch had been flicked and they were a unit again. The old swagger, the confidence they had so often lacked individually, but which came naturally to them as a collective, began flooding back.

Once the screening was under way, it was apparent the documentary was a hit with the invited members of the press. Afterwards, the band – ecstatic at their reception – partied the whole night at the after-show do, intent on savouring the moment for as long as possible. In the old days, it would have been Nigel telling them to make their excuses and go. Now it was Martin-Smith's turn to leave. During the show, Gary found himself looking in the manager's direction as the audience laughed at the digs and jokes made at Nigel's expense. Later, Gary would say that it looked like someone was driving a stake through Nigel's heart. But their decision simply to hang around and have a few laughs was not without its symbolism. Though not consciously setting out to do so, the four were quietly asserting their independence from Martin-Smith. Indeed, the old tensions between the band and their manager had never been far from the surface. Relations with Orange, who had long been at loggerheads with Nigel, reached such a low point that on the night of the premiere, he was barely able to look at Martin-Smith.

Nonetheless, when the programme was shown two days later on ITV, it scored seven million viewers, the highest viewing figures of the night. The following morning, Gary, who was due to take the train from Cheshire to London, found his phone was swamped by congratulatory texts and voicemails. For the first time he could remember, on his regular rail trip south he did not hide the whole journey under a baseball cap for fear he would hear those familiar giggles from his fellow passengers.

Not everyone was happy with the programme, though. Nigel, whose control over the production was not as all-encompassing as he had envisaged, was fuming over the way he had been portrayed. He told the *Daily Mail* at the time: 'The documentary was supposed to be the reality of what happened, but it was not. There was so much they didn't show or explain. When they asked Robbie why he was so angry with me and why, after ten years, he couldn't forgive me, they didn't show that he stuttered and stammered and hadn't got anything to say. He sees it as all my fault. Robbie has admitted that he took drugs. He said he was sacked and he only took drugs because of me, and the public bought that and so saw him as the underdog. What people don't realize is that Robbie was releasing singles when he left, but they were only reaching number ten. As soon as he came out with his sob story as the victim of a nasty manager, he started to sell records.'

For now, however, Rob had other things on his mind. As the Take That documentary was being filmed, he also had a new album to sell. *Intensive Care* was released in October 2005, and while it did not quite match the sales of Robbie's last outing with Chambers, the album, which took two years to come to fruition, was still a big hit, going to number one in a total of twelve countries, including the UK, Germany, Italy, Spain, Austria, Sweden, Portugal and Holland.

In what could have been construed as a further dig at Chambers, Williams was boldly asserting that it was his best record so far, but while the record was generally well received by the critics, it lacked – with the possible exception of the sweeping 'Advertising Space' – anything that would really last in the memory. Instead, in trying to mimic the sound of, for example, the Specials on 'Tripping', the first single from the album, he and Duffy only succeeded in pulling off a fairly flimsy pastiche of the ska band's 1979 hit 'Gangsters'. Likewise, his last single, 'Radio', sounded like cod Gary Numan mixed with a second-rate Human League take-off. Crucially, while some tracks, like the Lou Reed-inspired 'The Trouble With Me', started promisingly, they all lacked the huge anthemic choruses for which Chambers was renowned. There was no 'Millennium', 'Feel', 'Let Me Entertain You' or 'Angels' – i.e. the sort of songs that were likely to become favourites at his live shows for years to come.

Moreover, the signs were that the making of *Intensive Care* was not quite the plain sailing that Rob, who for the first time took a producer credit, had been suggesting. Quietly, EMI brought in the highly successful American producer Bob Clearmountain to mix a final version. The label was also disappointed when the record was knocked off the number-one spot in Britain after just a week. In America, it was not even given a release following the poor sales of *Escapology* over there. Two singles, 'Tripping' and 'Advertising Space', made the top ten, but a third, 'Sin Sin Sin', managed to reach only a very modest number twenty-two. And although the self-effacing Duffy would take over Guy's role as Robbie's director of music on the following year's world tour, named Close Encounters, their working relationship would only last one album.

The disastrous press launch of *Intensive Care* also gave a hint that Williams had been spending rather too long marooned on Planet Showbiz and, more pertinently, displayed the inability of those around him to temper his more excessive flights of ego. At an excruciating playback of the record to the media in London, Rob went armed with a wad of negative reviews of his previous records, which he had printed out the night before, the worst bits highlighted in marker pen. Embarrassingly, he then proceeded to read these out at length to the guilty parties seated before him. He was probably not expecting the music critics, annoyed at being berated for simply carrying out their job description, to argue back; in the case of one hack, in particular, with good cause, given that he had not even written the offending article for which Robbie insisted on rebuking him.

The reality was that even by the time of its release, the initial excitement within the Williams camp that *Intensive Care* could signal the beginning of a cohesive new direction for Robbie was already starting to wane. And in an unconscious admission that it was far from his best work, Rob was almost immediately making plans to go back into the studio to begin work on a follow-up.

All of which did little to suggest that Rob was in the best shape for the rigours of the coming months and the massive world tour he had planned. Not least because for some time he had been replacing his one-time drink and drug addiction with an ever-growing reliance on prescription drugs. On top of his use of the antidepressant Effexor and the sleeping tablet Ambien, he had added the powerful and highly addictive painkiller Vicodin, plus two further antidepressants, Seroxat and Xanex. In Los Angeles, he had already become adept at the practice of 'doctor-shopping' to ensure he could meet his need for his cocktail of medication. The method by which addicts obtain legal drugs involves the patient registering with several doctors at the same time and has become a serious problem in America, as physicians are persuaded to dole out drugs unaware that the patient is getting similar prescriptions elsewhere.

In the days after the screening of the Take That retrospective, frantic negotiations were taking place to agree plans for a Take That reunion tour, provisionally scheduled for April 2006. Behind the scenes, though, there were serious doubts that the project could work. The tense situation came to a head less than a week after the ITV show. Gary was in New York fulfilling a long-standing writing commitment. As he was waiting to board a plane at Kennedy Airport to return to London, he was called on his mobile by Jason. He sounded tense and wound up, but came quickly to the point. Jason said he couldn't work with Nigel any more. He'd had enough and called a meeting with the manager, he told Gary. It had not gone well. The upshot was that Jason told Martin-Smith that he wanted him to tender his resignation as their manager. Of course, the ultimatum had gone down particularly badly with Nigel, who told Jason in no uncertain terms that it was not his decision to make. Any decision to get rid of him would have to be jointly made by the four members of the band. Now Jason got to the point of the call. Fine, he had told Martin-Smith, it might be a band decision, but if the others decided that they wanted to keep him as their manager, then Jason would walk; he would be out. It was as simple as that. Orange told Barlow that he could not do the tour if Nigel was involved, and from that moment he would refuse to have any business dealings whatsoever with Martin-Smith.

Throughout the call Gary was being distracted by the annoying bleep of the phone's call-waiting alert. Finally, as Jason talked, he checked to see who was being so insistent. On the screen appeared the number of Nigel Martin-Smith. Barlow told Jason not to worry, that everything would be OK and that they would sit down and talk about it face to face when he got home. Suddenly, the adrenalin rush of the past few days gave way in Gary's mind to the harsh reality of just how hard it was going to be to bring the band back to life. He had allowed himself to get carried away on the wave of nostalgia and bonhomie that had greeted them in the previous week or so, but now the blinkers were off. How stupid they all had been to think they could simply pick up where they left off. Take That, he had to concede, had broken up for a reason. Rob had walked out because he could not take the environment any more; Mark had wanted out at the end; he, Gary, had become stifled and bored; and as Jason had so brutally informed him during their uneasy lunch the previous year, he still carried a burning resentment over Gary's behaviour inside the band.

Now came the issue of Martin-Smith. Nigel was as much a part of Take That as any of them. He had been the brilliant driving force behind them from the very beginning. There was a time not so long ago when Gary could simply not have imagined going on tour without having Nigel there as back-up; he was the Rottweiler, looking out for them and fighting their corner. Nevertheless, as he considered Jason's ultimatum on the flight back across the Atlantic, it surprised Gary that the more he thought about the possibility of Nigel being forced out, the more he was overcome by a sense of relief; with the dynamics changed inside the band, it might actually be enjoyable.

It goes without saying, of course, that the departure of Martin-Smith from the set-up would also offer the long-term hope that Robbie might eventually agree to return to the fold. But even before the band's decision to dispense with Nigel's services, a crucial change in the balance of power had already begun. Gary, perhaps because he was the father of two children, had extended his paternalism to the other members of the group. He was also determined that he would not make the same mistakes he had first time around, when ambition, desire for money and his vaunting ego had driven a wedge between himself and the others. If only subconsciously, he was already taking on the role of father figure, a position that had

previously been the exclusive preserve of Martin-Smith. This was
the new Barlow, chastened by his past failures, nurturing and
genuinely determined to make amends. In the eyes of the others,
Gary – always their creative force – now promised to be the benign
leader, the first among equals, something the band needed if they
were going to make the whole thing work.

His primary concern on returning to Britain was that, with less
than forty-eight hours left before they were due to reveal their tour
dates, they had still not resolved the issue of Martin-Smith. Gary
had been screening calls from Nigel, wanting to discuss with the
others what to do before talking to him directly. The four arranged
to meet in the luxurious confines of the Berkeley in Knightsbridge
the night before the press conference to announce their reunion
tour. But with little more than twelve hours to go, the Martin-Smith
question was not the only issue occupying Barlow's mind. The
concerns that Gary had about whether they would be able to pull
off reuniting for a tour had become a contagion. Before meeting
the others, he paced his hotel room alone, wondering what he had
let himself in for and whether it was too late to pull out. In their
exclusive quarters in other parts of the hotel, Howard, Jason and
Mark were having the same second thoughts. What if nobody
turned up to the press conference the following day? What if they
were accused of simply cashing in to make a quick buck for their
old age? What if they couldn't sell the tickets? Just to make matters
worse, the previous week Robbie had set a new Guinness World
Record by selling 1.6 million tickets for his upcoming 2006 tour,
estimated to be worth a total of £80 million, in a single day.

When the four finally met, they agreed that despite their mutual
reservations, it was too late to pull out. There was much to be positive about, they told each other – not least that the compilation

album had gone to number two and had sold 90,000 copies in the first week alone. They also took a vote and decided that Martin-Smith had to go. They had no contractual obligation to him, but he was part of their shared history and that would make getting rid of him all the more troubling.

The following day, the band sat before the press to announce live on Radio 1 that they would be embarking on an eleven-date arena tour of the UK and Ireland as a four-piece the following April. The eight-venue tour would begin at Newcastle's Metro Radio Arena, and two nights had been booked at Wembley Arena, with tickets going on sale the following week. The sense of impending doom was not alleviated by the press conference. Gary thought it had not gone well, that it felt ropy, and when he looked at the others as they sat in front of the cameras, they simply did not seem like a band any more. As the press exited the room and the four were left alone, Howard collapsed to his knees crying, with Jason – who again looked ill with the stress of the occasion – hugging him. Gary says that at that moment he truly believed that the tour could simply not happen, that they had all been away so long that not one of them – himself included – was ready for what was in store for them.

It was no surprise that after all this time they found the experience overwhelming. Like Gary, both Howard and Jason had given up performing and never expected to return to the spotlight. Howard, the oldest at thirty-seven, had spent his years away from the public eye making a living as a DJ in Britain, Germany and Spain, going by the anonymous stage name of DJ H.D. He had recently left the North-West to move to Southampton to be near his daughter, Grace, then six, from his failed relationship with make-up artist Victoria Piddington. He was also the father of a baby girl, Lola, from his relationship with German girlfriend Marie-Christine Musswessels. Donald had not coped well with enforced anonymity. As the band re-formed, he revealed for the first time that soon after they had gone their separate ways in 1996, he came dangerously close to breaking point. Robbed of the simple camaraderie of being with the band and cut adrift from the order that being in Take That had placed on his life, he quickly succumbed to depression and mourning. The low point for him came when he was staying in a London hotel. Lonely and miserable, he walked down to the Thames fully intending to throw himself in, but at the last moment talked himself out of it. He would later describe that low point as 'a mad ten minutes'. 'I thought, What an idiot. If I'm going to throw myself in, I'm going to get cold and then have to swim out again.' But despite the mental anguish he was going through, Howard did not feel able to share his suicidal thoughts with the rest of the band until several years later.

After his unsuccessful attempts to make a career as an actor, Jason had been splitting his time between Manchester and Ibiza, where he was regularly to be spotted driving round in his open-top Jeep. Rake-thin and unmarried, he had suffered for years with insomnia.

Mark was still attempting to breathe life into his misfiring solo career and had released an album under his own steam, called, aptly, *How the Mighty Fall*, earlier in 2005. His second single from the album, 'Hail Mary', only got to 103 in the UK charts. For several years he had lived in the Lake District, and since the previous year he had been dating actress and wife-to-be Emma Ferguson, with whom he would go on to have a son, Elwood, and a daughter, Willow Rose.

It was left to Barlow to break the news to Nigel Martin-Smith that he was no longer wanted by the band he created. In his 2006 memoirs, Gary wrote: 'He was in tears; his world had been taken away. Nigel had loved us boys. He'd gone further for us as a manager than anyone else would have done. He didn't only give us his undying attention and love, we'd been the sole focus of his career. He'd fought so hard for us, and pissed off so many people in the process, that when it was over, no one wanted to work with him again. With Nigel you're either for him or against him. For Nigel as a manager, it wasn't a case of moving on to the next young talent. We were his moment, his career, and now he wasn't going to be part of our future. It wasn't a decision any of us found easy or pleasant to make, but it's been part of us growing up. There was too much water under the bridge for us all to fall back in line and be dictated to.' (In fact, Gary's assessment of Martin-Smith's future prospects was overly bleak and Nigel continued to run his successful management company from his Manchester offices.)

Martin-Smith would later say it was Jason Orange who had loaded the bullets, and that it was Jason who had been the most resistant to the band re-forming. Now, in the absence of a manager and with a tour in the offing, Barlow was expected, in the short term at least, to take over the role vacated by Martin-Smith. He was about to discover that the job was going to be a bigger one than even he could have imagined. When tickets went on sale on Friday 2 December 2005, they sold out within six hours. Such was the incredible demand, the tour's promoters, SJM, doubled the number of gigs to twenty-six, as phone lines jammed with fans desperate for tickets. In Manchester, BT computers crashed and the phone network briefly went down due to the sheer number of people ringing the city's MEN Arena. Ticket brokers said their systems jammed because they could not cope with the demand. By the time the mad day was over, the promoters had sold more than 250,000 tickets, including 80,000 for the shows in Manchester and a total of six nights at Wembley Arena. Extra dates were added in London, Newcastle, Birmingham, Manchester and Dublin. Tracked down by the press on that day, a flabbergasted Gary said: 'We're all in shock. We always knew our fans were great, as they used to follow us around, but the response from them today has been over-whelming and we are so grateful for their loyalty and support.'

Despite the success, Gary's first day in temporary control of Take That was not exactly the most auspicious of beginnings. On the afternoon before the tickets were due to be released, he had been contacted by the promoter Simon Moran, who was already confi-dently predicting that the tickets would sell out as soon as the phone lines opened at 9 a.m. Moran told Gary he would need to keep an open line to him throughout the morning so that Gary could authorize additional venues and extra tickets could be released when necessary. Barlow took Moran's bold forecast with a pinch of salt. After a meeting in London, he went out to dinner with friends, returned alone to his flat more than a little worse for wear and crashed out still in his clothes, but not before drunkenly turning off his mobile. By the time he awoke at 9.25 a.m. and turned on his phone, his crashing head was further assaulted by the ping of twenty-eight missed calls and sixteen voicemails from an increasingly harried Moran. While Take That's new helmsman had been sleeping it off, Moran had been forced to take the deci-sion alone to add a further six nights at the NEC in Birmingham, less than fifteen minutes after the lines opened. Now he wanted Barlow's authority to add seven more dates to the nineteen that were already sold out. In the event the tour would eventually consist of thirty-two shows.

The following week, Moran added five dates at the new Wembley Stadium, the City of Manchester Stadium and the Millennium Stadium in Cardiff. This time the dates sold out in less than thirty minutes. In the process, the tour became the second fastest-selling ever – ironically bested only by Robbie's own upcoming record-breaking gigs. It meant Take That would be the first UK act to play at the yet-to-be-completed Wembley the following year, beating Robbie, who was due to play there in mid-September. As things turned out, however, building delays meant that both Take That and Williams's Wembley shows had to be moved to the Milton Keynes Bowl.

There's a question that Gary Barlow has returned to again and again in the intervening months and years: what kind of strange alchemy was at work during that period? Why, after so long, after all the knocks, the humiliations, was the time suddenly so right? Was it just that, like everything else in life, in the end it all comes down to a few key moments, that you just have to take your chances when they come along? But why, suddenly, did the fans want them back? Was it simply nostalgia? Maybe all those girl fans, many of whom had kids themselves now and were – like the band members – in their thirties, were simply at the age when they were starting to look back for the first time, that they wanted to feel what it was like to be that young again and were looking for a musical trigger to relive the old memories.

As in his career, Gary was undergoing some dramatic changes in his living arrangements. Earlier that year, Dawn had taken him out to dinner to celebrate his thirty-fourth birthday at a smart restaurant in the Cheshire stockbroker belt close to Delamere Manor. The place was stuffy, creaking and, except for one other couple, completely empty. Out of the blue, the realization came to him that he had been wasting the best years of his life locked away in his provincial ivory tower, with the cell keys jangling from his own Versace belt. After an evening of stilted conversation and the echoing sounds of metal against crockery, Barlow blurted out an announcement he had hardly even registered in his own mind before it came out of his mouth. He told Dawn he felt they were dying stuck out of the way in the shires. He had had enough and simply could not go on living there any more.

Later, Gary would ask himself whether the decision to put Delamere on the market had been the turning point when, subconsciously, he came to the end of the cycle of grieving for his lost career and was ready to shed his mourning clothes, leave his mausoleum and emerge blinking into the light. What he knew for sure was that he felt weighed down by the clutter, burdened by an existence that had left him out of touch with the living, breathing world from which he had retreated. Certainly he did not expect Dawn's reaction to his impromptu declaration. She immediately burst into tears and told her husband she had been feeling the same way for three years but had not felt able to say anything to him.

That night, the couple walked home and silently wandered from room to room of their palace. Now, suddenly, the veil was lifted and Gary was able to see it for the first time in all its preposterous excess. There were rooms he had hardly entered for two years, stuffed from floor to ceiling with the sort of high-end junk and pointless knick-knackery that can only be found in the finest auction houses of Paris, London and New York. There was stuff he did not even like, overblown gilded busts and marble statues he had bought from Elton John. Walking around the place, it felt less like a family home and more like a museum, albeit one with a random approach to curation.

Together they chose a few special pieces they knew they could not be parted with, and the rest were crated up and auctioned off at Sotheby's. The house, too, was eventually sold, and Gary and Dawn found a three-bedroom semi in Kensington, West London. It was without doubt a very nice house with a prestigious postcode, but it was not by any means your archetypal pop star's folly. It was just a home among the noise and hubbub of the city, among restaurants, shops, among people. The only downside was that by selling Delamere and the properties within its grounds that were home to his parents and his brother and his family, new houses had to be found for them nearby in Cheshire.

By way of following through his mission to simplify his life, after his arrival in London Gary dispensed with his silver Mercedes SL and even got rid of the family's modest Ford Focus. From now on he would make his way around the city on the bus and Tube with the aid of his latest investment, an Oyster card. But, as he was to discover, there is a price to be paid for freedom. On 7 July 2005, shortly before he made his move to London a permanent one, Gary woke up in his West London flat later than he had planned. Knowing he had to catch a train from Euston back to Cheshire by 9.20 a.m., he got ready hurriedly, threw his computer and a few things into a bag and headed out to catch his usual Circle Line train from Kensington High Street Station.

On board the Underground train, it was standing room only. As it approached Edgware Road Station, there was a shuddering bang and the sound of the train's brakes being slammed on. Those standing up were thrown onto the floor of the carriage. Other passengers on the same train later described panic setting in as it began to fill with smoke. In the darkness, people were shouting, crying, screaming in the long seconds before the watery emergency lighting kicked in.

Those there that day would tell how they were starting to have trouble breathing because of the smoke, that they thought they were all going to burn alive stuck down there. In the train carriages commuters were trying to force open doors or smash windows to get air. Finally, after what must have seemed like an eternity, cool air began filtering into the compartments. But Gary and the other passengers would wait another five minutes for the smoke to start to clear.

As the gloom lifted, Gary heard a cry from a woman who was sitting by the window. He turned and could see through the glass another train lying on the track next to them. It looked like a tin opener had been taken to it. The side and roof had been shredded and ripped away when Mohammad Sidique Khan detonated the bomb he was carrying in a rucksack at 8.50 a.m. in the second carriage of the westbound Circle Line train, number 216. The train, which had left King's Cross Station eight minutes earlier, had pulled away from platform four of Edgware Road Station on its way to Paddington. Khan, one of four 7/7 suicide bombers, was killed, along with six rush-hour commuters travelling in the same compartment as him.

A passenger in another part of Gary's train, teacher Tim Coulson, managed to get out on to the line and smash one of the windows of the stricken carriage. He climbed in to give first aid. Through the gaping hole in the side of the train those in Gary's compartment could see a badly injured woman lying on what remained of the carriage floor. Unable to get out to help, Gary and some others threw their bottles of water through a smashed window to the people in the wrecked train. After fifteen minutes, the first emergency services arrived, but it would be another thirty before the doors between the carriages were opened and he and his fellow passengers could escape. In the meantime, as they waited, some of them would describe breathing in the stench of burning flesh.

As the rescue services worked, Gary counted seven bodies. When, eventually, they were led out down some steps and on to the track at the front of the train, they saw the bodies covered with white blankets. Others – the injured and shocked – sat around, bloodied and bewildered. Gary, his face black with soot, emerged into the light, walked home through Hyde Park and borrowed a friend's car to drive home to Dawn and the children. Later, he jolted awake in bed as he felt that first hard explosion again in his sleep. He lay there, wondering what had happened to the woman he saw being pulled out of the wreckage, and realizing how easily he could have been on that other train, the one with the bodies, the blood and the death.

Several months before the beginning of what was due by Robbie's standards to be a fairly mammoth world tour, set to kick off in South Africa in early April 2006, members of the Williams camp had now become aware that he was misusing prescription drugs. His staff started to become alarmed that sometimes he was hard to rouse in the morning and regularly took to sleeping in so long that he would not actually emerge from his bedroom until it was dark. Privately, Rob was telling friends that he was terrified of going to bed at night because he had become obsessed by thoughts that he might never be able to sleep again and would die of exhaustion. At the same time, he was insisting that only by taking antidepressants was he finally able to drop off. They were also responsible, he said, for keeping at bay for the most part his terrifying panic attacks. Even so, he was still occasionally overtaken by episodes when, without warning, he would be reduced to a shaking and gibbering wreck. All the more embarrassing for him was that some had taken place in front of the girl fans he would invite back to his hotel room while travelling, or to the flat he had purchased in an exclusive block at London's Chelsea Harbour. Very often the outcome of such transient liaisons was not sex. Instead, Rob would announce vulnerably that he was simply lonely, frightened to be by himself and wanted nothing more than to talk to pass a few hours until he felt tired enough to sleep.

Unsurprisingly perhaps, Rob sought escape through music and soon after the release of *Intensive Care*, he began work on his next album, *Rudebox*, which would eventually be released one day short of a year after its predecessor. This time, with Stephen Duffy out of the picture, Williams chose to work with several producers, including Mark Ronson and William Orbit. He also collaborated with the Pet Shop Boys and production team Soul Mekanik, made up of Kelvin Andrews and Danny Spencer, who, like Robbie, come from Stoke-on-Trent. Much of the album was recorded in the bedroom of Rob's Beverly Hills house, which he christened Rockband Studios.

The sixteen-track album, which would feature covers of Duffy's 'Kiss Me' and the Human League's 'Louise', would signal a diversion into electro and dance music, and produce a record that Robbie himself still says is one of his best. It is fair to say, though, that his assessment of it does not by any means put him in the majority. It was recorded at a time when, according to those around him, Williams had been talking seriously about how he would never be able to make another album if he was expected to stick to the formula that had been so successful for him thus far. Privately, however, there was concern in the Williams camp that he was jumping headlong into the project in an effort to dispel his terror that he had lost not only the ability, but also the passion to write a record that he could be proud of and that would be a commercial success. Fearful that he was possibly staring at a future in which he had creatively stalled, and haunted by the tyranny of the blank page whenever he tried to write, he came to the conclusion that such a chilling inertia would be more likely to kick in the longer he waited between albums. It was not the ideal starting point for a record that, given the mixed reception that had greeted *Intensive Care*, needed to raise the bar several notches if it were not to be taken as further indication of a general downward trend in his ability as a recording artist.

Also worrying to those who guided his career was that, just as Guy Chambers had discovered during the recording of *Escapology*, Williams was becoming more and more adamant about what he thought was right for his career. To compound the issue, they found on occasion that he was inclined to displays of righteous indignation if anyone questioned his decision-making. In a sign of the petulance that now occasionally characterized his behaviour, he had reacted with fury when David Enthoven had informed him that he did not believe one of Rob's favourite songs, 'Ghosts', from *Intensive Care*, was strong enough to be released as a single. Now Robbie was insisting on forging ahead with a project that made those surrounding him increasingly worried.

According to one source, a feeling existed among several of those who would work with him on and off over the years that he was, ironically, easier to handle when he was drunk. 'From my point of view, I preferred Rob when he was drinking, simply because you knew where you were. This might sound like an absolutely terrible thing to say, but I believe that when he was drunk, there was a part of him that said to himself, I know I'm drunk and therefore I should listen to the people I trust, because my own decisions are coming from this alcoholic place and they may be totally wrong for me.

'I don't really know when his problems with prescription drugs got started, but I found personally that he became more and more resistant to opinions other than his own. I don't mean that he would wantonly ignore good advice; I just found that his attitude hardened. I think he was determined that he was going to be the artist he envisaged himself becoming and not what everyone else wanted him to be. In many ways, that is a healthy approach, because every artist needs a vision of where they want to be, but I think that Rob got off too much on being in control and stopped listening enough to some of the wise heads around him.'

At the same time, Robbie was telling anyone who'd listen that he was delighted by Take That's reunion and wished them well for their forthcoming tour.

CHAPTER ELEVEN

Relight My Ire

G iven the animus that was still evident in Robbie's attitude towards Barlow, it was stretching it a bit to suggest
that his disposition towards a resurgent Take That's
success was overflowing with quite as much sweetness and light as
he was keen to have us believe. Not least because Rob simply could
not resist taking a pop at Gary and was showing precious little sign
of the bonhomie towards his enemy that he insisted he now felt.
Indeed, in the privacy of his recording studio, Rob was already
planning his latest broadside at Barlow, a song called 'The 90s',
which he had written for his upcoming album, *Rudebox*. The track,
which would also infamously lambast Nigel Martin-Smith,
followed a fairly familiar pattern when it came to his continued
baiting of his old sparring partner. In the song, which chronicles
Robbie's life from failing his GCSEs to getting picked for Take That
and finally leaving the band, Barlow is described in the following
unflattering terms: 'I met the other guys. One seemed like a cock.'
While admirable for the stripped-down sparseness of the lyrics, it
is hardly likely to win any prizes for diplomacy.

It was not, it has to be said, the most magnanimous way to

respond to Gary's public open invitation to Williams to join Take That on their 2006 reunion tour. Nevertheless, the boys were still saying they would be keeping a spare microphone on the off chance Rob should decide to join them on stage during one of their shows. Clearly, their hopes of him taking them up on the offer were not especially high, given that as part of their spectacular hi-tech show, the band had enlisted the help of a twenty-foot-high hologram of Robbie, specially sanctioned by Williams himself, who sang an a cappella opening to 'Could It Be Magic'. The segment of the show, which was premiered at Take That's opening Newcastle gig at the end of April 2006, was to become one of the highlights of the tour.

Preparations had begun in January, when the four band members went on a bonding holiday to Las Vegas. It was, more than anything, a chance to get to know each other again, to see some shows for inspiration and generally to enjoy the calm before the storm. A month later, they went into a rehearsal studio for the first time in eleven years to work on the choreography for the upcoming shows. The brief high of the unexpected demand for tickets when the concerts were announced was now replaced once again with a sense of acute trepidation over what lay ahead.

Gary was feeling the anxiety more than most. He was keenly aware that he had always been the weakest dancer in Take That and that Jason and Howard in particular had been expected to make up for his shortcomings in their live shows down the years. Now he was faced with the added dilemma of just how fitting it was for a thirty-five-year-old bloke who – despite his best efforts on the diet front – was still carrying a few spare pounds to be prancing around the stage in a reheated boy band. Aside from the obvious apprehension about getting on stage again, Barlow was unnerved by how hard it had been for any real sense of brotherhood to return to his relationship with the others, and there remained the risk that the band would not be able to cut it as a four-piece. As preparations for the tour began, there was even discussion within the Take That organization that *Pop Idol* runner-up Gareth Gates might be brought in to fill the role vacated by Robbie.

In public, at least, all the talk from the band was of how stepping back into Take That had been a seamless process, that their shared history and fraternal bond was such that it was as though the intervening years had never happened. Behind the scenes, however, the old routines were simply not going to be an option if the band was going to survive the fissures, private grievances and unspoken animosity that had blighted it first time around. Central to this new dynamic was the tacit agreement between them that with Martin-Smith gone, Gary must find a new way of relating to the others. The transition was not an easy one.

The air of tension only intensified the closer they got to the opening night of the tour. There were the obvious concerns of any band making a comeback: would it seemed forced and silly to be back on stage doing the numbers they had first performed as teenagers and twenty-somethings? How would the fans react, and were they in for a mauling from the critics, who, they were well aware, could easily jump in with their size tens and accuse the whole shebang of being a cynical ploy to milk a final payday.

For Barlow in particular, there was, as ever, the spectre of Robbie's success, which threatened to overshadow everything they did. With that in mind, early on they had resolved that their live show – always a mainstay of their success – would be bigger and better than ever. The unexpected addition of the stadium shows meant they could push the boat out.

With a budget for the tour of more than £10 million, they brought in creative director Kim Gavin, who would later be chosen to oversee the closing ceremony of the 2012 Olympics in London. Together, they concentrated on choreographing a show that was a mix of pure pop and extravagant theatre. Along with eight costume changes came shooting flames and – for the finale – real rain, which flooded the stage and the first rows of fans, plus a mini-stage that put the band among the fans in the stalls. Thanks to some string-pulling by Gary, Dawn was also one of the dancers.

Cleverly, Gary set the agenda for the future when he officially called time on Take That's boy-band phase and announced before their first show in Newcastle: 'We're not a boy band any more; we're a man band – have you seen my stomach!' The show opened with the lads appearing at the back of the set and walking forward on a raised platform that gradually lowered them onto the stage. And if there was any doubt that women now in their thirties might be resistant to behaving like schoolgirls for the duration of the two-hour extravaganza, they had reckoned without the one significant addition to the reincarnated Take That experience – alcohol. There is, it would seem, nothing that helps roll back the years better than drinking your own body mass in Bacardi Breezers.

Even though it took them several shows fully to get into their stride, it was clear from the outset that this new version of Take That more than held its own when compared against the original. And if the hormones of the audience were not raging quite so out of control, to fill the gap came the warm glow of nostalgia and the unadulterated female joy of being on a hen night with a guest list of 12,000 and four blokes in the role of superannuated male strippers, for despite the passing of the years, sex was still very much on the agenda, with the band reverting to their S&M glory days, complete with flames and double-jointed dancers during a gaudy version of 'Relight My Fire'. On sale at the merchandising stalls outside were Take That-branded ladies' knickers, embossed with such saucy slogans as 'It only takes a minute' and 'How deep is your love?' Now even Gary found the fans throwing their thongs at him, rather than the Toblerones and cuddly toys he had had to make do with a decade earlier.

If the fans were wowed, then so too was Fleet Street. The clamour for seats meant that instead of the newspapers' usual music critics – who by nature might have been inclined to sniffiness – review tickets were usually bagged by those women journalists who had been dedicated Thatters in their youth. Gary had already spotted the tide was turning, that the media in general had tired of the notion of Take That as being good only for a cheap gag. Now there was a general mood of goodwill towards them. It tapped into the natural inclination in all of us to root for the punch-drunk slugger who takes his shots, heaves himself up off the canvas before the count of ten and puts his guard back up ready for the next round. There were exceptions, of course, to the air of bonhomie. The *Observer*'s reviewer was unimpressed with the dancing of Gary Barlow mark II. 'For "It Only Takes a Minute", a flamenco dancer comes on to smooch with the boys in turn,' she wrote. 'When she gets to Gary, it's like watching a swan dance with a people carrier.'

Amid the high campery, there was the occasional nod to the less harmonious elements of Take That's backstory. One video sequence symbolically showed the four as mannequins before gradually turning into real people. Later, as the band danced in black-and-white suits, they were addressed by the booming, disembodied voice of a pop manager telling them the commandments by which they must abide: that they must always be ambiguous about their sexuality, that they must not become friends in case one breaks down and has to be discarded. It was, of course, a not-so-subtle dig at Nigel Martin-Smith, but more than that, it was about asserting their independence, about acknowledging where they had come from and setting down a marker for the future, that from now on they would be their own men. It was also, perhaps, a subconscious and subliminal message to Robbie that they had broken with the past, had accepted their culpability in the way he had been treated within the group, and that in Martin-Smith they had removed the one person who had stood in the way of a rapprochement – and by doing so had removed Robbie's last excuse for staying away.

With the huge success of the tour, however, there were more pressing matters to be dealt with. Sony/BMG, the band's label during Take That's first incarnation, began making approaches to sign them up to a new record deal. The issue of whether Take That should make a new studio album was something of a no-brainer, given that there was clearly a lucrative market for fresh material. The question was, would Gary want to climb back in bed with them once more, given the way he had been so unceremoniously dumped by the label six years earlier? The situation was complicated by the fact that although Sony/BMG had no ongoing contractual relationship with Take That, it still owned the group's back catalogue of music. In normal circumstances, their old record company would have been the obvious choice when it came to signing a new record deal, but now the band, and particularly Gary, was holding all the cards.

According to those close to Barlow, there was also a sense that the label had underestimated Take That's ability to pull off its phoenix-like resurrection. While the promoter Simon Moran had confidently predicted from the start that he could sell out a big concert tour, Sony/BMG had been more circumspect, only offering a relatively small advance and predicting they would sell up to 100,000 copies of the greatest-hits album. In the event, it had shifted more than a million copies by the time the reunion tour kicked off, and there was more than a little irritation among the band that the company's executives had not taken them sufficiently seriously. By the end of the tour, Jonathan Wild, Mark Owen's manager, had taken over as the band's new manager, but for the time being Gary was in nominal control. He set up a meeting with David Joseph, MD of Polydor, part of the giant Universal Music Group. Within two days Polydor had made an offer, reported to be £3 million. At the last minute, Sony/BMG tried to salvage a deal, but it was a case of too little too late. Now, with delicious irony, it was Barlow's responsibility to deliver the news to his erstwhile label that neither he nor his band mates would be requiring their services. Fair to say, only the most forgiving of men would not have luxuriated in the moment.

This time the ground rules were already set. No longer would Gary be expected to write the music by himself. Instead, the creation of songs would be a collegiate process, each member pitching in their ideas to create the sound of Take That mark II. Crucially, the thorny and hugely divisive issue of Gary reaping the lion's share of the rewards when it came to publishing royalties was also resolved. In future, it was agreed, all new songs would not carry the name of the individual members who had written them, but would simply be credited 'Written by Take That'. Given that Gary and, to a lesser extent, Mark would remain the principal creative forces behind their future albums as a foursome, it was a magnanimous decision on their part. It meant that the band would no longer be divided by their vastly different financial fortunes, and that Gary would no longer have to carry the weight of everybody's expectations alone. Both moves were signs of Gary's maturity, and also showed that he had been listening to the others during the weeks when they were going about the process of becoming reacquainted. It was a symbol that Take That, now dispossessed of the divide-and-rule ethos that had contaminated their personal relationships during the Martin-Smith regime, were – more than they ever had been – a band in every sense of the word.

While Gary and the boys set about writing the record that was to make them more musically relevant than ever before, Robbie's latest album would leave some sceptics questioning whether his own relevance as a recording artist was in terminal decline.

Robbie had certainly been relishing the freedom to control fully his musical output, even to the extent of using multiple producers on *Rudebox*, which became his seventh studio album in October 2006. He loved the idea of not being tied down by someone else's notion of what the record should be. The result, however, was a mishmash of ideas that lacked any of the coherence of his work with Chambers. And becoming more involved in all aspects of the recording process also carried the potential for expensive mistakes. A case in point was the track 'The 90s', the latest get-even assault on Gary Barlow and Nigel Martin-Smith.

Even after more than ten years, the singer still bore a grudge, in particular over the bitter and highly expensive lawsuit that the Take That manager brought against him following his departure from the band. He continued to refer to Nigel in interviews as the 'spawn of Satan', and the vitriol wasn't merely for public consumption. Songwriter Ray Heffernan told me that during his friendship with Williams, the vexed subject of Take That's manager was one that

Robbie would return to again and again. 'The situation with Nigel came up a lot,' says Heffernan. 'He always referred to him as "Satan". There was still a lot of anger about the way he had been treated in Take That.'

The lyrics to 'The 90s' contained yet another rabid attack on Martin-Smith, but this time one notorious verse would prove to be Rob's undoing. Previously Williams, guided by his management team, had been careful that his lyrical volleys at Martin-Smith went no further than goading him with a stick. Now Robbie upped the ante. His rapping about Martin-Smith on the song was calculated to cause offence. Worse, it implied Take That's manager had ripped him off when he was in the band. When word of the song reached EMI executives, there was undiluted panic over the potential for Martin-Smith to take legal action over the lyrics, but Rob stood firm over the song and insisted it must appear in its original form on the album. With its release imminent, the internal toing and froing continued, with the singer refusing to budge. When promotional copies were sent out to radio stations and the media, EMI executives ordered that the offending track be removed. Meanwhile, with the threat of legal action from Martin-Smith, the planned release of his new album was thrown into disarray as EMI took steps to jettison the song altogether or, at the very least, bleep out some of the lyrics. Williams's own lawyers were readying themselves for a £1-million libel writ, and sources within Robbie's camp revealed that the singer had been specifically advised by his legal team that he should make no further reference to the dispute with Martin-Smith for fear of inflaming the row.

Rob, however, was in no mood to bow to the warnings of his record label or his attorneys. Finally, with the album's release less than a month away and EMI refusing to release it with the offending track in its current form, Robbie launched a public rebellion against his masters. In a moment of wanton defiance, he went on stage at the Milton Keynes Bowl in September 2006 and rapped an impromptu version of the highly defamatory song in front of 65,000 fans. Hardly surprisingly, there were gasps of horror from Robbie's management and the invited record-company executives as he sang of Martin-Smith: 'He's such an evil man. I used to fantasize I'd take a Stanley knife and go and play with his eyes.' Suffice to say, it was all decidedly unpleasant stuff. Later, as members of the audience joined in and yelled abuse about Martin-Smith, Williams told them with mock incredulity: 'I don't know what he is upset about.' Predictably, of course, as his lawyers squirmed in case a recording of that part of the show should become public, a female fan who had filmed the unscheduled rendition of the song on her mobile phone posted the clip on YouTube.

The following month, Martin-Smith launched the inevitable lawsuit for libel while EMI edited the track to remove references to him. The legal battle would drag on for another fourteen months before Robbie was forced to make a humbling apology in the High Court to Martin-Smith and agree to pay undisclosed damages to his ex-manager amid reports that the total cost of the action to him was £500,000. Williams's counsel, David Sherborne, told Mr Justice Tugendhat in court: 'Robbie Williams wishes to make it clear to his fans, and the public at large, that he did not intend these lyrics to be taken at face value or as a serious statement by him of the views which he holds of Nigel Martin-Smith. Specifically, Robbie Williams did not intend to allege that Nigel Martin-Smith has ever stolen any funds from Take That or anyone. Robbie Williams wishes now to apologize publicly and unreservedly for the distress that the original publication of those lyrics caused to Nigel.'

Robbie's solo career really took off from 1997 onwards and he repeatedly performed at sell-out shows over the next decade. The zenith was his record-breaking shows at Knebworth in 2003, for which he chose a novel entrance.

Robbie's success resulted in repeated awards nominations and wins, including the 1998 Brit Awards which saw his leather-clad duet with Welsh legend Tom Jones.

Robbie's personal life did not always run as smoothly as his professional career. He had a tempestuous relationship with All Saints' Nicole Appleton to whom he was engaged. Their relationship suffered not only from prolonged absences due to their respective careers, but also from the tensions that came from their partying and Robbie's addictions.

Robbie was pictured with a number of high profile women, including Rachel Hunter and Geri Halliwell. It was claimed that he used his relationship with the former to deflect press attention and the latter apparently to attract it.

Robbie met American actress Ayda Field in 2007 and the pair married in 2010.

Below Gary began dating his dancer wife Dawn Andrews in 1996 and the pair have been together ever since. They married in a private ceremony in 2000 on the Caribbean island of Nevis and have since had three children.

Opposite page:
(*Top*) Jason, Mark, Gary and Howard pose after reforming in November 2005. The boys appeared relaxed and happy during the press conference in London (*middle*). Back stage, however, there were nerves and tears.

(*Bottom*) Howard and Mark are greeted by excited Thatters outside London's Coronet cinema at the premiere of the documentary *Take That: For The Record* in November 2005. After their nine year hiatus, the band was surprised and relieved by the positive media and fan response.

ORANGE　　GARY BARLOW　　MARK OWEN　　HOWARD DONALD

Before the band reformed in 2005, Gary had been pursuing a successful writing career off-stage, and he increasingly found a natural role as mentor to up-and-coming artists. He began his own record label in 2009, to which he signed budding artists such as Camilla Kerslake (*left*), and his mentoring also put him in the perfect position to replace Simon Cowell on the *X Factor* in 2011 (*below*).

In 2010 Robbie and Gary publicly celebrated their surprise – and effusive – reconciliation which led to Robbie rejoining the band for their latest album *Progress* and the related 2011 tour.

(*Below*) Back together after fifteen years, the newly reformed Fab Five performed at the Royal Variety Performance in December and the Brit Awards in 2011; here they are together at the Q Awards in October 2010.

Robbie and Gary perform their duet 'Shame' on stage, which was one of two songs Gary co-wrote with Robbie for the latter's 2010 album. The Country and Western inspired single was notable for its tongue-in-cheek video that was a spoof of the gay romantic tragedy, *Brokeback Mountain*, and a playful nod to the teasing their burgeoning bromance was attracting.

At the same time, Martin-Smith was revealing openly that he would have been willing to drop the action if Williams had agreed to meet him. 'I told Robbie I didn't want damages and that I would happily waive them if he would meet me face to face to chat about what has happened and put all this negativity behind us,' he told the *Manchester Evening News*. 'I said we should just be friends again, but he refused to meet me. It's a real shame it has come to this.'

Nigel was not the only one attempting to persuade Rob to put his bitterness and grievances behind him. Elton John, who had heard the rumours of Williams's increasingly self-destructive behaviour from mutual friends, chose the same moment to go public with his own concerns. 'Robbie is the number-one star in the world,' Elton said. 'He should let the other shit go, and if he can't, then he needs to see someone and talk about it. All he is doing is burning a hole inside of himself, eating him up, making him angry and miserable.' Given Robbie's state of mind, however, he was not in the mood to heed Elton's warning.

In truth, the relationship between the two men was also going through a period of strain, caused by Rob's decision to go public in his book *Feel* about how Elton had 'kidnapped' him during his early drinking and drug-taking days and put him in rehab. Meanwhile, in late 2006, Elton provoked the ire of Rob when they were sharing a hotel in Sydney while Williams was completing the final dates of the Close Encounters Tour. The 'Rocket Man' singer sent a note to Robbie about the re-formed Take That's recent success in which he wrote: 'Take That, number-one album, number-one single – funny how things work out. Elton.' Rob, in a touchy mood, took the missive as a personal dig. Later, in his 2010 picture-led book *You Know Me*, Williams wrote: 'I read that and I thought, What a bizarre way to think about things. When the boys had a number-one album and a number-one single, I was stood in front of 60,000, 70,000 people a night myself. I'm trying to think if there was even a part of me that wasn't pleased for them, and I can't recognize me having that. So when I read that note, I just thought, Well, you live in a world that I don't live in.'

Even before *Rudebox* was released, the knives were out. When Robbie premiered the album's title track to the audience at his Hampden Park gig in Glasgow in September, the reaction was not good. Later, Robbie would say: 'In my mind, it was, It's going to be another glorious victory for the boy Williams, who reinvents himself so majestically again and again and again, but when it started, the whole stadium kind of took one step back and just looked at me with bewilderment, just a lot of Scots with puzzle-ment on their faces.'

The run-up to its launch was overshadowed by the row with Martin-Smith over 'The 90s', but there was worse to come. Suddenly, the *Sun*, which had until that point been one of Williams's most resolutely loyal cheerleaders, turned. Victoria Newton, the then editor of the *Sun*'s influential 'Bizarre' column, launched a scathing attack and pronounced the album's title track 'not only the worst track I've heard by him, it's the worst I've EVER heard (and believe me, I've had to listen to some shite in the past)'. She added: 'Try to imagine you and your mates messing around in your bedroom with a drum machine while comedy "rapping" over the top. The only difference is, Robbie is actually allowed to release this rubbish because he has a record deal. It shouldn't be allowed on grounds of taste.'

She was not the only critic who was unimpressed. The *Guardian*'s Alexis Petridis gave the album a disappointing two out of five, and his verdict on the album's closing 'hidden' track, 'Dickhead', was:

'A woeful sub-Eminem rant, it features Williams gallantly threatening to set his retinue of bouncers on anyone who dares to criticize
his music. By the time it concludes, puzzlingly, with the singer
shouting, "I've got a bucket of shit! I've got a bucket of shit!" one
feels less inclined to say the kind thing than the cruel thing: you
don't need to tell me that, pal. I've just spent the last hour examining it.'

Without doubt, it was a strange record with a disparate array of
musical styles and genres. There were the faithful, almost karaoke,
eighties cover versions of the Human League's 'Louise' and Stephen
Tin Tin Duffy's 'Kiss Me'. Then we had the Pet Shop Boys pastiche 'She's Madonna' and the electro of 'Rudebox'. 'Viva Life on
Mars' sounded slightly too reminiscent of the melody of Bruce
Springsteen's 'I'm on Fire', while 'Lovelight' was distinctly R&B in
flavour. Indeed, it is tempting to conclude that the involvement of
so many people, including producers Neil Tennant and Chris Lowe,
Mark Ronson, William Orbit and Soul Mekanik, left the whole
project lacking any recognizable direction. The title track had no
less than eight writer credits listed on the sleeve notes.

It was also becoming plain that Rob had begun to tire of being
Robbie Williams on record. Publicly, too, he was being explicit
about his dissatisfaction. 'I've got to take a view over the next
eighteen months and see if I want to be part of the machine any
more,' he said at the time, 'because I don't see me singing again.
It's a question of what I want and where I want to be. I don't know
where I stand with it all at the moment. Do I take things into my
own hands and dismantle this monster and have a nice life?'

The problem for the album was that his ambivalence was all too
obvious, and this was no more evident than on the track that had
caused him so much aggravation, 'The 90s'. It is simply impossible

to come away from listening to the song without the clear impression that Robbie is doing a fairly barefaced impersonation of the Streets' Birmingham-born rapper, Mike Skinner, and while it could be argued that imitation is the sincerest form of flattery, it does leave you scratching your head somewhat given the relative success of the two men. After all, when the Streets' third album, *The Hardest Way to Make an Easy Living*, came out earlier in 2006, it made international sales of somewhere in the region of 600,000. By comparison, even the maligned *Rudebox* would go on to sell more than two million copies in Europe.

The title track, however, struggled to reach number four in the UK singles chart. The follow-up single, 'Lovelight', which was released in November, could make it only to number eight. Elsewhere, the single fared even worse. In Germany, traditionally home of some of Robbie's most loyal fans, 'Lovelight' got no further than a very disappointing number twenty-one, while in Sweden, Ireland and Austria, it failed even to break into the top twenty.

Although the album itself went to number one in fourteen countries, including Britain, Germany, Australia, Italy, Mexico and Spain, by Williams's own high standards sales of *Rudebox* were disappointing. While *Escapology* had gone six times platinum and the new album's immediate predecessor, *Intensive Care*, had garnered five platinum discs, *Rudebox* managed only two. In the run-up to Christmas, it was shifting around 38,000 units a week, when earlier albums, like *I've Been Expecting You*, notched up nearly ten times that number. Amid the fallout of its lower than expected figures, rumours began circulating in the music business that two EMI executives who were involved in the album's development had been fired as a result. Within two months the head of

EMI's music division, Alain Levy, was also sacked after the company issued a dire profits warning.

The figures were doubly disappointing considering that the album had been given a massive sales lift by the fact that Robbie had spent most of the year on his biggest tour to date. By the time the gruelling 2006 Close Encounters Tour was due to conclude in Australia, just before Christmas, it was planned that it would have taken in South Africa and Hungary in April and travelled through Europe during the summer, before moving on to Argentina, Hong Kong and the Far East. But given his personal problems, notably his increasing reliance on prescription drugs, Rob was far from fighting fit. Just to complicate matters, as the start of the tour approached, he was showing the symptoms of a new and virulent form of stage fright that would be about to threaten his capacity even to get up on stage.

Even the opening of the tour was inauspicious. By the time he reached Dublin, in June, Robbie was jittery and depressed. The show at Croke Park was an early low point and brought back to him the painful memories of his appearance seven years previously at Slane Castle, County Meath. On stage, Rob, in a black three-quarter-length coat and bright pink scarf, was again pulling off the charade that he was enjoying the experience of being in front of a 70,000-strong audience. The reality, however, was decidedly bleaker. He spent the show stifling curses as he berated himself for the quality of his voice and brooded about the sound quality at the stadium. Just to further disturb his equilibrium, the highlight of the night's light show went spectacularly wrong when, for the finale, he was supposed to descend a hundred feet onto the stage while suspended in a specially designed 'gondola'. At the crucial moment, a computer glitch meant that he had to abandon the contraption and instead run around the stage in a blind panic as a series of timed firework explosions went off frighteningly close to him.

He was in no mood to try to put a gloss on the night's inadequacies. 'When the man standing behind you says, "It's fucked," in front of 70,000 people, you panic,' he told the audience. 'You'll never know how much panic went through my mind up there. You've been much better than me. I've not been very good tonight. I will come back and do it for free.' Once the concert was over, he was seething – ranting backstage about his own poor performance and the technical cock-ups.

His gloomy outlook was not lifted by the sapping schedule that meant he would have to complete a six-month block of gigs before he could return home to California. It was a new and sobering reality for Rob. While other artists and bands think nothing of performing 200 shows a year, Williams had never previously committed to performing for any longer than a month without a suitable break. And this time, the usual diversions on offer during a tour were much harder to come by. Once, he had been able to go out clubbing with the other members of his band. Now, he was faced with the prospect of being confined to his hotel room. Often even the lobby and the bar of the upmarket places he stayed in were no-go zones, as they were inevitably invaded by scores of fans. His sense of dislocation and rising panic were now joined by the inescapable conclusion that never had he felt more like the quarry, never had he been so trapped. One thing that did not change, however, was the carousel of female fans, whom he would send his minders to collect and escort to his room. They would offer one of his only chances of release.

Unsurprisingly, Rob wanted an extensive support network around him. So, along with David Enthoven and Josie Cliff, Rob's boyhood friend Jonathan Wilkes joined the tour to perform a camp nightly version of 'Me and My Shadow' with Robbie. The pair, who christened each other 'Flank' and 'Spank', allowed themselves to be filmed semi-naked by a documentary crew in a paddling pool, jokily discussing whether the singer might end up settling down with a man.

Robbie's performance at Milan's San Siro Stadium remains a career highlight, so the tour wasn't all doom and gloom, but while publicly Robbie was boldly claiming he had never performed better, privately he was nearing the precipice. Members of his circle say that the hours before some shows came to resemble a kind of Mexican stand-off, with Williams stubbornly refusing to go on stage and his closest handlers trying to cajole him into performing. It became a fraught, sometimes nightly routine that left not only Rob, but his entire support group exhausted and depressed.

By the time he began the UK leg of the tour, which included five nights at the Milton Keynes Bowl, he had been on the road for three months and was reaching breaking point. His rows with EMI over 'The 90s' came to a head with Williams mounting his bitter attack on Nigel Martin-Smith on stage. Meanwhile, his depleted physical and mental state was even obvious to those attending his shows. Fans began going on online sites to question his health. At the same time, Robbie himself was having trouble keeping up the illusion that all was well. As reviewers began commenting on how he looked ill, stressed and was sweating profusely from the very beginning of his shows, Williams told the 65,000-strong audience at one Milton Keynes gig that he 'felt like shit'. One newspaper described him as 'looking bloated and dishevelled'. 'There wasn't a glimmer of the star who lit up Knebworth,' it reported. 'The show felt unrehearsed and at times akin to Butlin's.'

By the middle of September critical mass was reached. Robbie had a near meltdown while staying in the luxurious confines of the Grove Hotel in Hertfordshire, from where he would helicopter nightly to his Milton Keynes shows. One afternoon, he launched into a four-letter-word-strewn stream of consciousness, ranting and raving at his retinue, whom he had summoned to his sumptuous suite. For several minutes, as they sat around in nervous and embarrassed silence, he did not pause for breath as he railed about everything from his constant energy-sapping insomnia to how he was convinced that his fans did not appreciate him enough. Privately, his management team began calculating the potentially enormous cost of cancelling the remainder of the tour, which was due to move on to the Far East and Australia.

Rob's father, Pete, saw his son's fragile condition at first hand and told him he needed to rest. I remember talking to Pete that week and it was clear how concerned he was about his boy's health. 'He is absolutely exhausted,' Pete said. 'He's hardly been home for ten months and he just needs to sleep in his own bed.' By now others within the Williams organization were also openly saying that, despite the financial implications, there was no way he should submit himself to completing the full tour. A compromise was reached. His upcoming £10-million tour of the Far East, which was due to take in Shanghai, Bangkok, Singapore, Mumbai and Bangalore, and stretch throughout November, would be cancelled, giving Robbie a chance to recuperate before fulfilling his commitment to play six dates in South America in October. He would then take a month off before travelling to Perth at the end of November, followed by shows in Adelaide, Sydney and Brisbane, and finish the tour in Melbourne a week before Christmas. Finally, IE Music put out a statement, saying: 'It became clear that the stress and exhaustion of the Asian tour coming shortly after the end of the European dates would seriously impact on his health.' By the time the news was released, Rob had already been put on a flight back to Los Angeles, where he would attempt to get well for two weeks before heading to Santiago, Chile, to begin the South American shows. Nevertheless, the exertions of the tour were still about to exact their toll.

CHAPTER TWELVE

Everything Changes

Considering that the traffic had been exclusively in the other direction during the previous wretched decade, with the opportunity now presenting itself finally to kick Williams when he was down, just what was Gary to do? In truth, in his position not even Mother Teresa of Calcutta herself could have resisted hitching up her stripy habit and delivering a dusty sandal to the nuts. So obviously, Barlow was not going to pass up the chance for some long-awaited retribution. As the critical knives came out for 'Rudebox', Gary waded in as well. Like almost everyone else, he came out to say he didn't like the single, that he didn't understand it and thought it was not 'classic Robbie'. Clearly having decided to take the moral high ground, he resisted the temptation to turn the tables and do what Rob had done all those years before and take the record back to the shop and demand a refund, but he hinted he was aware that his old adversary was not in a good place. 'I'd hate to see him go through what I've been through,' Gary told reporters. 'I don't think he'd come out of it the other end.' Only Barlow himself would have known if those comments were a case of twisting the knife or whether he was genuinely concerned about Rob's welfare. What is without question is that Gary was now in a position to crow.

By early December 2006 the success of Take That's Ultimate Tour had been joined by a number-one single, 'Patience', and a number-one album, *Beautiful World*. It was the first time the band had topped both charts simultaneously. When 'Patience' was released the previous month, it had gone to the top of the UK chart in its second week, where it stayed for four weeks. It was also a number-one single in Spain, Germany, Denmark and Switzerland. The band's first studio album since *Nobody Else* eleven years earlier would go on to sell more than three million copies worldwide and go eight times platinum in Britain, platinum in Germany and Ireland, and gold in Italy and Switzerland. It was also noteworthy in that it was the first time all the members of the band were given lead vocal duties, with Jason breaking his duck on the folky 'Wooden Boat'.

Barlow stuck to his word that he would cede control to others during the recording of *Beautiful World*. In Los Angeles, at the suggestion of Polydor, Take That hired American Grammy-winning producer John Shanks, who had worked with the likes of Bonnie Raitt, Alanis Morissette, Bon Jovi and *American Idol* winner Kelly Clarkson. Shanks, who was born in New York, had lived in LA since he was a teenager and was thoroughly versed in the slick, if safe, realm of American MOR (middle-of-the-road) music. Prior to the tour, the four members of the band had come up with the ballad 'I'd Wait for Life' during a two-week writing stint in London studio the Townhouse. However, with just ten weeks to make the album once the tour finished at the end of June, the recording sessions in

California and later in London had much riding on them. Thankfully, Shanks proved to be a skilled technician and inspired co-writer, eventually sharing writing credits with the band on six of the twelve tracks.

For once, Barlow, whose love of recording always trumped his relative unease on stage, was not looking forward to making the album that would define whether the band had a future as relevant music-makers or were destined to see out their careers as a super-annuated novelty act – a top night out, for sure, but nothing more substantial than that. Gary's sense of anxiety was not helped by his concerns that he might not be able to work with Mark in the studio, given that in the intervening years Owen had become used to calling the shots on his own records. It took only three days in LA for the jitters to subside. That afternoon, they came up with 'Patience' and Gary knew they had their hit record.

Crucially, as Barlow et al waited for the album to be released that autumn, they would be the beneficiaries of a terrific piece of good fortune – or wanton act of self-sabotage, depending on how you look at it. With the release of the incomprehensible *Rudebox*, Robbie Williams, their biggest rival for pop's polished middle ground, deserted the territory on which he had appeared to own the freehold and left Take That and Barlow staring gratefully into an open goal. It was the most mouth-watering of all ironies.

Other than the Beatles-like singalong of Mark Owen's 'Shine', this was an album that, for all the genuine collaboration that went on in the studio, was a testament to Gary's unerring ability to write the most gargantuan of big choruses. Nowhere was his stellar talent for the sweeping and anthemic more apparent than on 'Patience', which builds slowly from its initial simple guitar arpeggio intro to the sumptuous strings, recorded later at Abbey Road Studios in London, and pitch-perfect harmonies of the classic Barlow chorus. Ironically, too, it was everything Williams had been so clearly lacking since his split with Guy Chambers.

Nobody was underestimating the significance of the first single, least of all Gary, who was under no illusion of how key it was. As far as he was concerned, it was a make or break situation and the positive responses he had from people before its release were heartening.'

As with the tour, the album also benefited from a sense of goodwill towards the band, and Barlow in particular, that had previously been noticeably lacking. It tapped into the very British trait of willing on the underdog, as well as for forgiveness. Even those who did not like Take That first time around, or had little interest in their new music, wished them well.

Publicly, at least, Robbie was sending out the same positive vibes, saying how he had excitedly gone on YouTube to catch a first listen to 'Patience'. In reality, though – as Robbie's song 'The 90s' was so starkly to illustrate – the divisions between him and Gary were far from resolved, despite the fact that the two men had overcome the hurdle of their first meeting in ten years.

On a May evening earlier that year, Robbie sat nervously biting his nails in the bar of Chelsea's Conrad Hotel as he waited for more than an hour for Gary and the rest of the boys to return from the second night of their three-night stint at Wembley Arena. During the previous days, various diplomatic cables had been exchanged between the Williams and Take That camps, with Jason, who had met Rob at the end of the previous year to make peace, acting as intermediary. After deciding to rid himself of his house in Notting

Hill, Williams had bought a penthouse flat in the Belvedere building adjacent to the trendy Thames-side hotel and the flat would act as home on his semi-regular trips back to the UK. Rob had been due to meet the band the previous night, who as usual when they were in London were staying at the Conrad. At the last minute, however, after taking the lift from his apartment and making the short walk to the hotel, Rob panicked, turned round and virtually ran home. How could he face Gary after all these years, after everything he said about him, after all the needless rancour? Overcome by terror at the prospect of what could have become an unpleasant show-down with Barlow, Rob texted Jason saying he was feeling tired and would not be coming.

In the climate of suspicion that remained, Robbie's decision to cry off at the last moment was viewed by some of the more fragile egos in the Take That camp as Williams pulling rank, him playing the big-star card to let them know who was boss. There was some evidence, too, that at this point – six months prior to the triumphant release of *Beautiful World* – Rob still felt very much in the ascendant. Indeed, some of those close to him say that for days Williams had been in two minds about making the effort to accept the invitation to see all four of his ex-band mates together for the first time since he walked out of the Stockport rehearsal studio eleven years previously. One minute he would be telling friends he was excited about meeting them again and discussing what he should wear. The next he was saying: 'You know what? I don't think I can be arsed.' It would not, after all, have been the first time, as far as the members of Take That were concerned, that he had rejected the hand of friendship.

Understandably, Gary, too, was – to say the very least – ambiva-lent about the prospect of seeing Robbie again. At some point during the previous months and years, the others had all been in contact with Williams and had, to some extent, if not quite reached forgiveness, then come to an accommodation with him. Gary, with his particular history with Rob, would be a different matter altogether. What would make it all the more awkward for Barlow was that he knew he would be going into any meeting with Rob as very much the junior partner, so it was greatly to his credit that when Jason floated the idea of meeting Rob again, he was prepared to bite the bullet and say yes. His magnanimity would also prove in the long run to be crucial in the eventual return of Robbie to the band. Had their first meeting come only a few months later, when Take That were again riding high in the charts, how much easier would it have been for him to have concluded, with some justification, that they no longer needed Robbie?

It says something about the fundamental contradictions in Rob's make-up that at the same time he was prevaricating privately about seeing the boys again, he was making arrangements to have a giant bunch of flowers delivered to Take That's hotel prior to their first Wembley show. And by the time he and the others did meet, the evening after his no-show, it was clear that his failure to turn up was far less about posturing than his genuine nervousness about being in a room with them all once more. His anxiety wasn't helped by the fact that after the second show at Wembley Arena, the members of Take That had stayed on at the venue to attend a party being thrown for the band and their families. After waiting for more than sixty long minutes in the bar of their hotel for them, Robbie was jittery. Gary says that one of the first things he noticed about Rob at that time was how he was constantly twitching and fidgeting in his seat. In truth, the issue of Williams's uncontrollable twitching had been a cause of concern to those around him for some time. Not least because in the past the singer has been candid about the fact that his friends were always able to spot when he was back on cocaine, because it caused the same telltale physical tic. Hardly surprisingly, then, there were those in his circle who were unaware that it was prescribed drugs that were leading to the familiar muscle spasms and so assumed he was back on coke.

When Gary, Jason, Mark and Howard finally walked into the hotel, there were the prerequisite showbiz hugs all round, but as soon as the others joined Rob at his table, it was obvious that both he and Gary were ill at ease. It did not help that as they made small talk about that night's show, the eyes of everyone in the bar were watching the momentous meeting of the principal combatants in pop's most famous feud. After a few minutes of stilted conversation, Jason suggested they all go upstairs and carry on the reunion in the room of Take That's new manager, Jonathan Wild, so they could have some privacy. According to those who were there, however, Rob, who is admittedly never at his best in small groups, or one-on-one situations, was no less nervous once they were upstairs and away from prying eyes. Gary says that throughout their time together Robbie was nervous and twitching and 'eating and drinking non-stop'. Of course, given that from his point of view, Robbie must have felt like he was outnumbered four to one, he had every right to seem edgy.

What did Gary feel as he saw his nemesis sitting opposite him, eating French fries and sinking cans of full-fat Coke? Initially, he felt nothing: not the rush of rage he imagined would come unbidden when he had played out this very scene in his mind during the dark times; not the urge to blurt out every snide remark, every gag that Williams had said about him that – despite his attempts to cleanse his mind – he still kept in unwanted storage. For his part, Rob was keen to talk about anything other than their problems. He wanted to know all about their gigs, the lighting, the choreography, the set and how the fans reacted to them after all this time away. Most of all, though, he wanted to know how the lads felt to be together, not just up there on stage, but behind the scenes. What was it like in the dressing room before the shows and afterwards? How did they get along with each other on the road? Did they have a laugh? Did they feel like brothers again?

It was not hard to see where he was coming from. After all, Rob had been candid with them about how much he hated touring, how he was now terrified to go out on stage and face his fans, how he felt he could no longer cope with everything revolving round him and him alone. He listened as Gary told him he made a point now of looking after himself, of eating right and exercising. Rob replied that being Robbie Williams meant he could not get ill because without him there would be no show. Typically, though, the contradictions at the heart of the Williams psyche were not far from the surface. After telling the boys of his dread of performing live, Rob was saying in the next breath that he would have to pass up their offer of coming to see one of their shows because he would not be able to resist jumping up on stage with them.

Now, as Gary watched Rob, he saw for the first time the emotional muddle he was in. How, despite the entourage of hangers-on, he still obviously felt completely on his own. And in that moment he allowed himself to feel genuinely sorry for a man who, for everything he had achieved, was clearly as unhappy as ever in his own skin. Up until then Barlow's feelings towards his adversary had not allowed for pity. He wrote in *My Take*: 'Time may be a great healer, but still, whenever I thought of him I thought, You absolute fucking cunt. I've never had anyone do so much damage as you've done. No one has said or done such awful things as you have said and done to me. No one has even come close.' But as they sat talking, the anger subsided. 'I looked at him,' says Gary, 'and thought, You're just a bloke like the rest of us. That person I'd seen on TV and detested for so long was just ordinary and no different from the lad I met all those years ago. There was still tomato sauce all down his top from dinner.'

But it would be naive to expect more than a decade of acrimony simply to melt away over a shared drink in the impersonal, if luxurious, confines of a London hotel room. Both men were, understandably, still wary of each other, still choosing their words carefully. The band was due to leave the following morning to continue their tour in Dublin, so one by one they disappeared to go and pack ready for an early flight. At one point, Gary and Robbie were left alone. Neither man had banked on being by themselves without the comfort blanket of the others. Rob wanted to hear some tracks from Take That's yet-to-be-released album, but Gary – reminded perhaps of Williams's damning and very public critique of Barlow's last album – was unwilling. Gary also recalled his unease at seeing how Rob could not wait for Howard to finish talking about the hard times he faced during the wilderness years, so he could ask Gary about his low point. Was Robbie a little too eager to hear Gary's version of being dropped by his record label, or of the twin scourges of public ridicule and apathy?

Likewise, Rob would later tell friends that talking to his one-time enemy did not magically lift the veil of mistrust and hurt between them. It was a step, but no more than a step in the right direction. If Gary should not be expected to take Rob in a giant man-hug and announce to him that the slate was now clean and his prior sins expunged, then why should it be incumbent on Williams to do the same? Rob, with his preternatural disinclination to let bygones be bygones, would need longer to forgive and forget Gary's part in his miserable Take That years. He told a friend shortly after the meeting: 'I went there to see Gary as the man he is, not the one he used to be, but it was hard because he sounds like the old Gaz and looks like the old Gaz and I couldn't get all the negative thoughts about him out of my head even though I really tried.'

What was crystal clear to the rest of the band from the meeting was that Rob was not in a good place. He looked drawn and pale, and despite his genuine happiness at seeing the others, he bore the look of someone struggling to cope with the situation in which he found himself. Why, then, would Williams not look at his four ex-band mates and want what they had? Wouldn't being with the band again solve his problems? After all, for the past four years Rob had been talking about breaking up Robbie Williams, about how he wanted to start his own rock band so he would not have to stand in the glare of the spotlight by himself. What better way to ease those stomach-churning, pre-show jitters than to know that with the boys he would have safety in numbers, that no matter how he felt up there, he would not be alone? More than that, nobody would blame him if he did not feel more than a touch of jealousy when he watched the four of them together and saw how they were on their way to becoming genuine friends in his absence. Why would he not feel a gnawing resentment, alongside his sincere happiness for them, when he saw the new camaraderie they had and realized that, yet again, he was the odd one out?

If Gary had needed a wake-up call about the potential pitfalls of falling back into the same mistakes he had made first time around, he needed to look no further than the man sitting opposite him. Seeing Rob again brought home to him the way he himself had once been – obsessed by his work, driven by it and damaged by it. Robbie was a reminder to him in the early days of the band's second coming that there must be no going back, that although Rob might still not be able to see past the self-centred, self-contained Gary of the old days, he was a different man now and would never again allow his life to be subsumed by the vaulting ambition that characterized his younger self.

The following night, Rob was sitting in the same seat in the bar of the hotel when the band arrived back from the gig, ready to pick up where they had left off. But though the process of fence-mending had been started, there was no indication that a return to Take That was on the cards anytime soon for Williams – not least because there was still open resistance to the idea from some of the senior voices in Robbie's circle. David Enthoven's party line throughout had been that Rob should never go back, that no good could come to his career by returning to Take That when he had spent so long trying to shake off the tag of ex-boy-band member. There were also legal potholes standing in the way of a reunion, namely Robbie's deal with EMI, which still had two albums to run. There was cause for some doubt that the label would be happy for their star act to begin putting out material with Take That under the umbrella of EMI's rivals Universal, particularly as Take That would be going after the same market as Williams. Publicly, too, Gary was unequivocal, telling music journalists at the end of 2006 that he believed there was 'no place' for Robbie in the newly re-formed line-up.

And those close to the two men were openly saying that, despite them getting over the hurdle of their first meeting in years, they had far from put their differences aside. Elton John, who remained close to Barlow, had tried to play peacemaker in the past without success. Now he went public by identifying the man he felt was responsible for the continuing froideur: Williams. 'I wish he would drop the whole Gary Barlow thing,' Elton said three months later. 'It's like, Robbie just let it go. It doesn't matter. I'd like to sit down with Gary and Robbie and say, "For fuck's sake, get rid of it. You don't need to go on about it any more. Get the monkey off your back."' Meanwhile, Lulu, who had made a guest appearance on Take That's 1993 high-camp number-one hit 'Relight My Fire', was also saying she had offered her services as mediator in a bid to help the two build bridges. Rob, however, had more pressing issues to deal with.

CHAPTER THIRTEEN

In and Out
of Consciousness

For nearly a week the phone had gone unanswered. The shades were drawn all day long, and around the once airy rooms of the vast Beverly Hills house lay long-abandoned plates of half-eaten food. Strewn over the plush carpets was the detritus of the addict: discarded pill bottles, empty blister strips and plastic bags containing a few forgotten tablets. In the cavernous kitchen, Robbie Williams lay naked and delirious on the floor in the foetal position, his knees pulled high up to his chest, tattooed arms hugging them for comfort. For the last seventy-two hours his world had consisted of nothing more than this and the living-room sofa on which he had slept away the previous days in a drug-induced haze of confusion. Day and night had become conflated in his mind so that he had lost his bearings. Somewhere in his altered state of consciousness, he recalled a frightening scene – of him shouting, crying, screaming – but the recollection flickered and faded like a Polaroid in reverse and now he wondered if he had dreamed this starring role in his own nightmare.

Alerted by the fact that Rob had gone worryingly off radar, various ever more panicky phone calls had taken place between his managers, David Enthoven and Tim Clark. They were already deeply concerned about him. He had finished his tour six weeks earlier only thanks to a mixture of uppers and adrenalin. Since then he had been on a downward spiral as his drug-taking reached a new, almost suicidal nadir. On top of his addiction to the anti-depressants he was taking a nightly hit of twenty tablets of the powerful and addictive painkiller Vicodin and Adderall, the equally habit-forming treatment for attention-deficit disorder. Now, to supplement the list of prescription medicine, he had included sativa, a form of cannabis that can lead to hallucinogenic episodes similar to LSD. The cumulative effect over the previous dark weeks was that, day by day, Rob had further retreated from the world he sought to escape through his nightly forays into oblivion. In some vaguely lucid part of his mind, he knew beyond doubt that he was killing himself. The only difference now was that he had stopped caring. Checking out would be a relief. It was 13 February 2007, his thirty-third birthday.

Enthoven had a long-standing appointment to meet Williams to check on him the next day, but with Robbie refusing to pick up the phone on his birthday, it was obvious it couldn't wait until then. Concluding that they would have more success dealing with him if they both turned up on his doorstep, Clark and Enthoven decided to bring their visit to Rob forward by twenty-four hours. It would probably save his life. A day later and Rob is convinced they would have found a dead body. As it was, when they arrived, he was in a pitiful state. In his few moments of clarity he told them that for eight straight days he had eaten nothing but box after box of chocolate eclairs, and he admitted to bingeing on drugs. Finally,

Rob told them resignedly: 'You've come to take me to rehab, haven't you?'

Indeed, Clark had been busy making a flurry of frantic calls and had a private jet prepped and ready for take-off at a nearby airport. The two managers told Rob to pack and he would be flown to a clinic in Arizona, where, once again, he would begin the process of getting clean. He was loaded into a car and they accompanied him on to the plane. On the flight, Williams was in a blind fury, kicking and headbutting the seat in front of him. He would say later that he was incandescent with rage for allowing himself, after working so hard to get straight, to fall back into the cycle of desperate addiction followed by the inevitable horror of having to go through rehab. How could he have let this happen again? Why had he not seen the warning signs months ago and agreed to seek help? He was scared too. Scared of getting clean, of being without the one thing that had made his existence bearable. Scared of going through withdrawal.

He was also frightened about the people he would be forced to meet and live with during his time drying out. Would they hate him? Would they be dangerous and want to kill him? Most of all, though, he felt embarrassment. Embarrassment that he had been through this so publicly before. He had been rightly proud of his achievements in getting off the bottle and drugs. He had been protective of his success, threatening newspapers and magazines with his lawyers if they even so much as implied he had fallen off the wagon. Now, as far as the rest of the world was concerned, he was just another addict who had blown his recovery, who had been too weak to resist the urge for one more high, one more hit. How his enemies would be laughing when they found out. It was the same old story all over again – Robbie could always be relied on to fuck up.

Less than an hour later, the plane taxied to a halt on a small runway 60 miles north of Phoenix, Arizona, where a car was waiting to take him to the Meadows clinic on the outskirts of the small desert town of Wickenburg. The admission process would be the first of many humiliating comedowns during his stay at the hospital. The pop-star pampering he was used to was, for the time being at least, a thing of the past. Like all patients he was required to stand and watch as his luggage was searched by a member of staff. Prior to his arrival, his managers had been told that any drugs, scissors, mobile phones, cameras, food, computers or musical instruments would be confiscated if they were found in Rob's case. He was told he would be allowed to smoke, but only the cigarettes he had brought with him. Then he was shown to the dormitory he would spend three weeks sharing with three other male addicts on small single beds.

A former patient at the clinic described to me the daily routine of the recovering addict. The clinic, he says, is set in beautiful grounds, where the days were wonderfully warm but the nights freezing cold. The facility has a swimming pool and a gym, but is fairly basic. 'The beds, in particular, are really uncomfortable and everyone was complaining that it was just like sleeping on the springs,' says the source. 'So it did have a feeling of boot camp and was nothing like the health spa people might think it is.' Both men and women are admitted, and there is a smoking room and a common room where they can meet, but otherwise there is strict segregation of the sexes. The clientele was exclusively white and came from all over the world. Most were well off, although some poorer people had their stays subsidized by the clinic. Patients were expected to submit to regular blood tests to ensure they were not secretly taking drugs, but they were prescribed medication by doctors at the facility to help keep them calm during their stay.

Although mobile phones are banned, inmates were allowed to use a payphone for up to two hours a week. The food, he says, was excellent, but the patients were expected to rise early for a buffet breakfast, which was served between 6.30 and 7.30 a.m. From 8 to 11 a.m. he would be expected to attend group therapy sessions with others suffering from drug addiction and alcoholism. After a break for lunch, they would attend specialist meetings where patients with specific problems, like an addiction to cocaine or prescription drugs, would listen to talks by guest speakers and be encouraged to recount their own history of substance abuse. Those being treated were also encouraged to sign up for day trips to nearby places of interest like a local museum and air force base.

After his release from rehab, Rob would admit how close his addiction had come to killing him. 'I might have been a couple of days or twenty-four hours from dying,' he said. 'At the time, you don't give a shit if you pop your clogs. I must have been very, very close. I would have carried on, to be honest. You get to the point that far into your addiction, you're not bothered if you live or die, because that's where it takes you. I was on my way out. It was the American addiction: prescription drugs. I'd do colossal, heart-stopping amounts. There was other stuff that I cannot mention because of the amount of trouble it would get me into.' Of his spell in rehab he said: 'They're all nutters, including myself. I was in a hospital ward. It's absolutely horrendous in there.'

Given his limited access to the outside world at that time, Robbie would not have known quite what a stir the news of his readmittance to rehab would cause. Or the fury it would stir up in the Take That camp. On the day he was admitted, Williams's management made the somewhat odd decision to make an immediate press statement announcing he had checked into the clinic. Given that the decision to admit him had been taken at the last minute, there seemed little immediate risk of the news leaking out to the press. And while the media would surely hear about his hospitalization sooner rather than later, why did his people feel the need to invade his privacy, particularly about a medical matter, so pre-emptively? Surely if the press had found out about it through their own channels, Robbie's PR representatives could have argued – as several other show-business personalities have successfully done – that it was a private situation that the singer did not want to be revealed. Whether the strategy would have worked is open for debate, but it seemed strange that they did not even attempt to keep a lid on the news.

Could it possibly have been that the timing of the statement was a crafty attempt to steal the limelight from Take That and Gary? Was it mere coincidence that the morning papers would carry the story on the very day the band were due to make their headline appearance at the Brits in London, where they were expected to walk away with the Best Single Award for 'Patience'? Certainly, Gary was seething that Williams had managed to upstage him yet again, and Barlow was not the only one spitting tacks. Among the wider team surrounding Take That there was unbridled anger. Dark rumours began circulating that it was Robbie's revenge, particularly because for the first time in years Williams had not been nominated in one of the major categories. On the night, he would also fail to win the one prize he was up for, that of Best British Live Act, which went to guitar rockers Muse.

Rumours of Take That's fury were not dampened by the fact that when they appeared on stage to collect their award for Best Single, the boys made no mention of Robbie in their acceptance speeches.

Their failure to wish him well from the stage was widely interpreted as a fairly blatant snub to their one-time band mate. And although when they were questioned later on, they did send him a get-well message, Gary gave every impression of a man who was beside himself with anger that his big moment had been overshadowed. As he left the show, Barlow tersely told the waiting reporters: 'There are some people who will never be happy, and I fear Robbie is one of them. We haven't heard from him in ages, but the boys and I hope that he is OK.' Later, Barlow would suggest he had taken a cynical view of Williams's decision to make his hospitalization public. 'If I was going into rehab, you'd never know,' he said. 'I'd be embarrassed. But a press release giving all the reasons why? What a coincidence!'

Who could blame Gary if he was completely hacked off by the turn of events? After all, the night was supposed to be about a celebration of the best, and possibly the most unlikely, pop story of the decade – the triumphant return of the band that so recently had been good for nothing but a few 'Where Are They Now?' features in the tabloids. More than that, winning the Brit for 'Patience' was Gary's personal vindication that he was still a great songwriter, that even if Take That was now a thoroughly democratic and collaborative effort, those people who mattered in the music business knew it was Gary steering the creative ship in the studio, that it remained to a great extent his vision. Now, yet again, here was Williams – whether intentionally or not – raining on his parade, showing how effortlessly he was able to switch the media's focus back on to him. It was some kick in the teeth. Not least because while Gary and the others had been making the critically acclaimed *Beautiful World*, Robbie had been indulging in the madness of *Rudebox*. No wonder that on what should have been their proudest night since their reunion, Gary had cause to repeat a phrase that had become something of a mantra during his personal wilderness years: 'Talent,' he sighed, 'has nothing to do with it.'

There was some reason to think that if his latest descent into addiction was a personal tragedy for Rob, the publicity surrounding his admission to rehab was not the worst possible outcome. After all, there remains in the eyes of the public more than an element of kudos attached to stars who so wantonly overdo the staple rock-'n'-roll indulgences, and Williams could certainly do with the focus of attention turning from his problematic recording career back to his colourful personal life. But would he or the people advising him really be so cynical as to exploit his very real problems in such a way? It does seem unlikely. What is certainly the case, however, is that Robbie, his management team and record company were desperately searching for a way to nullify the damage that the almost universally derided *Rudebox* was doing to his career and reputation. Prior to his drug-induced collapse, Rob was openly saying to those around him that he was convinced his career as a pop star was over. He was shaken to his foundations by the fact that he had got it so spectacularly wrong with the album, that he had so misjudged what his audience was prepared to accept as a Robbie Williams record.

Even more worryingly for some senior figures at EMI, while Rob admitted that the record had been misjudged in terms of its appeal to his market, he refused to accept it had been woefully substandard. In fact, he maintained, and still does, that it was his best work. What he was prepared to concede, however, was that it was the wrong album at the wrong time. That he had been so convinced he was on to yet another winner with *Rudebox* was what really worried him. If he could make such a dreadful misjudgement, Rob concluded, he must have lost his touch. And once you fail to connect with your listeners, it is as good as over. It may sound a rather overly pessimistic assessment of what was still just one misfiring album, but such was the delicate state of his mind, he convinced himself the day he had long predicted – when his life as a pop star would be over – had finally come.

This sombre air of resignation was not confined to Rob alone. All around him the signs were not promising. Days after leaving rehab, he released the follow-up single to the disappointing 'Lovelight'. The song, 'She's Madonna', was a collaboration with the Pet Shop Boys and was written about Rob's ex Tania Strecker, who – so the story went – was dumped by her former boyfriend Guy Ritchie for the Material Girl with the immortal brush-off line 'I love you, baby, but face it, she's Madonna.' By way of giving the song a publicity boost, PRs involved in the promotion of the record fed the press the fanciful story that Williams had lined up Madonna herself to appear with him in the video, but that Ritchie had put the kibosh on it. However, the ploy did not help sales of the single and 'She's Madonna' reached only as high as a depressing number sixteen in the UK chart.

Perhaps because of the scale of Robbie's problems, Gary could begin to afford to be magnanimous. By the spring he was admitting that in spite of everything – not least being upstaged at the Brits – he was at last in forgiving mood. 'I mean, he said some horrible things about me, but I'm old enough to get over that now,' Barlow said. 'I think that's the beauty of having kids as well – it teaches you that there are things in life that just aren't important.' It was a newfound sense of Zen at odds with the old driven and uncompromising Gary.

CHAPTER FOURTEEN

Earth to Robbie . . .

On the basis, presumably, that if it was good enough for Howard Hughes, it was good enough for him, Rob set about growing a suitably impressive beard with which to signal his segue from international recording star to seriously rich recluse. The reality was that a break from the pressures of work, particularly because of the toll the Close Encounters Tour had taken on him physically and psychologically, was an absolute necessity if he was to get well. Williams, however, was ambivalent about the upcoming period of rest and relaxation. Rationally, he knew he had pushed himself way beyond the limits he was able to bear, but given his glum certainty that his career as a pop singer was dead and buried, he did not relish the idea of an eternity spent twiddling his thumbs.

Nonetheless, in the spirit of making the best of a bad job, Rob began preparing for a life incognito. On the upside, he was beginning to think he might not have to start it alone. In January 2007, shortly before his admission to rehab, Williams met twenty-seven-year-old American actress Ayda Field at a party in Los Angeles. It had not, fair to say, been the most auspicious of first meetings. Their introduction came by way of a semi-blind date, arranged by a mutual friend, who persuaded Rob that he should take Ayda back to his house so they could get to know each other better. Once they were alone together chez Williams, Rob was working out how he could get her back to the party as quickly as possible and beat a hasty retreat. Later, he would say: 'I thought she was a mentalist at first and I thought, I've got to get her out. I was going to take her back to this party, drop her and go home. Then I fell in love, there at the party.'

Considering Robbie's fragile state during the early part of their courtship, their nascent relationship was not by any means plain sailing. Typically, Rob was telling his friends within days of them meeting that he had found the woman he planned to spend the rest of his life with. Their reaction, however, was not exactly the sort of unbridled excitement one would expect to greet such a momentous announcement. Of course, they had been here many times before. It was not uncommon for Rob to make similar wide-eyed assertions on a Monday and by Friday be adopting fake accents when answering his phone to inform the woman in question that he was sorry but Mr Williams was out of the country indefinitely.

Likewise, he and Ayda – who had had bit parts in TV shows *Will & Grace* and *Days of Our Lives* and had recently landed a part as a weathergirl in the ill-fated Kelsey Grammer sitcom *Back to You* – appeared to be following the usual pattern of Robbie's romantic entanglements, which normally involved periods of apparent domestic bliss, followed by blazing rows, break-ups and tearful reunions, before Rob finally lost interest. Indeed, they were going through an early period of estrangement when his emergency airlift to the Arizona drying-out clinic was called for. Nevertheless, Ayda, whose father is Turkish and mother American, successfully passed an early test that most of the women in his life have to take sooner or later. After the brief break-up, Ayda – unlike so many of his former paramours – did not go running breathlessly to the press to pass on the details of their short-lived relationship. Such shows of loyalty are, understandably, meaningful to someone who has been on the receiving end of more tabloid kiss 'n' tells than most. She also fitted neatly into the category of his 'type': tall, striking and leggy.

Despite the early hiccups, Rob was soon excited about spending his extended period of unemployment with his new girlfriend. Certainly, there was no imperative to work anytime soon. His accountants had informed him that his earnings for 2006, largely made up of the world tour, were just over £69 million. Such phenomenal amounts of money are prone to lead to displays of conspicuous excess, and three months after his release from rehab – and for no reason other than he fancied it – Robbie threw a Christmas party at his house in the middle of July. A specialist firm was hired to build a Santa's grotto, complete with full-sized sleigh and Father Christmas. Snow machines were brought in to turn the lush summer lawns into a winter wonderland and a pair of ten-foot-high toy soldiers were stationed at the front door to welcome seventy guests into the yuletide-themed house. Once inside, the partygoers ate Christmas lunch, sang carols and opened presents with their host.

Similarly, when one has money to burn, virtually no childhood ambition is beyond reach. Despite decent ability and a good left foot, Rob's desire to play professional football had never been more than a pipe dream. So, if Manchester United, Arsenal or his beloved Port Vale would not have him, he would simply start his own team. That way, like the kid at school who owns the only football, he could never be dropped or put on the subs bench. After building a full-size pitch on a piece of land he owned near his house, complete with floodlights, stand and dressing room, Rob went one step further and created LA Vale FC. Adidas was contacted to make the kits, a designer was brought in to create the shirt emblem, and Williams – captain, manager, box-to-box midfielder and owner all rolled into one – hired a private jet so he and the group of team-mates he had assembled from friends and ex-professional football players could travel to friendlies with American pro soccer teams. At the time, Robbie said: 'I've always wanted to be a member of a gang, so really I've bought a gang.' The whole thing said a lot about the lonely predicament he found himself in.

Inevitably, with his release from the drug clinic still so recent in the memory, Williams soon tired of such flights of fancy. Indeed, those around him remained concerned that his eccentric behaviour was an indication that he had not left all his problems behind in the Arizona desert. It was also the feeling of some within his circle that, with an abundance of leisure time at his disposal, he was turning to the wrong type of people to help him overcome the boredom of inactivity. After all, many of the so-called friends he was hanging out with, and who treated his luxury home like a hotel, had been nowhere to be seen when his addictions took him over and he needed them most. It was the case with more than a few of the hangers-on who had attached themselves to him. And it is a sad fact that there have been times, particularly since moving to LA, when he has fallen prey to people to whom he has offered friendship who were actually only looking for a meal ticket. The realization that he has misplaced his trust in people has, on occasion, led to considerable angst on his part.

The LA Vale FC experiment ended after it dawned on Rob that

his involvement had laid him open to a contingent of chancers and wasters who'd fastened themselves to him and the team. He therefore announced he was disbanding the team and scrubbed from his website the photos he had posted, including what he jokily called 'male-bonding sessions' in his Jacuzzi.

Meanwhile, his new girlfriend was keen that they should use his time away from the music business to travel together. In truth, the idea of holidaying had never rated particularly highly on Rob's agenda, in as much as he was quite candid in admitting that the idle time he spent at home in the sunshine of Beverly Hills was as close to a holiday as he cared to get. The idea of travelling to a beach somewhere also held negative connotations in the Williams mind, given that in order to get him focused on writing songs for his earlier albums, his management team had always insisted on him jetting off in the company of Guy Chambers, where he would be expected to put in a daily shift on the music and lyrics front.

Nonetheless, the remainder of the year was marked by a series of holidays. Given his later admission that sativa cannabis had been part of his cocktail of drugs, eyebrows were raised among his handlers when he announced he was hiring a private jet to take himself, Ayda and a group of friends to Amsterdam. They were entitled to ask if it was totally wise for Rob to put himself in the way of the temptation offered by the Dutch city's scores of cannabis cafes. In all honesty, Williams's disguise of bushy beard, beanie, shades and puffa jacket meant he was able to meld seamlessly with the legions of potheads pitching up with the express purpose of getting completely off their trolleys. Nor was the news, issued by Dutch radio, that Rob had been browsing, though thankfully not buying, in one of Amsterdam's so-called 'smart shops' – legalized emporiums that sell psychedelic drugs over the counter – exactly welcomed by his handlers back in the UK.

From Holland, he and his entourage travelled to Morocco and Egypt. In a classic piece of entertaining Robbie madcap, he was telling friends he had come to the conclusion that by exposing himself to the spiritual aura surrounding the Pyramids, he might find a connection with the aliens he believed had been responsible for building them and thus make himself a vessel for their thoughts. This way, he hypothesized, he might find the inspiration to write the huge-sounding instant classic that he would need to record if he was to resurrect his career.

Deep down, though, it seemed Rob suspected that, rather than a little green man from a distant galaxy, a bloke from Frodsham might offer him a more realistic hope of securing just such a hit. In August 2007, he contacted Gary and Mark Owen and invited them to meet him – not at his Beverly Hills home, but at the neutral venue of the Sunset Strip hotel Chateau Marmont. After the bad feeling over the timing of his announcement that he was going into rehab, it was a conciliatory gesture on the part of Williams. Given that it had been fifteen months since he had last set eyes on the two of them, it was a chance to catch up, chew the fat and discuss their widely differing fortunes in the intervening period.

Williams was nervous about facing Gary again, particularly in such a small group. As the clock ticked down to when he would have to leave for the meeting, he panicked. To make matters worse, he had toothache and did not want to go in mumbling like Marlon Brando. He told Ayda he was cancelling. She spent the next fifteen minutes talking him round.

Robbie could be forgiven if, by meeting up with Gary again, he was hoping that some of Barlow's stardust would rub off on him.

Following the success of *Beautiful World*, Take That had written a new song, 'Rule the World', for the Matthew Vaughn film *Stardust*. The single, which would eventually be released in October and get to number two in the UK, was an instant classic with its archetypal Barlow powerhouse chorus. It represented the pinnacle of the group's creative work in their second incarnation thus far and featured Gary, who performed the lead vocal, at the very height of his powers. When they wrote the number in Spain earlier that year, Gary knew instantly this was a song that would join 'Back for Good' and 'A Million Love Songs' as one of his finest creations. The strength of their new output also won them a deal with the American label Interscope Records, home of U2 and Sting, which would release their album in the US and Canada. With that in mind, it was a very different Gary who sat down for dinner with Rob and Mark that evening in the restaurant of the hotel. The previous year, he had been reserved, guarded, defensive even. Now he projected a markedly more relaxed, confident demeanour. He was entitled, after all, to believe that for the first time since Williams had released 'Angels', he was able to view Rob as an equal.

And whereas Gary was confident that some of his best work was still ahead of him, it was clear from the moment they sat down and he began talking that Williams had no such faith in his own future. If it might be too simplistic to suggest that Gary's new self-assurance gave him the edge in the always complicated dynamic of his dealings with Robbie, it at least allowed him the opportunity to view his former adversary as a man rather than a back catalogue. With Mark acting as an impartial and sensitive buffer, the evening was a success. Rob told Gary he loved *Beautiful World*, and 'Patience' in particular, and said he sincerely believed the band was better than ever. Afterwards, Gary was buzzing. It was one thing to make a major step in putting the bitter years of animosity and backbiting behind them, it was quite another for him to know that he had won the genuine respect of someone whose undoubted talent had long provoked in Gary the conflicting emotions of grudging awe and undiluted, raging envy.

Barlow was full of the meeting, happily telling the *Daily Mirror* it had been 'the best we've had since 1996. Yes, we met, had a great chat. Robbie's really well and we're good buds again.' Predictably, perhaps, the news was met with conjecture that Take That and Williams were on the verge of reuniting, with the newspapers speculating that he could even join their upcoming Beautiful World Tour, starting in October and running through to Christmas. Ironically, though, and in spite of the dramatic thawing in the relationship between the two men, the prospect of Take That becoming a five-piece was, if anything, further away than ever. The tumultuous recent months had convinced the band, and Gary especially, that Robbie was no longer needed. The realization had taken rather longer to arrive at than one might imagine. Even by the end of the previous year's Ultimate Tour, there was still the nagging doubt among Barlow, Owen, Donald and Orange that the revival would lack a sense of permanence until Williams was returned to the fold. The success of their album and singles changed all that, and supplied a mainline confidence shot.

As if to hammer home the point, Barlow chose to sign off his autobiography, *My Take*, by saying: 'Since *Beautiful World* came out, I look at pictures of us and I no longer see anyone missing from the band; that's something I never felt before.' Symbolically, too, as they began preparations for their upcoming arena tour – which would take in six German cities and Holland, Spain, Italy, Denmark, Switzerland and Austria before finishing with nine nights at the O2 in London either side of eleven at Manchester's MEN Arena – the Robbie hologram was dropped from the show.

In the event, four would briefly become three when Howard suffered a collapsed lung during a show in Vienna, missing seven of the European gigs. Nonetheless, the tour, which cost £4 million to stage, was an unmitigated success, selling out in forty minutes and culminating in a barnstorming New Year's Eve show in London that was filmed for a live two-disc DVD set. By way of confirming their position as budding national treasures, the band was chosen by Marks & Spencer to front a multimillion-pound advertising campaign for the store.

Even in the Williams camp there remained scepticism about whether a return to Take That would be a good move, but such qualms did not extend to Rob's mother, Jan. She came out publicly just before Christmas to say she believed it was only a matter of time before he re-joined the group. 'On the question of him doing something with them, I feel that will happen,' she said. 'It would be something he wanted to do. I'm thrilled that out of all the negative stuff that happened there's now something great happening. Take That were excellent when they were all together and they are excellent now.' Jan's intervention was significant. She was, of course, more aware than most of the creative malaise her son was in the midst of, and was also acutely aware that boredom and the creeping return to drugs had in the past been frequent bedfellows. More than that, as a smart and shrewd woman who had from time to time acted as unofficial PR for her son, she was highly unlikely to make such bold predictions without at least the tacit approval of Robbie.

Even so, if Williams was quietly angling for a call-up back to the Take That ranks, he was no longer in the position of power he had formerly occupied. As if to prove it, within days Gary slapped Jan down, saying he felt there was now 'no place' for Robbie in the line-up. 'When it comes down to it, he's just not going to be in the band again,' he said. Even Mark joined in, saying that Rob had been given the chance before but had decided to 'walk his dogs instead'. They would not have been human if thoughts of payback did not come into the equation given the previous snubs, the unre-turned calls and Williams's intentional or otherwise high-handed response to their earlier entreaties to him to re-form the band. What was unspoken, however, was the strong opinion among some in the wider Take That set-up that not only was Williams still clearly in no shape physically or mentally to come back, but his return would risk diverting the hitherto smooth upward curve of Take That's trajectory. Why take the chance that Robbie, who had been unable to finish his last tour, would upset the highly profitable apple cart?

In terms of his solo career, things were about to go from bad to worse for Williams. In August 2007, the struggling EMI, which had posted losses of £260 million in the last financial year, was sold to private equity firm Terra Firma. With the takeover in the offing, Paul McCartney left the label, and soon afterwards Radiohead jumped ship as well. The relationship between the new owners and Williams did not get off on the right foot when Terra Firma's owner, Guy Hands, gave an interview to the *Financial Times* in which he claimed that some unnamed EMI artists needed to work harder. By the following January the situation had deteriorated to all-out war. Williams's manager Tim Clark made the unprecedented decision to give an interview to *The Times* in which he effectively announced that Robbie had gone on strike. With two more albums still due to the label as part of the deal, Clark said Robbie would not supply them with another album because he could not be sure how EMI would handle it. 'The question is, should Robbie deliver the new album he is due to release to EMI?' he told the paper. 'We have to say the answer is no. We have no idea how EMI will market and promote the album.' Meanwhile, Rob went on his official website to tell fans there would be no tour anytime soon, saying: 'The last one nearly killed me.' Bizarrely, he was also floating the idea that he might put an album of B-sides from his next album out on the Internet.

Despite Williams's hard-line stance with his label's new owners, however, his decision to withhold his labour was a purely technical argument – not least because, regardless of the state of his relations with his bosses, the simple fact was that he had nothing that sounded remotely like an album to give them. In the breaks from his holidaying he had been half-heartedly looking for the writing partner he hoped would provide the inspiration to reignite his creative juices. He began working with various musicians, including Chaz Jankel, a former member of Ian Dury and the Blockheads, and was reported to have entered into discussions with Guy Chambers about resuming their partnership. The net result, however, was that precious little new material had been produced. For the most part, Rob's once formal writing sessions with Guy had been replaced by him hanging around the bedroom cum studio of his LA home, strumming an acoustic guitar with a bunch of friends/hangers-on and putting hours of the unstructured and mainly lacklustre bits of songs on hard disk, never to be replayed.

In the absence of any meaningful work, Rob decided to indulge further his increasing interest in all things extraterrestrial. In early 2008, he phoned journalist and author Jon Ronson out of the blue to ask him if he would like to accompany him on a trip to Nevada to meet some people who had been abducted by aliens. The two men had corresponded three years earlier after Rob read the author's book on conspiracy theories. At the time, Williams told him he was keen to stay in a haunted house and asked Ronson to contact some members of the aristocracy on his behalf to find out a) if their stately homes were inhabited by ghostly apparitions and b) whether they would mind if Robbie Williams came to spend the night. Surprisingly, there were several offers, but in the event Rob announced he was too busy to take up the opportunity of being scared witless by things that go bump in the night in some of Britain's best houses.

This time, Rob excitedly told Ronson he had been doing some research on the Internet and had discovered a conference on UFOs was taking place where a whole family who claimed they had been transported into outer space by creatures from another planet would be available to meet. They quickly decided that Ronson would record their trip for a Radio 4 documentary and Williams arranged to hire a private jet to fly himself, Ronson, Ayda and a record-producer friend called Brandon Christy from LA to the conference in Laughlin, Nevada, the following Thursday. 'I want to do something,' Rob told him. 'I want to go out there and meet these people. I want to be a part of this. I want to do something other than sit in my bed and watch the news.'

The singer would blend in anonymously with his fellow delegates. Since the end of his last tour more than a year earlier, he had put on weight. Now, to add to his disguise of bushy and greying beard, he had longish collar-length hair and wore a Fidel Castro-style army-issue canvas cap, matching fatigues jacket and a large pair of bright blue sunglasses. It was a safe bet that nobody would recognize him.

The guest speakers at the conference could be described as a colourful collection of individuals. One delegate was Ann Andrews, from Lincolnshire, who claims her son, Jason, has had disturbing experiences at the hands of many different alien species. Another, American surgeon Dr Roger Leir, says he removed 'non-earthly metallic' implants from fifteen of his patients. Robbie, it seemed, had his own theories on why spaceships were visible to only a chosen handful of believers. 'I think the shield comes off by mistake and they were there all the time,' he told Ronson. 'I don't want to hear any debunking because I want to believe.'

According to Ronson, Williams listened rapt to an audio-visual presentation Mrs Andrews gave to the conference at a large hotel in the desert town, in which she explained that when her son was a toddler, he began being abducted by aliens during the night and taken to their spaceship, where they experimented on him so they could send him back to earth to be a psychic sage. She said she had seen the extraterrestrials taking her son off and tried to photograph them on several occasions, but only had a cheap disposable camera so the images were just fuzzy blurs. Later, when Robbie went to talk to her and buy her latest book, she told him her son had no friends because he had been shunned in their small village shortly after she wrote her first book about his nightly rendezvouses with creatures from other planets. Williams subsequently told Ronson he did not believe her story was made up.

The trip to Nevada was not Robbie's only attempt to make interplanetary contact. Later that year, Rob, Ayda and a group of friends travelled to Washington State to meet a team of employees from an American website called AboveTopSecret.com. The site is full of outlandish conspiracy theories and claims that the US government has covered up contact with aliens. One typical post involves its claims that the changeover to digital television has nothing whatever to do with clearer pictures, but is instead a sinister government plan to plant microphones and cameras in set-top boxes so they can monitor and record the goings-on in every household in the US. Another claim repeated on the website is that not only does the FBI have spy satellites that can see through brick walls to watch people in their homes, they can also read the minds of members of the public and scan the brains and memories of humans as if they were computers.

Rob had been an avid member of the site for more than year, signing on to discussion groups under the usernames 'cyar' and 'chrisonabike' to chat with other members about his interest in UFOs. On the trip, and much to the chagrin of his management and record company, Rob even gave a radio interview to the AboveTopSecret operatives, in which he discussed what he believed were alien visitations to him in Los Angeles. One incident happened, he said, when he was lying on a sunlounger with a friend one night looking at the stars while staying at the Beverly Hills Hotel. He claims they saw a black-and-yellow striped flying saucer flying over their heads.

The second incident happened in 2007 at around the time he was admitted to rehab. Rob told them he was with some friends in his bedroom cum recording studio at his LA home. They were listening to a recording of a song called 'Arizona', which he said he wrote about UFOs, when a ball of light appeared over his house. It was followed a few seconds later, he told his interviewers, by a black 'negative' light about three inches thick and twenty feet long, which shot into the room through a balcony door and out through another window. By way of explaining what he had seen, he added with apparent seriousness: 'All this could be government ops – they want to cover it and we might be getting in the way.' He began inviting the website's founder, Mark Allin, over to his house, and the two started taking what Allin described to me as 'expeditions' to investigate unexplained UFO sightings.

The singer turned the visit to Washington State into a road trip, hiring a giant camper van and spending the evenings with Ayda and his friends sitting round a campfire playing the guitar. The purpose of the jaunt was to visit the headquarters of the ECETI (Enlightened Contact with Extraterrestrial Intelligence) Research Center, which is located in the foothills of Mount Adams. For more than a week they joined other UFO aficionados in photographing and logging what they believed to be alien activity in the night sky above the mountain. During the trip, Rob became firm friends with the research centre's founder, James Gilliland, a middle-aged Californian real-estate worker who claims he started seeing UFOs after nearly drowning while surfing.

Gilliland, an amiable if off-the-wall individual, told me: 'Robbie was here when we filmed some large triangle ships going over. The alien spaceships dock inside Mount Adams in a massive underground base, then link up on a nightly basis with craft from other star nations. Robbie told me he had his own experiences, and coming here reaffirmed what he already knew inside. He was very open to what he was seeing. He really believed he had seen UFOs. Ships did appear and he was part of our crew, playing with the instruments and helping us document the activity.' Indeed, the research centre's website carried pictures of the singer, in puffa jacket and trucker's cap, watching the sky through a telescope with other UFO enthusiasts. Gilliland added: 'Robbie was really inspired, and he and his friends created their own little recording studio and did some writing and put together a lot of music while he was here, just sitting around a campfire and sleeping in a mobile home. We kept his visit under wraps and didn't tell anyone he was coming. I think part of it was that Robbie was trying to get the creative juices flowing again. I heard the music he wrote and it was beautiful. He told me his album was going to be inspired by what he saw during his investigations here.'

It is difficult not to draw the conclusion that what Rob was really looking for was not likely to be found at the end of a telescope lens or buried on the conspiracy-theory websites he spent his nights scouring. Of most concern to those whose living depended on him, however, was the fact that while Williams was on this strange odyssey to find himself – and, if at all possible, intelligent forms of extraterrestrial life – he might just make matters far worse by chronicling the whole adventure for an album he planned to unleash on an unsuspecting public.

As Rob looked towards the heavens for inspiration, Gary's focus was on the far more down-to-earth business of making the follow-up to *Beautiful World*. In February 2008, the band was again successful at the Brits, winning Best Single for 'Shine' and also taking home the award for Best Live Act. Now the focus was on building on their achievements. Gary was already finding himself much in demand away from Take That. He began writing for the soundtrack of the ill-fated ITV musical drama series *Britannia High*, and co-wrote *X Factor* spoof 'The Winner's Song' with comedian Peter Kay, which went to number two in the single charts in December. Take That once again brought in the American John Shanks to produce their second album, *The Circus*.

The record would pick up where its predecessor had left off when it was released in December 2008. It was a consolidation, once more chock-full of Barlow's classic mighty choruses and ultra-slick arrangements – even if tracks like 'Hold Up a Light' and 'Said It All' were, with their soaring falsettos and Open University philosophizing, more reminiscent of Coldplay than Take That. The title track, 'The Circus', showed off Barlow's skill for show-tune ballads, but there was also the odd dud moment. The Eurovision-esque 'Up All Night', with Mark Owen on lead vocals, sounded like a cross between Oasis and the Brotherhood of Man. If anything, though, the album was more mature, more assured than *Beautiful World*, with Gary again coming up with the prerequisite towering ballad on which the record would ultimately be judged. The song in question, 'Greatest Day', went straight to number one when it was released at the end of November. Meanwhile, the album would top the charts in Britain and Ireland, selling more than two million copies in the UK alone and going seven times platinum. Like *Beautiful World* before it, the record outsold all Take That's albums from the Robbie era.

At the same time, the band announced that the Circus Tour would take place the following summer. The staging would be the band's most ambitious yet, featuring a giant elephant, big top, hot-air balloon and acrobats. Again, there was an unprecedented clamour for tickets when they went on sale at the beginning of November. More than 600,000 were snapped up in just five hours as promoters added more dates to keep up with demand. In the end, the stadium tour would stretch to twenty dates, including the 80,000-venue Croke Park in Dublin, plus five shows at Old Trafford cricket ground in Manchester and four nights at Wembley Stadium in early July.

While Take That were making the album with Shanks in Los Angeles, Gary and the others used the time to renew contact with Rob. As further evidence that a thaw was now firmly under way between the two men, Rob invited Gary to spend time with him at his Beverly Hills home, with the plan that he would play Barlow some of the tracks he had been producing during his self-imposed period of hibernation. Instead of simply being an opportunity to listen to Robbie's records, however, for the first time it was a chance for the pair to put their cards on the table. Rob, with the security of being in his own home, was more confident, more willing to open up and tell Gary the way it had been for him when he left the band. Crucially, though, he wanted Gary to know that he had come to the realization some time ago that he had to stop blaming Gary and the others for what happened to him, that he would never overcome his many issues if he continued to use his anger and hurt as a way of avoiding facing up to the things he needed to resolve in his life.

Gary, too, was at last ready to speak without constraint, without the fear that by laying himself bare in front of his one-time enemy, by admitting the mistakes he made with Rob and the other boys first time around, he would find his words being used against him at some future point when Robbie's present goodwill had turned back to bile. Gary talked about his kids, and how they had changed him, and Rob told him that being with Ayda had made him think for the first time that he might one day do what he had always thought would be impossible for him and settle down with one person. The sense of liberation they took from the simple act of talking freely and face to face was palpable. Then something neither man was expecting occurred. Chatting in Robbie's kitchen, they spontaneously flung their arms around each other and seconds later were laughing and rolling around on the floor in a man-hug, drunk on the overwhelming sense of relief and instant euphoria.

It was a spontaneous and unabashed reaction to the ending of the feud and surprised Rob and Gary just as much as it did those around them. It was the signal, too, for both men to fall for a time headlong into a sort of quasi-romantic, if non-physical,

relationship that was as heady and all-encompassing as any traditional first flush of love. Gary became a regular visitor to Rob's
house, hanging out in the kitchen, talking as the pair got to know
each other again. To those observing them at close quarters, their
burgeoning relationship had all the hallmarks of a courtship – or,
to be more accurate, the rediscovery of affection between a
divorced couple whose emotional force fields have drawn them
back to each other years later. Typically of Williams, his reawak-
ened brotherly love for Barlow – and, to a lesser extent, his former
band mates – came for a while that summer to be all consuming.
For both men, the feeling of a weight being lifted off their shoulders was the trigger for an outbreak of soppiness that would have
been vaguely comical were it not so touching. It said much about
how theirs was a relationship of extremes: from the pure, uncut
hate of the previous years to the billing and cooing of their fast-
developing bromance.

Even so, their rapprochement was cause for genuine celebration.
As Gary began promoting *The Circus* with the others, he couldn't
stop talking about how he and Rob had hung out in LA and were
in constant email contact now Barlow was back in the UK. 'It's
really fun getting to know each other again, I must say,' Gary said.
'The five of us are rebuilding our friendship and that's really the
only place to start.' For the first time he was admitting he could
now see the day when Robbie might return to Take That. 'As long
as we're alive people are going to ask if we're going to get back
together, and I do believe we will one day, but I just don't know
when,' he told a press conference in Paris.

For his part, Williams was publicly circumspect about the chances
of a reunion. That same week, he wrote on his personal website:
'I'd love to be in the band again, but I've got some unfinished

business of my own.' Nonetheless, he could barely hide his fervour for the idea of taking up his old berth in Take That. 'The thing that struck me was how much fun they're having,' he went on. 'It's more rewarding when you're in a gang. Ever since I left Take That I've wanted to be in a band. We've all matured a lot since we parted. I'm really pleased to say the differences we had just melted away. I'm proud to know the boys and I'm proud to have been in the band.' In their honour, he announced he had added a new tattoo to his already impressive collection of body art. It consisted of a circle on his right forearm, enclosing the classic double-T symbol of Take That. As job applications go, it was hardly subtle.

Gary was also saying nice things about the new songs Williams had played him during their getting-to-know-you sessions in LA. Whether he was just being kind, we will never know, because if Gary, who was also saying that he thought *The Circus* was 'the ultimate Take That album', really liked them, not everybody shared his high opinion. Indeed, the consensus of at least two of those I spoke to at the time who had listened to the tracks Williams planned to put on his long-awaited new album was that they were nigh on career-ending stuff. His UFO interest and ad hoc approach to recording had resulted in songs that, according to one who heard them, were 'a mush of navel-gazing, la-la-land psychobabble and downright weirdness'. If that were not bad enough, they also said the melodies were rubbish.

For all that Gary was keen to sound complimentary about his new best friend, he was already using his influence to suggest that a change of scene was needed if Robbie was to get back the creative spark his career so desperately needed. Barlow began counselling him that while he knew from his own experience of living there that California had much going for it as a place to lay one's head, it should only ever be seen as a passing fancy, a metaphorical spa retreat of a city. It was somewhere to go and hang out in a fluffy bathrobe, somewhere to be pampered for a while, but equally, it was the type of place that would be likely to drive you insane after only the briefest of stays. Gary told Rob bluntly that it was time to put his interrupted six-year Tinseltown sojourn behind him and come home to where he was loved – and, more importantly, where he was understood.

In reality, Barlow was not the first person in the Williams circle to point this out. Many had long been of the strong opinion that while the climate might have been great and the lifestyle agreeable, Los Angeles had had a soporific effect on Rob. Beyond that, there was also the feeling that his dislocation had thrown him off his axis, that as an expat he had lost touch to an extent with his Britishness, and therefore his market. Rob himself was convinced that his move to LA had saved his life by removing him from his ordeal as the hunted fox back home. He was also unapologetic that he liked the sun and enjoyed the fact that on virtually any day of the year he could sit around in the garden or play with his growing pack of dogs by – and frequently in – his swimming pool. Yes, living in California was at times little more than an extended holiday, but as someone who suffered with depression, the weather made life bearable during the bad times. On top of that, he liked the air of positivity that suffused life in Hollywood. He knew it was sneered at by outsiders as shallow and fake, but he liked the American 'can do' spirit, the 'have a nice day' platitudes, and the childlike clinging to the 'anything is possible' pipe dream.

If anyone could persuade him that a return to these shores would be in his best long-term interests, however, it was Barlow. As a sign of how close they had become in the intervening few months, Gary and Rob made their first appearance in public together for twelve years when they attended a match between Arsenal and Manchester United at the Emirates Stadium in early November 2008, posing for photographers with their arms around each other. As part of his campaign to persuade Robbie to make a full-time return to Britain, Gary went public with his hopes in an attempt to ratchet up the pressure on his friend. 'I don't think the US is the best place for him to be,' Gary told the *Sun* at the end of the year. 'I've always loved working here and wouldn't want to be anywhere else, and I've been telling Robbie for a while now that he needs to move back. I think the time is right for him to come back now. This is where he thrives and it's the best thing he can do for his career. He's got a lot of unfinished business here and he'll be back to his best in no time if he comes home.'

Barlow's intervention was typical of the new nurturing approach of Gary mark II. No longer the self-seeking egotist and puller of strings, he had given up jealously guarding the creative process with Take That. Moreover, he had successfully transformed himself into an unofficial mentor to the others in the band, encouraging and cajoling them into producing their best work during writing sessions and in the studio. Now in his role as enabler, he was focusing his attention on sorting out Robbie.

Suddenly, after years of saying privately that he could never imagine living in his homeland again, Rob came round to Gary's way of thinking. He began telling those around him that Barlow was right. After all, it was obvious to any fool that Gary knew what he was talking about when it came to the British record-buying public; just look how he had tapped into the musical zeitgeist with Take That. If Gary was saying he needed to come home, then he must have a point. That Rob was prepared to put his faith so wholeheartedly in Gary was indicative of how he was already prepared to defer and accept without question the judgement of someone whom he not only instinctively looked up to, but believed without doubt had his genuine best interests at heart.

Within weeks Rob's people were instructed to begin hunting for a suitable house in England. Meanwhile, Rob, with all the zeal of the recent convert, was wistfully telling the Los Angeles-born Ayda of the magical British winters, of log fires, cosy pubs and bracing country walks. He told his management team to find him somewhere in the West Country near where his friend Jonathan Wilkes now lived with his wife, Nikki, and young son, Mickey. By early February he and Ayda had moved into a £7-million seventeenth-century French-style chateau in the Wiltshire village of Compton Bassett. Set in seventy-one acres, it came complete with formal gardens, tennis courts, gym, swimming-pool complex, eight bedrooms and – naturally – its own helicopter hangar.

Nevertheless, only days after moving in he was already having regrets. Firstly, he and Ayda found themselves at the mercy of a particularly cold British winter. Then Robbie was to find within twenty-four hours that much as he had hoped his time away would have dissipated the craziness that had surrounded him when he last lived here, things were, sadly, pretty much as he'd left them. The first time he ventured out, he was mobbed in the street by his fans and followed around by the seemingly ever-present paparazzi. Just going to nearby Swindon to buy a couple of bicycles proved to be an exercise in crowd control for his hassled minders. Rob, who had reverted to his habit of going out in a disguise, this time a black ski mask and oversized shades, glowered as he found himself trapped in a shop doorway. The whole unpleasant experience led to one of his bodyguards issuing an impassioned entreaty for him to be left alone, telling his baying fans: 'Is there any chance you could not hassle him so he can have his first day back in peace?' Needless to say, his plea fell on deaf ears.

It was not simply a case of having to suffer the constant attention of his fans and the arrival of what seemed like the complete massed ranks of the photographic press corps on his doorstep. Ayda, who after years of struggling for roles had finally found her career beginning to gain momentum, told him that while she was happy to visit, she would not risk her Hollywood acting career by placing herself 5,500 miles away from the action. Alone for much of the time in his lavish new home while Ayda stayed in the Beverly Hills house, Rob quickly became isolated and bored. He began attending a rather unglamorous casino in Swindon, where he would join strangers to bet £20 on a midweek game of poker. He also hired a local sports hall so he could go with his minder to kick a ball against the wall.

His depressed state of mind was not the only cause of concern for his management. Now into his third year since making an album, Robbie's earnings had dwindled dramatically from the vast profits he had made on his 2006 tour. Accounts filed by Robbie's firm, the In Good Company, showed his earnings had fallen by £65 million in a year. His income in 2008 dropped sharply to £3.7 million, compared to £69 million the previous year. And after paying himself £5.5 million in wages, his profits slumped from £15.7 million to less than £500,000 after tax. None of which exactly meant he was on his uppers, but with two expensive homes to maintain on either side of the Atlantic, he was no longer in a position to rest on his laurels. Finally, Williams sent the songs he had recorded in his bedroom for the comeback album, so his handlers could listen to them.

They did not like what they heard. In fact, so horrified were they by what Rob told them ominously was an 'experimental album' that all copies of it were immediately put under lock and key, for fear they would somehow end up on the Internet. They should, perhaps, have realized what they were in for when Rob began describing the material he had recorded as a series of 'bleeps and blobs'. Williams was eventually told in no uncertain terms by his team that if the album was released, it could wreck his career. Thankfully, after an initial stand-off, Rob saw sense and agreed to can it. He would later concede that the shelved album was what he described as 'Robbie gone mad . . . career suicide'. Robbie's handlers, IE Management, decided to start again from scratch. An experienced head was called for and they quickly hired the renowned English record producer Trevor Horn, who had worked with Frankie Goes to Hollywood and the Pet Shop Boys and had his own 1979 hit as lead singer of the Buggles with the novelty song 'Video Killed the Radio Star'.

It says something about the quality of the material on offer that when the album – jokily titled *Reality Killed the Video Star* in Horn's honour – finally appeared at the beginning of November 2009, it included a track, 'Blasphemy', that had been written six years earlier by Williams and Guy Chambers, and had been collecting dust ever since. That said, after the debacle of *Rudebox*, at least the new album was fairly recognizable as a Robbie Williams record. In fact, songs like the hummable 'You Know Me' and 'Won't Do That', both of which were written for Ayda, were resolutely middle of the road and commercial. The issue for the record was that they simply did not sit comfortably with some of the other more left-field material – most notably the incomprehensible 'Bodies', which would be released as the first single from the album that October. The song, with its references to Jesus, the Bodhi tree, cemeteries and entropy, had worrying echoes of *Rudebox* about it. The fact that the song was featured alongside the show tune-like 'Somewhere' and the very George Michael-esque 'Starstruck' made the record either catholic or schizophrenic, depending on your point of view. This was hardly surprising considering that along with Williams himself, there were no fewer than seventeen writers involved on the thirteen tracks.

At its release, Robbie was talking it up. 'I want people to feel elated,' he said. 'I want them to dance. I want them to forget about who they are and where they are for fifty minutes – and, within those fifty minutes of forgetting who they are, I also hope people relate to the songs. This is a record that I'm very proud of. I think it's fucking brilliant. I want it to be the record that if people think of Robbie Williams, they go, "Yeah, *Reality Killed the Video Star*."'

Less than a year later, however, he was revising where the album stood in the Williams canon. Of 'Bodies' he said: 'A great track, but the lyrics are fucking gibberish. You look at them and go, "Stop watching documentaries, you knob,"' he told *Q* magazine. 'Who knows what I was going on about? I was fucking stoned. The edge had gone.' The album, he claimed, was a reaction to the panning *Rudebox* had received. 'When suddenly you're not on top of the wave any more and the imperial phase is over, you panic,' he added. 'You're left to compromise, basically. The album was schizophrenic – it was like, I'll put "Morning Sun" on it because I know the fans will like that kind of thing.' He admitted he had not wanted to promote the album, saying: 'I was gutted about it. And unfortunately for EMI, disinterested.'

Nonetheless, 'Bodies' still managed to reach number two in the UK singles chart and number one in Germany, Holland, Austria,

Italy and Hungary. Meanwhile, the album went three times platinum and got to number two in Britain, topping the chart in seven countries, including Germany, Australia and Croatia.

The reason for Rob's reluctance to go out of his way to support the album was that, in his own mind at least, he had bigger fish to fry. For the previous few months of 2009 he had secretly been working with Take That on their first material as a five-piece in fourteen years. The delicate negotiations to allow Rob to retake his place in the band had been going on for much of the year. As early as January, Gary was laying the groundwork for Williams's return by finally admitting publicly that he and the band had been culpable in not spotting Robbie's problems with alcohol at the time he left Take That. Two months later, Rob made his most blatant and most public pitch yet to get his old job back. 'My head's in the right place, so the timing could be right if Gary calls,' he said. 'I think it would be fun and it's looking more likely by the week. It would make sense for it to happen sometime over the next year.'

By naming Gary as the man in whose hands his fate rested, Robbie was unintentionally giving an insight into the balance of power that now existed in the band. Nevertheless, the decision did not solely need Barlow's ratification. In reality, there had been some discord for several months within Take That over the question of Robbie re-joining them. And although Jason Orange had built a close relationship with Rob in the three years since meeting him during their comeback tour, he – more than any other member of the band – was resistant to him returning. According to members of Take That's inner circle, while Jason – and to a lesser extent Howard Donald – were prepared to forgive Williams for the things he had said about the band, both were sceptical about whether Rob could be relied upon. As possibly the member of the band who is

most protective of the institution of Take That, Jason told the others
he was concerned about the consequences if Robbie returned to the
fold and then walked away again just as an album was about to
be released, or on the eve of an expensive tour. Rob had walked
out before, he reminded them, so what was to stop lightning striking
twice?

CHAPTER FIFTEEN

Progress

The vexed question of whether Rob's head was in anything like the right place for the coming fray would be something the other four members of Take That would all soon come to ponder. As, reluctantly, he set about the task of promoting *Reality Killed the Video Star,* he did not exactly look in the best possible shape for it. After three years away, a series of public appearances had been planned by EMI, the most high profile of which was Williams being booked to perform 'Bodies' on ITV's *The X Factor* in early October 2009. In the minds of his PR team, it would be the perfect opportunity to herald his triumphant return to the limelight after his self-imposed exile from the music business. That may have been the plan, but the reality was that Williams gave one of the car-crash performances of the year in front of the talent show's fourteen million fans.

From the start it appeared the Fates were conspiring against him. As a giant set of doors on the stage began opening to reveal Robbie in all his glory, they suddenly jammed and he was forced to wrestle his way through the gap as though he were making a dash to catch the last Tube home. The technical hitch seemed to throw him and for the next three and a bit minutes he gave the impression that – given the choice – he would have preferred unanaesthetized colorectal surgery to staying on stage a second longer. Towards the end, as if to convince himself as much as anyone else, he shouted: 'It's good to be back!' It clearly wasn't. He looked not so much ill at ease as terrified by being on stage and live television after so long. By the time he finished the song and was submitting to an interview with the show's host, Dermot O'Leary, a sweating Robbie was wide-eyed and wired-looking. It was excruciating to watch and impossible to feel anything but heartfelt sympathy for him.

Predictably, almost as soon as he left the stage, the traffic on Internet message boards went into overdrive. 'It's totally disgusting that he was allowed to perform in such a state,' one contributor wrote. Others suggested he was on drugs and the spokesman for the singer was forced to issue a denial to the media that he had taken anything before the show. 'The truth is, he hasn't performed in the UK for ages and he was excited to be on the show,' his PR told the press. 'That's the reason his performance was so spirited. He was excited to be there and to perform the single live for the first time. He was not on anything.' Now, instead of building on his comeback appearance, Williams's panicking team was forced to begin a damage-limitation exercise.

He was hastily booked to appear on the BBC's *Friday Night With Jonathan Ross* to explain himself. 'The doors got stuck,' he told the chat-show host. 'I thought, What are the words? I get incredibly nervous. It wasn't drugs or drink, just deer in the headlights. I've always been very nervous on stage. It's an unnatural thing to do. You don't know what's going on in my head. It's traumatic, really scary.' As if to prove the point, when he returned to appear on *The X Factor* again in December, he fluffed the opening to 'Angels' during a duet with contestant Olly Murs. A nervous Robbie missed his cue, began singing the second verse by mistake and had to be helped out by call-centre worker Murs.

On the personal front also, his return to live in Britain had been an unmitigated disaster and only nine months after buying his vast Wiltshire pile, he was putting it on the market and returning to Beverly Hills. The house would remain unsold for two years and in a bid to cut his losses he was forced to knock £1 million off the asking price.

Is there any question, then, that if Rob still harboured doubts about whether re-joining Take That was the right thing to do, he now had his answer? In fact, it was arguably his only credible option. The simple state of affairs was that he had developed such a terror of appearing alone on stage that he was now under no illusion that his only hope of coping with it was by going for the safety-in-numbers option. Maybe, he convinced himself, he could deal with the white-knuckle dread, the killer shakes before a show, if he had the prop of four friends. Somehow their force field would be his protection; he could feed off their collective strength. Beyond his fear of performing, however, Rob was also convinced that he had simply run out of things to say on record. If anything, his latest solo album had only reinforced that opinion in his mind.

The only logical conclusion to draw was that, given his multitude of problems, Robbie needed Take That more than they needed him. Thankfully, now he found that the member of the band who was most championing his return was none other than Gary. As early as spring 2009, the circumspection Barlow had been displaying in public had been replaced privately by an active desire to make Robbie's return a reality.

While the benefits to Williams of becoming part of Take That were obvious, and were now – crucially – also accepted by Rob's team of managers, what exactly was in it for Gary? It is necessary to understand at this point that the heartfelt mea culpas the men had issued to each other at Rob's house the previous summer had made huge strides towards them being able to leave their previous animosity behind. And seeing how fragile Rob was emotionally and physically over the months they had been back in touch had stirred Gary's paternal and nurturing instincts. In the middle of January, he had become a father for the third time when Dawn gave birth to their daughter Daisy, and increasingly he was playing the role of father figure to Rob.

Aside from his genuine desire to help Rob, who was about to be free of his contractual obligations to EMI, Gary was, and is, a pragmatist at heart. For all that he had loathed Williams during their long estrangement, he was in no doubt about his huge talent. He was equally convinced that Williams's creative malaise could be cured if he was prepared to allow himself to submit to Barlow's tutelage. The combination of Robbie's undoubted ability as a wordsmith and his own as a writer of instantly memorable melodies would be a potent one, Gary was convinced. What's more, he felt, according to those around him, that *The Circus* had been rather too similar to *Beautiful World* and that it was time for Take That to break, at least for the time being, from the fairly predictable and unthreatening sound of their most recent albums.

Subconsciously, perhaps, Gary also got off on the image of himself as the spiritual and creative force behind Robbie's redemption. And to adopt the cynical approach for a moment, would it not be possible to speculate that Gary had, at long last, achieved the upper hand in his dealings with his erstwhile enemy? Now Robbie's faltering career was in his hands, given over to him by a man who, for all that he had sold in excess of fifty million records, was prepared unquestioningly to put his faith in him. After all the years of obscurity and humiliation, what could have been more flattering to Barlow's once shattered ego than to know that the world's biggest male pop singer had come to believe that only his extraordinary talent could save him?

It was no wonder Williams was in no mood to go out on the road to promote the substandard *Reality Killed the Video Star*, considering that as he was waiting for the album to be released, he was already secretly back in the studio with Take That. The neutral venue of New York was chosen for their first recording as a quintet in fourteen years. To be strictly accurate, the first of the new era of Take That songs had already been written by Gary, Robbie and Mark before Howard and Jason arrived at the Electric Lady Studios in Manhattan a few days later in September 2009. As far as Gary and Robbie were concerned, the creative spark they were hoping would develop between them was evident from the very outset of their writing sessions. Within two days they had come up with the opening verses and chorus for 'The Flood', which would prove to be the standout track on the album and the first Take That single as a five-piece since 'Never Forget' in summer 1995.

Given everything that had gone on before, however, they could hardly be expected seamlessly to fall back into the old routine – particularly as the old routine, with its battles for supremacy, backbiting and bitterness, was somewhere no one was keen to revisit. Instead, they would have to create a new band dynamic on the hoof. The traditional way, of course, would be for a group to begin their reunion with a tour, as Take That had done in 2006, but they had chosen the potentially far more problematic route of locking themselves – and their respective egos – away in a small recording studio. There, they would each offer up their ideas, their melodies and their lyrics for the scrutiny of the others – risking the possibility of rejection by the newly democratic Take That quorum.

As the outsider, Rob was especially nervous at the prospect. For two weeks before the New York studio get-together, he had locked himself away writing lyrics day and night so he would feel like he had something tangible to offer on day one. Such dedication was, by his own admission, something of a novelty considering his notoriously short attention span. Clearly, Williams felt on the back foot. As they began recording, Rob was describing the lyrics he had brought along as his 'artillery' to the documentary film crew hired to record his reunion with Take That for posterity. It was a strange use of the word, conjuring up obvious thoughts of warfare or a battle – of something from which a victor might emerge. At the same time, Robbie was letting slip that, despite their outwardly lovey-dovey demeanour, the tensions in his complicated relationship with Gary were not yet fully resolved. On camera Williams said, 'My problem's always been with Gary,' before quickly correcting himself to 'My problem always was with Gary.'

Rob was also implying that the group's current unrivalled success was not a factor in his decision to come back. 'This is the perfect time and the perfect moment for that something other than being Robbie Williams to happen,' he said. 'And it just so happens that they're massive, and that's the way it's worked out.' It might have been stretching it just a touch, however, to suggest that he would still have happily jumped on board if – instead of being the biggest band in the country – Take That were about to top the bill on a Saga Holidays summer cruise.

For his part, Gary was, apparently, well aware that the reconciliation had only been made possible by the massive success of

Take That since their revival. 'If we hadn't have come back as a band, we wouldn't have seen Rob again,' he said. 'We needed to meet again as equals, with equal success, back in a great place. And we're equals at the moment.'

Nonetheless, the careful balance of the Take That ecosystem was undoubtedly disrupted by the addition of Williams. Jason was still the one who was struggling most with the situation, and matters were not helped by the fact that by the time he and Howard arrived in New York, a camaraderie already existed between the other three as they brainstormed song ideas. At times, Jason's body language was defensive. In the studio, he was invariably to be found on the opposite end of a sofa to Rob, his arms crossed, and leaning as far away from Williams as possible when they talked. Or he would avoid eye contact by putting on sunglasses when they disagreed about Robbie's choice of lyrics on the highly self-referential album track 'Eight Letters', which charted the demise of the band in its first incarnation. More often than not during the sessions, which took place in New York, LA and London, Gary would be required to step in to defuse the situation – often, it has to be said, by taking Rob's side.

In fact, as a symbol of just how selfless both Barlow and Williams were to become in their dealings with each other, Robbie, who wrote the emotive lyrics to 'Eight Letters' and recorded a highly impressive vocal of the track in Los Angeles in February 2010, would eventually gift the song – one of the standout numbers on the record – to Gary for him to sing on the final version of the album, which they had fittingly titled *Progress*. And it soon became apparent to those around the band that although Stuart Price, the Grammy-winning British producer renowned for his work with Madonna, had been brought in to oversee the record, creatively it was being driven by Gary. He had a hand in every aspect of the record, from writing, playing keyboards and singing to stationing himself in the control room to cajole singing performances out of Mark and, particularly, Robbie. For his part, it was touchingly evident that Robbie was revelling in his role as Barlow's student and protégé.

In October 2009, a month after the recording of the album got underway, Gary's seventy-one-year-old father, Colin, died suddenly from a suspected heart attack. Barlow pulled out of the press launch in London for an upcoming Children in Need concert and travelled up to Cheshire to be with his family. On stage at the BBC's Electric Proms, Robbie sent him his condolences, saying: 'About fourteen months ago, we all got together and I got a new best mate. Gary, I'm sending my love to you. I know it's been a tough week.'

On 12 November, the two momentously shared a stage when Take That and Robbie appeared separately on the bill at the Children in Need Rocks the Royal Albert Hall. As Take That opened the show with 'Greatest Day', Rob stood in the wings embracing Ayda and singing along at the top of his voice. It was a telling moment. He gave every impression of hanging on to his girlfriend for dear life, as though she was the comfort blanket he needed at the thought of following the band on stage and having to perform alone. How he must have wished he could simply be out there with the band, of which he was now secretly a part, instead of having to be Robbie Williams for one more night. As the other four took their bows following their performance, Rob briefly joined them on stage before they made their exit, and at the end of the show, while Paul McCartney led the evening's performers in a singalong of 'Hey Jude', Gary and Rob stood swaying with their arms around each other.

Afterwards, Robbie was buzzing with excitement and admitting he'd been tearful before joining the others on stage. 'I started tearing up just before I came on and the lads were singing,' he told reporters, 'knowing it was just about to happen and knowing what the reactions were going to be like. And then all my team were like, "Please don't cry." I think we should have milked it for a lot longer than we actually did. I think Gaz, in his wisdom, went, "Right, we should get off now – let the lad do his singing." That was probably what was in his head, because I was trying to get them back to do a bow. That's the first time in fifteen years; we should have at least stayed there for ten minutes. I'm not nervous any more because we've seen each other. The bitterness and resentment has completely gone and I'm just left with four other lads that I just love to pieces. That's why I was so bitter and resentful in the first place because I loved them then and love is all that's left now, and that's what you see tonight.'

Less than a week later, Robbie announced to the band that he had had a change of mind and no longer wanted to be in Take That. Gary heard the news as he was about to fly off on holiday with Dawn and the children. He was utterly shell-shocked. How could the euphoria of just a few nights ago have paled so quickly for Rob? How could he have sat in a room with Gary and the others only the previous week and talked so excitedly about the record they were making, and how he felt he was going through a healing process and was enjoying recording for the first time in years? Was he simply talking crap when he told them he was actually looking forward to coming into the studio each day to work with the band? It was a personal kick in the teeth, too, for Barlow, who had gone out on a limb for Williams and had fought his corner when those within the wider Take That set-up were saying the whole thing was too risky, that Rob was just a flake, a recovering druggie, a prima donna, an accident waiting to happen. Worse, much worse, was that Gary, with his finely tuned musical ear, knew they had already written hits – and big ones at that – in the few recording sessions they'd had. What a terrible waste of something that, in Gary's mind at least, seemed to be going so well.

Other members of Take That were less surprised that Robbie had jumped ship. Several weeks earlier, Jason told the film crew following their reunion: 'I've been sceptical about him coming back in the band, and I'd like to think he would be cool and everything would be fine and it would be tight-knit, but from what I've experienced, Robbie's got a very changeable mind.' In the wake of his decision to walk, Howard sent Rob an emotional email imploring him to think again, and Jason called Williams to tell him in no uncertain terms that his whims were affecting the rest of the group, that he needed to understand that in a band it was all for one and one for all. If he chose not to come back, that was his decision, Jason told him, but he needed to know the impact his capriciousness had on the rest of them.

Finally, Mark, in his allotted role of peacemaker, made two trips to see Rob. Williams told him he was sorry for letting everyone down, but things were going too fast for him. In their excitement they had already begun talking about a tour together and Rob realized the prospect terrified him. He just did not feel in the right frame of mind for everything that entailed. Mark told him he understood how daunting the thought of touring and promotion could be, and he knew it could take up to a year of their lives, but there was nothing to stop them just doing the album and putting it out, letting it promote itself. To finish recording it, Owen told him, would involve thirty days of work over the next twelve months.

Did Rob have thirty days free, and did he want to do this album? Mark asked him finally. The answer from Williams was yes. He was, for the moment at least, back in.

By January 2010 he and the rest of the band were back in the studio, with the agreement that this time they would shift recording of the album to Los Angeles so that a still-wobbly Robbie could put in short stints in the studio before returning home to Ayda or playing a game of football with his friends. Later, Williams would say of his decision to walk out of the band for a second time: 'I wasn't very well physically. I just didn't feel as though I had the energy to do it. It was a scary prospect to be out there among something that would be so huge when you're feeling depleted of life force.'

Given how much time and energy they had committed to the project, the rest of the band were happy and relieved to have him back, but the nagging question of whether they could really rely on Robbie was at the forefront of their minds. If he could bail twice, what was to stop him doing it a third time? What would happen if – like fifteen years earlier – he just announced he'd had enough and wanted out on the eve of the major tour that everyone, including Robbie, was talking about so excitedly? This time, though, it would be different; this time it would be the reunion tour with Robbie. How can you have a reunion tour when the person the whole reunion revolves round doesn't turn up? How embarrassing would it be for the other four, who would be left to pick up the pieces? More to the point, how much would such a monumental calamity be likely to cost them?

For the time being, though, they each – Robbie included – did their best to put their doubts into storage. From his perspective, Gary was just happy to have Williams back. He had found the experience of their recording sessions as a five-piece the best of any period of his career. His mistakes during Take That mark I had made him purposely shy away from taking too much of a hands-on role in the production of the previous two albums, but now he felt confident in his ability to handle the role of leader in a more equitable way. Crucially, too, he had proved to the others that he was up to the task. Arriving at the LA studios each morning, he would be so excited at the prospect of another day of recording he had to force himself not to run from the parking lot to the building.

For his part, Rob found himself more than willing to put his trust in Gary, who, as the sessions progressed, became as much a father confessor to him as a musical sounding board. Away from the studio, Barlow began spending more time just hanging out with Rob at his Beverly Hills house.

In July, Take That and Robbie called a press conference in London to announce publicly what was by now the worst-kept secret in pop – that they were re-forming to release their first album together since *Nobody Else*. But the line being toed by the band was that Williams would only be on board for one album and the tour, which would involve eighteen months' work, after which he would go back to his solo career and Take That would return to being a foursome.

A month later, Rob married Ayda at his Californian home. Sixty guests, including his parents, Jan and Pete, and Ayda's mother, Gwen, and stepfather, Vance, saw the couple take their vows in a thirty-foot marquee before Rob broke into a spontaneous perform-ance of 'Angels'. He had decided against having a best man, but Ayda chose Rob's former PA and current manager, Josie Cliff, to be her maid of honour. The role of the couple's eight dogs was to act as bridesmaids, with the pets, including Poupette, their Maltese-poodle cross, wearing specially made garlands of miniature roses as collars. Meanwhile, the entrance of the house was made to resemble a Las Vegas casino, and a huge heart, made of hundreds of roses, was erected under which the couple took their vows, with Ayda stunning in a strapless silk taffeta gown by designer Monique Lhuillier and Rob in a tuxedo and white bowtie made by Savile Row tailor Spencer Hart. Later, Rob, Pete and Jonathan Wilkes took turns to sing numbers backed by a swing band in a Moroccan-themed marquee before a traditional English breakfast of bacon, beans and eggs was served at 1 a.m. when the newlyweds changed into his-and-hers stripy pyjamas.

Strangely, neither Gary nor any of the other Take That members was present, although a team from *Hello!* magazine was there to chronicle the expensive extravaganza. In fact, two months earlier, in the studio in London, when Gary had been mildly ribbing Robbie about when he and Ayda were going to tie the knot, Williams told him they were planning to get married soon. As Barlow angled for an invite, saying, 'I'm really good at weddings,' Rob was caught on camera pulling a sceptical face.

The wedding had indeed been a long time coming. The couple were due to get hitched on Valentine's Day, but Williams called it off after the date was revealed to the press. Likewise, they had been making arrangements to have the ceremony on the Californian holiday resort of Catalina Island until news leaked out at the very last minute. The proposed venue was highly symbolic. As part of Robbie's continuing interest in all things otherworldly, he, Ayda and some friends had recently hired jet skis to travel the 33 miles from LA's Marina del Rey to the island. The reason for the trip was so he and his party could peer below the waves as they skimmed across them in the hope of seeing marine aliens or USOs (unidentified submerged objects – the underwater equivalent of UFOs).

Even so, as an example of how close they had become in a relatively short period of time, Robbie asked Gary if he would help him write some new songs he was contracted to add to a greatest-hits album that would signal the end of his problematic deal with EMI. The record, *In and Out of Consciousness*, would eventually feature two songs co-written with Barlow when it was released in October 2010, the maudlin 'Heart and I' and the country-inspired duet 'Shame'.

The latter was released as a single at the beginning of the month, the first time the two men had appeared together on record in fifteen years. The song itself was a pleasant enough ditty, with hints of the Beatles' 'Blackbird', and told the tale of their successful personal reconciliation. However, the video to accompany the single was more noteworthy than the song itself. Filmed in the Los Angeles suburb of Chatsworth and also at Malibu State Park in June, the promo was an as-camp-as-Christmas spoof of the big-screen story of the two lovestruck cowboys in *Brokeback Mountain*, with Robbie and Gary hamming it up, staring into each other's eyes, touching tenderly and eventually stripping off. The only thing missing was the original's man-on-man action under canvas. It was all a bit of fun, and their way of playing up to the leg-pulling they were getting from the other members of Take That about their burgeoning bromance.

Gary flew in from London for the two-day shoot and hung out at Rob's house in the evenings, Rob watching TV comedy shows while a jet-lagged Gary nodded off on the sofa. The pair debuted 'Shame' live at the Concert for Heroes at Twickenham Stadium in September. As Robbie introduced Gary on stage, he told the crowd of 60,000, which included Prince Harry: 'This is one of the most amazing moments of my career. It's been fifteen years in the making. My wife calls him my boyfriend. I call him my captain. To you, he's Mr Gary Barlow.' Not that the campery of their performance was to everyone's taste. When they sang the single live on the BBC's *Strictly Come Dancing* at the beginning of October, the station received complaints. One mother posted a message on the *Strictly* website commenting: 'I'm not sure how appropriate it was for Robbie and Gary to be making goo-goo eyes and singing a love song to each other.' Another wrote: 'I was expecting tongues.' Nonetheless, 'Shame' reached number two in the UK, while the album got to the top of the charts at home, in Germany and Austria. Even so, it was merely the undercard for the main event.

The long-awaited *Progress* was released on 15 November 2010. The recording of the album had been held up by the admission of Mark Owen into rehab in March to deal with his drinking problems after reports that he had cheated on his wife, Emma, and confessed to up to ten affairs. He also admitted to having a five-year relationship with twenty-four-year-old accounts manager Neva Hanley. They were said to have carried on the affair up until weeks before his marriage to Emma in March 2009.

Bizarrely, there had been serious talk during the latter days of the album's recording about changing the name of the band from Take That to the English. The thoroughly illogical plan was dreamed up and proposed by Robbie, who was concerned, he said, about the emotional baggage that went with the band's name. It says something about how accommodating the others were that they did not immediately shoot the idea down in flames.

The record immediately went to number one, becoming the fastest-selling UK album of the century and the second-fastest selling of all time. It sold an amazing 235,000 copies on the day of its release, a million copies in twenty-four days, and went six times platinum in the UK in the first six months. At the same time, it went to number one in Germany, Greece, Denmark and Ireland.

In preparation for its release, Gary was saying of the album: 'We decided it couldn't be us sounding like Robbie's last record, and it can't be us sounding like our last record. We've had to adopt some of what Rob does, adopt some of what we do and move this forward, with a new producer on board, and take on a bit of a new sound.' He was certainly right that *Progress* was a departure from the sound of the band's last two albums. In fact, there were only really two tracks on the record that were recognizable as Take That songs. Symbolically, perhaps, the numbers in question – 'The Flood' and 'Eight Letters' – bookended the record. Much of the rest could easily have been taken for a post-*Rudebox*, synth-pop Robbie Williams record. It was fun, but bonkers fun. An offbeat, quirky collection of paranoiac, often unintelligible streams of consciousness.

'Happy Now', for example, sounded like the sort of rambling year-eleven English essay that persuades form teachers to ask little Johnny's parents if everything's all right at home. The bolted-on Bee Gees-like chorus didn't fit with the dark feel of the verse, either. Williams's distinctly madcap approach appeared to have rubbed off on his comrades. Mark Owen kicked off the lead vocal on the apocalyptic 'SOS', while 'Kidz', with its marching jackboots and dystopian lyrics, was a laugh-out-loud conspiracy theory set to music. When Mark tried to snarl: 'What you looking at?' after the chorus, he sounded about as threatening as Wallace from Wallace and Gromit.

But during its more mainstream moments, the addition of Robbie took the band to a new level, particularly his soaring opening of the radio-friendly first single 'The Flood', which got to number two when it was released in the middle of October. Elsewhere, there was a notable dearth of the classic Gary Barlow ballads that had defined past Take That albums. In fact, Barlow seemed content to play a bit part on the record following the return of the band's prodigal son. Was it simply the case that Gary had realized, cleverly, that their fans would expect the first record of Take That mark III to be Robbie-heavy, or was there another reason why the shrewd Barlow was so easily converted to the idea of dramatically changing the band's sound to the quirky, retro eighties feel of *Progress*? If, as Rob was promising, he would be jumping ship before the next Take That record, would that not be the perfect opportunity to revert to the band's middle-of-the road heartland? With a suitably long break between their records as a foursome, their audience would surely be chomping at the bit for a slice of the classic Take That they know and love. *Progress*, meanwhile, would be seen as a pleasing but passing phase, an off-the-wall interlude before the band returned to more familiar territory.

Two weeks before the album was released, tickets for Take That's reunion tour with Williams went on sale and the band smashed its own UK first-day record. More than 1.35 million tickets were snapped up on day one, and promoters added ten more shows because of the phenomenal demand, with fifty tickets being sold every second. Some fans queued for seventy-two hours at box offices to make sure of a seat, and those trying to buy them on the Internet tried for hours just to log on to the ticket sites as operators reported their highest ever traffic in a single day. The tour would start at the end of May 2011, with four shows at Sunderland's Stadium of Light, followed by eight at the City of Manchester Stadium. After

Cardiff, Dublin, Glasgow and Birmingham, the Progress Live Tour would then pitch camp at Wembley Stadium for eight nights, breaking the previous record of seven nights held by Michael Jackson's Bad Tour in 1988. The bandwagon would then move on to Europe, with dates in Italy, Denmark and Holland, and three shows in Germany at the end of July.

Given his previous change of heart, however, could the others count on Robbie being there?

Words and Music

Given the genuine doubts about whether Williams could truly be depended on, it may have been a simple, unconscious case of his own self-defence mechanism kicking in that made Gary stick rigidly to the party line that Robbie's inclusion in the band was still being viewed by all involved as very much a temporary situation. As preparations began for the shows, which Gary was confidently predicting would change the face of live stadium concerts for ever, he was promising, publicly at least, that Take That would revert to a foursome once the Progress Live Tour was over. As if to prove the point, the band performed without their newest recruit at a private party in Barbados on New Year's Eve. Robbie, who had been due to appear with the others at the event, was reported to have pulled out a month before the gig because of family commitments. At the same time, he was also rumoured to have ducked out of a Christmas party held by Take That's management in Mayfair.

In January 2011, Gary celebrated his fortieth birthday by throwing a charity gig in his own honour at London's Shepherd's Bush Empire. Under a huge backdrop that spelled out 'GB40' in red and white lights, he took to the stage with Mark, Howard and Jason, as well as pop starlet Ellie Goulding and Coldplay's Chris Martin, in front of a celebrity audience that included Gwyneth Paltrow, Peter Kay, Claudia Schiffer and David Walliams. Elton John, who could not make the event, sent a congratulatory message, as did Rob, which he recorded in his LA home. Given the ongoing speculation over whether Williams was up to the rigours of Take That's upcoming high-profile tour, the video Robbie made, which was beamed onto a giant screen at the birthday bash, could be seen in one of two ways: as a classic piece of Robbie slapstick, a bit of knowingly self-aware vaudeville; or, conversely, as a signal to the moneymen financing the reunion extravaganza that they really should start to be concerned.

Williams appeared naked before the camera with his genitals tucked out of sight between his legs. 'I just want to put your mind at rest about the tour, as I know you're a little bit worried,' he said in his tongue-in-cheek message to Gary, 'but I'm going to be absolutely fine, buds. I'm on the meds.' It was a limelight-stealing display that naturally dominated the newspaper coverage of the occasion the following day. It might also have been, had the relationship between the two men still not been in its touchy-feely honeymoon period, a tad irksome to Gary, who was – lest we forget – supposed to be the star of the show. What was also evident was that while Gary may have made the decision some time ago to put the past behind him, certain Take That fans were not quite so prepared to offer their forgiveness on his behalf: an admittedly small number in the crowd could be heard booing Robbie's filmed appearance. It was evidence that some of the group's fans remained far from happy about the prodigal son's return.

Those Robbie-hating Thatters may, then, have been buoyed by

the fact that after the event, Gary was admitting he was still doubtful of Williams making his stay in the group permanent. 'This is a very extraordinary situation,' he said. 'When the five of us are on stage, there are three acts there. Take That are a four-piece band. We can exist and be successful as a four-piece band. Right now we are a five-piece band, and we really don't know where that is going. Then you have got Robbie Williams the solo artist, and he is still desperate to be a solo artist. I know we're back with Rob now, but we still see our future as a four-piece.' Just to muddy the waters further, however, sources were revealing that Robbie was already writing material for a possible new album with the other band members.

Indeed, the mixed messages from Gary were being echoed around the Williams camp as well, with even some of those closest to Rob still in the dark about what he planned to do once the Take That tour was over. Moreover, there remained a nagging doubt, though it can be put no stronger than that, among some in his entourage that despite all the assurances from Rob that he felt himself to be in the most positive frame of mind for years, he might yet have a change of heart about going on the road with Take That. It is fair to say that the more pessimistic in his circle were keeping their fingers crossed that the old demons that had blighted him in the past would be held at bay, at least until the conclusion of the tour at the back end of July. The sense of trepidation was not helped by the bookmaker William Hill offering 10–1 that it would go ahead without him. Meanwhile, Williams himself was talking about wanting to take an extended break once his commitment to Take That was over in the summer so he and Ayda, who would be thirty-two that May, could begin thinking about starting a family.

*

While Rob had been a no-show at Barlow's birthday celebrations, the band united in February to celebrate Williams's thirty-seventh birthday with an alcohol-free dinner at the Ivy in London. A couple of nights later, Take That won Best British Group at the Brits, bringing their Brits total to eight. The five opened the show at the O2 Arena performing 'Kidz', the second single from *Progress*. The band, appearing for the first time at the awards as a quintet since 1994, had been due to perform the song on *The X Factor* final two months earlier, but the show's overlord, Simon Cowell, had decided the performance, which featured dancers dressed as riot police and holding steel shields bearing the Take That logo, was too provocative in the wake of the recent clashes between police and students over tuition fees. As it was, the cop-themed routine at the Brits only helped 'Kidz' to struggle to an unsatisfactory number twenty-eight in the UK singles chart.

It was not the only disappointment. For the first time there was talk, if only privately within Take That's close circle, of growing tensions between Robbie and his band mates. Since the turn of 2011 some in their camp had been whispering that despite the all-smiling, all-dancing image the five members had been projecting since Robbie's return, there had been several key moments of distinct and concerning disharmony among the group's ranks. The word was that tensions between them had come to a head during the Brit Awards and had consequently put a huge dampener on what should have been a night of celebration.

The first signs that something was amiss that day came when the band made a pig's ear of what was supposed to be their glamorous arrival at the O2 aboard a white Sunseeker yacht on the Thames. As they were helped onto the landing stage by deckhands at Docklands, the band were not exactly projecting the glitzy rock-god aura that must have been part of the thinking when the PR stunt was being dreamed up, though officially, their spokespeople said they had taken to the river to avoid traffic jams in the capital. Mark, in a duffel coat, scarf and carrying a satchel, looked to be only a pair of NHS specs away from provoking a call from Harry Potter's lawyers asking for his image back. Gary, meanwhile, came sporting an ill-judged Fair Isle cardy in various shades of sepia that looked like it had been handed down to him by Grandpa Barlow. More significantly, however, Jason decided at the last minute to jump ship and make his own way to the venue separately from the other four. To add insult to injury, the band were still late for rehearsals and were forced to race through a soundcheck, which did nothing to alleviate their pre-performance nerves.

Later, when they were backstage, the tensions, which those who were there say seemed to materialize from nowhere, came to a head. Rob ended up having a blazing row with the others. In subsequent days, as the five came to terms with the fallout from what was the first major rift of Take That mark III, each would stick to the agreed line among their friends that it had blown up so suddenly that they simply couldn't remember what had sparked the row. What was undeniable, however, was that they were all shaken by how quickly they had been at each other's throats. It was a sobering reminder to the band members themselves, as well as those around them, that despite the unforced public shows of camaraderie, their relationship might not have been built on quite the sound footings they had all allowed themselves to believe. According to Rob, the bad feeling lasted no more than a week. Nevertheless, it was a wake-up call to everyone.

Without a record contract, Robbie began negotiations with Take That's record company, Universal, about agreeing a solo deal. At the same time, a select group of rival labels were queuing up to try to persuade him to sign with them. In March, as the preparations for the tour stepped up another level, Gary, Mark, Howard and Jason visited Rob in Los Angeles, where Barlow and Williams – as competitive with each other as ever – made a bet to see who could shift more excess weight by the time they went on stage for the first time at the end of May. (In the end, a draw was declared.)

From Gary came a shift in emphasis too. By the end of March he was reassessing his earlier circumspect predictions about whether Rob would remain in the band beyond the tour. 'We really want this and this is our dream come true,' he said. 'At the beginning, we all said it was going to last for one album, but we've started to write again, so we don't know now.' Gary was also mulling over a reported £1.5-million offer from Simon Cowell to take over as the chief judge on *The X Factor*, with Cowell announcing at the same time he would be relinquishing his seat on the talent show's panel to launch the show in America. Cowell had previously approached Rob about joining *American Idol*. Rob thought about it and turned him down. While Gary considered the offer, the rehearsals moved to a 700-foot aircraft hangar in Cardington, Bedfordshire, where the tour's director, Kim Gavin, began putting the band through up to twelve hours a day of dance and singing practice, while the 275 technicians, who would be employed by the band on the road, were also coming to terms with the sheer scale of the task ahead of them.

Inevitably for Rob, with the countdown to the gigs came the first stirrings of that familiar negative rush of the impending stage fright he knew was not about to loosen its grip, in spite of the comfort blanket of having the four others with him. The impression that the pressure was getting to him was only ramped up when he was photographed looking scruffy and exhausted at a casino in Swindon a few days before the £15-million tour was due to start. He was not the only one panicking. Mark was also admitting that he had gone through a 'meltdown' lasting two days as the pre-tour jitters set in hard.

They need not have worried. The opening night of the Progress Live Tour, which took place in front of 54,564 ecstatic fans at a rainy Sunderland's Stadium of Light on 27 May, was an unmitigated triumph. Taking the stage after a set by support act the Pet Shop Boys, Gary, Mark, Howard and Jason had to try to persuade the delirious multitudes to quieten down before launching into a communal version of 'Rule the World', followed by 'Greatest Day', 'Hold Up a Light', 'Patience' and 'Shine', the latter seeing Owen being carried around the stage on the back of an enormous multi-coloured caterpillar. For the moment at least, the audience would have to wait for Robbie. In a classic case of understatement Gary told the crowd: 'We've got someone else joining us later.'

When Williams did eventually make an appearance, it was – typically – with a bang. Suddenly, from the top of a giant screen displaying images of him, the man himself exploded out of the centre, to be catapulted 30 feet down onto the stage on harness wires, where he proceeded to roar out 'Let Me Entertain You'. With the others taking a breather, for another four songs it became a Robbie Williams gig, as he moved on to 'Rock DJ', 'Come Undone', 'Feel' and 'Angels'.

His solo set and the band's earlier appearance minus Robbie meant effectively that they were their own warm-up acts for the main event. Finally, the five, all dressed in black and with Rob at the centre, trooped on to begin 'The Flood'. The rest of the set, featuring such technical marvels as a 20-metre-tall robot called Om and dozens of abseilers negotiating torrents of cascading water, was split between songs from *Progress* – 'SOS', 'Underground Machine', 'Kidz' and 'Pretty Things' – followed by early Take That, including 'A Million Love Songs', 'Babe', 'Everything Changes', 'Back for Good' and 'Pray', with Gary seated at a piano for the trip down memory lane. They also performed 'Love Love', which had been recorded for the newly released soundtrack of *X-Men: First Class*. After 'Never Forget', the others then poignantly joined Robbie in the song he wrote about their split, 'No Regrets', before a rousing 'Relight My Fire'. The night concluded with the band doing a walk-about among hyperventilating fans during 'Eight Letters'. The press was as smitten as the audience, with the *Independent* saying the gig 'shattered the bar set by other artists for an intimate show in a stadium'.

Backstage afterwards, the mood was one of undiluted ecstasy. Robbie, whose past reaction to such mass displays of adoration had invariably – and perversely – been one of sadness, now joking he wanted to go back out and do the show again that very night. Gary, meanwhile, was backtracking about Robbie's future with the band. 'It felt great having Rob back up there,' he said, 'and I guess after that, it would be unnatural now for us not to work together as a five.'

By way of promoting the tour, which, in truth, scarcely needed any more publicity, Robbie was making the strange confession that for two years he had been injecting himself twice-weekly with the male sex hormone testosterone. In an interview with *Esquire* magazine at the beginning of June, he said he had been put on the drug after a blood test in Los Angeles diagnosed that he had extremely low levels of the hormone. His doctor, he revealed, told him he had the sex drive of a hundred-year-old man. Aside from the obvious conclusion that Williams's no doubt expensive medic might want

to think about working on his bedside manner, it was hardly the
most welcome news for someone with such a virile reputation as
Rob. He told the magazine he was using the drug, which boosts
the male sex drive, to tackle what he described as crippling lethargy.
Friends told me at the time that he was also crediting the injections
with helping him keep his depression in check.

Along with the oddly personal admission about his low sex drive,
however, came an altogether more worrying disclosure. During the
same interview, Robbie revealed that the diagnosis had only been
reached after he visited his doctor because he wanted to be
prescribed the hugely controversial human growth hormone. 'To
cut a long story short, I went to get some HGH,' Williams said.
'It's what all the old fellas are on out there in LA that's making
them look forty instead of sixty. It's improving their health, their
memory, their hair, skin. Could give you cancer. I weighed that up.
Thought I'd have it anyway. Went to see a Hollywood doctor. Had
my blood tests. Went back. He said, "You don't need HGH. You've
got the testosterone of a hundred-year-old man." And then everything made sense. It was kind of an epiphany that day. It has
changed my life. I feel I'm getting a second wind.'

Given his history of drug addiction – both illegal and prescribed
– what was Rob thinking in trying to get his hands on human
growth hormone in the first place? It is normally used to treat children and adults with growth disorders and those with multiple
sclerosis, and can have some pretty nasty side effects, but has
become known as 'plastic surgery in a bottle' because its devotees
claim it reverses the ageing process.

Nonetheless, it has become the wonder drug du jour of the
celebrity set, with doctors in Beverly Hills and Harley Street doling
out £500-a-time prescriptions that are said to aid weight loss, build

lean muscle, improve fitness and generally make you feel a million dollars. The big question, however, was, why was Rob willing to take the risk? Was it simply a case of the narcissism his detractors had perennially accused him of? Or was it a sign of something more pitiable, that despite everything he had achieved, despite his recent marriage and his public pronouncements of his newfound contentment, the Rob he woke up with every morning was never slim enough, never youthful enough, never good enough? Sadly for him, it seemed this fundamental self-loathing would not disappear as quickly as the track marks from injecting some synthetically produced elixir.

Five months after the Brits, Rob was the first to break rank and admit publicly the hitherto private tensions within the band. Of the backstage falling-out that soured the awards ceremony in February, he said: 'It was so disappointing, because stuff had been going horrendously well. It's completely sorted now, but it does put a different light on things. Until then I was just walking along in a marshmallow land going, "Isn't this great?"' He added: 'Am I a member of Take That? Well, it has gone swimmingly. It has been a load of fun. I've enjoyed it and I'd do it again. Whether that's in three or four or five or ten years, I don't know. Whether the boys will be up for it, I don't know. Whether there will be a Take That after this tour, I don't know. It's all up in the air.'

As evidence of the totality of Barlow's public rehabilitation – not to mention his prodigious work ethic – while the tour continued, Gary took over Simon Cowell's role as *The X Factor*'s head judge. At the beginning of June, he made his first appearance on the panel at auditions in Birmingham. From the point of view of the ITV show's producers, Barlow's arrival added the much-needed musical gravitas that had been so lacking in ex-judges, like the recently

departed Dannii Minogue, Sharon Osbourne and – for all his
populist genius – Cowell himself. However, Gary's appointment was
to some extent overshadowed by the ongoing media storm over
Cheryl Cole's supposed sacking from the new American series of
the talent show and the speculation over whether Cole, with whom
Gary had scaled Mount Kilimanjaro two years earlier for Comic
Relief, would re-join the British version.

As he began filming, Gary was saying of Cowell: 'I haven't spoken
to Simon and I haven't taken advice from him. I will do things my
own way. It's time for a new generation. Simon's had so many years;
it's time he moved over.' It was exactly the sort of headline-
prompting stuff of which the arch media manipulator Cowell would
have been proud. Nor was Gary, it seemed, shy of taking on the
former head judge's mantle as the show's pantomime Mr Nasty.
During early recordings, Gary, who was joined on the panel by
Louis Walsh and fellow newcomers former Destiny's Child warbler
Kelly Rowland and N-Dubz singer Tulisa Contostavlos, was said
to have told one female contestant she looked like a man and
lambasted others for their song choices and dodgy voices. There
were even reports that he had been asked by ITV executives to tone
down his criticism after one hopeful he laid into was supposed to
have admitted to feeling suicidal backstage. All of which was exactly
the knockabout tabloid material that the producers of the show
had no doubt been looking for when they hired him.

Aside from the mandatory hype, those close to Barlow were
saying privately that as well as the obvious personal boost to his
ego and profile the X Factor gig would offer him, he was motivated
by the real desire to mentor the new talent he was hoping to
discover. It was a course he had earlier embarked on by signing
classical singer Camilla Kerslake to his own independent label,

Future Records, in 2009, but it was his ongoing and expanding role as musical guide to Robbie that would continue to be of most significance. As the Progress Live Tour kicked off, Rob was announcing that even though he was yet to sign a new solo record deal, he and Gary were already close to finishing the next Robbie Williams album, with Barlow taking on the role of producer and co-writer. 'Gaz is great for me,' Rob said, 'because he knows how I should sound. He wanted to make a Lennon and McCartney-type album. That was his big idea – big, standard records. At the minute, it's just me and him finishing the album, and I love it. Love my friendship with him. Love that he regards me as an equal. Gary is kind of unemotional about stuff; I'm emotional about stuff. He's solid; I'm fickle. He gets stuff done; I don't. It's incredibly impor-tant that the next album I do is a big album. It's incredibly important that it's successful, that it ticks all the boxes. At the same time, it's not the be all and end all. I'm not going to throw myself off a cliff if it's another *Rudebox*. It's exciting. There's a possibility it will have a similar impact to things I've done in the past. And before I wander off into the retirement home of the pop world, I'd like to have another fistful of hits to play to people. I believe I've got one last stab at global success. I want to right some wrongs. Make up for how I've looked and behaved. There's a place I'd like to go for a bit of redemption, for myself. Just to do a good job. I just want a few more hits and then I'll gladly go.'

Of course, for 'global' what Williams really meant was 'American'. And given his previous ego-sapping disappointments when it came to his attempts to crack the States, it was testament to the new vigour evident in Rob that he was once again prepared to put himself through that particular emotional wringer. It was proof, too, of how far his career, which had seemed moribund and floundering just a few months earlier, had been given fresh legs by his association with Barlow.

The replacement Williams had been searching for since he had dispensed with the services of Guy Chambers nine years earlier had been found. Now it would be Gary to whom Rob would look to deliver him the holy grail of the transatlantic stardom he still so desperately coveted. It was not, clearly, a relationship that had come full circle, but an altogether new friendship and working partnership, hewn from the rock of their mutual respect, ambition and shared conviction that the scars from past cauterized wounds should be allowed to fade of their own accord. And in doing so, they had both gained a sense of renewal and liberation that would be their reward for their joint acts of forgiveness.

At the same time, neither man was naive enough to think that amid the rosy glow of their reconciliation, there would not be, in all likelihood, perilous hazards placed in the way of the warm and fuzzy Tinseltown ending that we wanted for them. It would also be equally naive to imagine that amid their genuinely fraternal feelings towards each other, there was not also the hard-nosed business sense that each was the conduit to the other's ultimate ambition. In the case of Robbie, that would involve him conquering the one elusive territory that stood in the way of him being able to proclaim himself a bona fide worldwide star without male equal. For Gary's part, in his mind, the prize had become the creation of a songwriting partnership with Robbie that could place them up there with the pop immortals. It goes without saying, of course, that there would be those who were ready to denounce the presumptuousness of Barlow and Williams comparing themselves to Lennon and McCartney. In fact, Rob would later regret the comment, though it was meant only as an indicator of the pure excitement at what they were creating together and as aspiration, rather than a comparison in any real sense.

Surely both men knew in their heart of hearts that the failure of such lofty objectives would only serve to place the relationship under the same sort of irresistible pressure that eventually did for the partnership of Williams and Chambers. Similarly, the burden of being the living embodiment of a latter-day parable for the power of forgiveness and reconciliation was not a weight that could be borne easily by anyone – particularly, in Robbie's case, by someone so aware of their human failings. And we hardly need to remind ourselves how the once brotherly relationship between John and Paul ended in the kind of acrimony and public vitriol that acted as a precursor to Robbie and Gary's own drawn-out feud.

The newfound friendship between them would, no doubt, be subject in the future to the whims of Williams's changeability, but it would only be with the inevitable bumps in the road that the relationship could truly be tested. Only that way could Robbie and Gary discover if the seams of hatred and mistrust, which they had once mined to spur on their respective bids to dominate the other, had really been abandoned for good. Time would tell if the ground on which they had built their unlikely rapprochement was solid enough to bear the weight of their own expectations of each other, or whether the fault lines that had so blighted them in the past would ominously reappear.

For now, though, they were rightly proud of a rare achievement. This was not a time for neat endings. It was the closing of a scene, not the final act. In this allegorical tale of salvation and redemption, it would be down to the two principal characters to write their own ending.

Acknowledgements

I would like to express my thanks to the many people who generously gave up their time to give me so much assistance in researching this book.

My thanks also go to my agent Dorie Simmonds, and to my wife Alison for her good advice. I would also like to thank everybody at Pan Macmillan for their support, particularly Ingrid Connell and my editor Natasha Martin whose guidance and expertise have been invaluable.

Finally, my eternal gratitude goes to Kathy Hodges who kept me fortified during the long days of writing with her incomparable cakes!

Sources

This is by no means an exhaustive list, but it represents a selection of sources I found most useful in writing the book. I would also like to thank everyone who gave me their time and thoughts.

Books:

Robbie Williams, *Somebody Someday*. Ebury Press, 2001.

Paul Scott, *Robbie Williams: Angels and Demons*. André Deutsch, 2003.

Robbie Williams and Chris Heath, *Feel Robbie Williams*. Ebury Press, 2004.

Gary Barlow with Richard Havers, *My Take*. Bloomsbury, 2006.

Take That, Take One. Penguin Books, 2009.

Take That, Take Two. Penguin Books, 2009.

Robbie Williams and Chris Health, *You Know Me*. Ebury Press, 2010.

Television:

Nobody Someday. Century Films, 2002.
The Truth About Take That. Channel 4, 2004.
Take That: For The Record. Back2Back Productions, 2005
Look Back, Don't Stare. Pulse Films, 2010.

Publications:

Attitude Magazine, July 1996.
Advocate Magazine, May 2003.
Esquire Magazine, August 2011.

Picture credits

Getty – pages 3 (top), 4, 6 (middle), 8 (bottom right), 10 (main), 13 (middle), 14 (top), 15 (bottom right), 16

Mirrorpix – pages 5, 6 (bottom), 7, 9 (top), 10 (bottom), 13 (top),

Press Association – pages 1, 2 (top), 3 (bottom), 6 (top), 9 (bottom), page 11, page 12 (top), page 13 (bottom), page 15 (top)

Rex Features – pages 2 (bottom), 8 (bottom left), 12 (bottom), 14 (bottom)